20TH CENTURY FARMER'S BOY

FIRST EDITION
published in 2001
by
WOODFIELD PUBLISHING
Bognor Regis, West Sussex PO21 5EL, England.

ISBN 1-903953-01-4

ISBN 1-903953-01-4

9 781903 953013

The Life & Times of a

20th Century Farmer's Boy

*The trials and tribulations
of one Sussex farming family
through 100 years of rural change*

NICK ADAMES

Woodfield Publishing
~ WEST SUSSEX • ENGLAND ~

Key to Owners and Tenants. 1844.

O. Thomas Sanctuary
T. Benjamen Haydon Gulliver

O. Thomas Sanctuary
T. Himself

O. Thompsons Charity (Petworth)
T. Ephraim Bulbeck

O. Ephraim Adames
T. Himself

O. Hussey & Titchener
T. Ephraim Adames

O. William Bridger
T. William Meaden

O. William Allin
T. William Tupper

O. Duke of Richmond
T. Thomas Cozens

O. Joseph Coote
T. Thomas Coote

O. Kenneth Cozens
T. James Boiling

O. Thomas Cozens
T. Himself

O. Richard Ibbetson
T. Edward Green

O. Richard Coote
T. Himself

O. Charles Duke
T. Himself

O. Stephen Farndell
T. George Farndell.

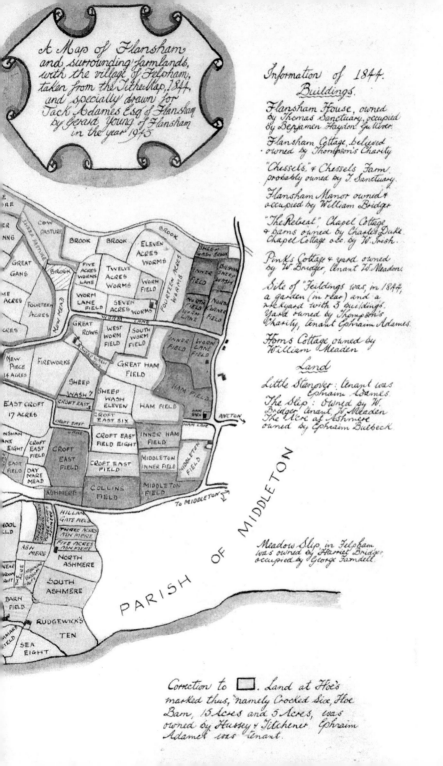

A Map of Flansham and surrounding farmlands, with the village of Felpham, taken from the Tithe Map, 1844, and specially drawn for Jack Adames Esq of Flansham by Gerald Young of Flansham in the year 1945

Information of 1844.

Buildings.

Flansham House, owned by Thomas Sanctuary, occupied by Benjamin Haydon Gulliver.

Flansham Cottage, believed owned by Thompson's Charity

"Chessels" & Chessels Farm probably owned by T. Sanctuary.

Flansham Manor owned & occupied by William Bridger

"The Retreat" Chapel Cottage & barns owned by Charles Duke. Chapel Cottage occ. by W. Irish.

Pinks Cottage & yard owned by W. Bridger, tenant T. S. Meaden.

Site of "Feildings" was, in 1844, a garden (in rear) and a brickyard with 3 buildings. Yard owned by Thompson's Charity, tenant Ephraim Adames.

Hom's Cottage owned by William Meaden.

Land

Little Stanover: tenant was Ephraim Adames.
The Slip: owned by W. Bridger, tenant, T. Meaden
The Acre at Ashmere owned by Ephraim Bulbeck.

Meadow Slip in Felpham was owned by Harriet Bridger, occupied by George Farndell.

Correction to ☐. Land at Hoe's marked thus, namely Crooked Six, Hoe Barn, 15 Acres and 5 Acres, was owned by Hussey & Titchener. Ephraim Adames was tenant.

Nick in the Oat Field.

Gay & 'Milkmaid'.

Contents

Introduction

This little book of reminiscences has been put together primarily as a way of recording what life was like in a small Sussex hamlet around and after the second world war. It tries to travel through time with me, with my family and my many friends. It attempts to chronicle my sporting interests, both on numerous golf links around Britain, and also forty years spent skiing in Murren, a small mountain village in Switzerland.

The Adames family is one of the oldest recorded farming families in Sussex and, with no direct successor to follow me into farming, the name will die with me. The irony here is that the first recorded family member, also Nicholas, who was purportedly washed up on nearby Pagham beach in the 1600s, was the only other of the male line to carry the name Nicholas. The first and last. The beginning and the end.

The present surviving local branch of the family has farmed within three miles of Bognor all this time and in every generation at least one male has stayed loyal to the family farms and kept the name and interest firmly in farming.

My first love, after the land and our cattle, shows I hope clearly, my love of the countryside. And here I have some very strong views on where rural England is going, and where those in charge are leading it astray. I remain a traditional farmer who farms primarily to earn enough money to improve the farms, and also to finance a long time interest in a variety of sports and all wildlife but particularly my beloved wild birds.

My name may be familiar to some people in West Sussex since as a writer I, contributed for many of years, to a regular Farm Diary column in the *West*

Sussex Gazette and, more recently, to a similar and regular offering in the popular *Downs Country* magazine.

Never the less all the time I have tried to remain, primarily, as a working farmer, with a fair knowledge of the practical side of stockmanship. I hope you find it some gives some interesting insights to the intricacies of the art and of my involvement with several long gone characters.

One of the old names that recurs regularly is that of Gerard Young. Gerry, who lived close by in Flansham and was a close friend of the Adames family, was a writer and historian of note in West Sussex in the middle of the twentieth century, and one whose gift for writing and art fanned this young lad's enthusiasm. Interestingly, my own family formed the basis of the three books Gerry himself wrote about this little hamlet, and the Adames family, including myself as a three year old, appear regularly throughout the books.

I have no shame in admitting that my schooling was a self-inflicted disaster and that I left that miserable period 'being able to do little more than bowl a cricket ball'. A low starting point yet one that rapidly developed an enormous interest in sport which runs right through this account of my growing up, and indeed even past middle age.

However, taking a tip from my father Jack's example, I began in 1952, as a thirteen year old, writing a daily diary, and have kept this fascinating record up, without fail, every day since. This, with father's own diaries running back to 1922, forms the outline of much of the following chapters.

I would be the first to admit that, while never a star at anything, my participation, understanding of, and enthusiasm for sport, has been enormously helped by the luck of having had, as friends, fellow competitors of the highest standard. And as such, they have given me an acute awareness of how sports should be played, and in what spirit.

What has been called by others my hard, unflowery, and quite direct manner of writing is, I hope, softened and enhanced by the addition of numerous old family photographs, many of which go back in the 1890s and give a unique flavour of those hard but happy old times.

With the wonders of modern technology readers are invited to communicate with me by e-mail (my address is **n.adames@btinternet.com**) to discuss any points of interest or direct the expected criticisms.

I really hope you enjoy this undramatised and unsensational 'trip' back down memory lane, and that you finish with a flavour of what those times were like, away from the rush and aggravation of the modern world.

The work is dedicated to the two strong and understanding women in my life. My late mother Betty, for what she gave me in the way of a rather 'lateral' outlook on life, and most importantly to my 'rock', my beloved wife Mary, to whom nothing is too much trouble, and who is the same lovely happy soul, every day, through thick and thin.

Nick Adames

Flansham, September 2001

Nick and his father, Jack Adames 1943.

Flansham in 1901 during lane repairs. George Stoner's cottage on the left; Flansham House's gated drive is on the right.

Loaded wagons waiting in the farm drive ready to be uploaded in the rickyard c.1937.

~ Chapter One ~

THE EARLY DAYS

George Stoner woke me up on most of my childhood mornings as his steady footfall crunched in the loose gravel of the lane below my bedroom window. George rented a one-acre allotment given him by a grateful, or perhaps guilty, government after he had survived the trenches of the Great War. Twice a day since then he had walked the 500 yards each way from his cottage to see his motley collection of chickens, ducks and geese and collect their eggs. His first visit, every day of every season, was at 7am, and my Father swore he never varied.

"Set our clocks by old George," he said, on many occasions.

At the time I first noticed George, our small hamlet was just emerging from the dark days of the Second World War. The Battle of Britain was behind us, and apart from the seemingly constant drone, day and night, of military aircraft, friend or foe, our life on the farm passed happily and quietly. At least it did for a five-year-old.

I had just been joined in the household by a tiny sister, Gabrielle. Born prematurely at under 2lbs and not initially expected to survive, she spent the first three months of her life in an incubator at Bognor hospital and then, when she could be taken home, many more hours in the warmth of the linen cupboard, near the hot water tank, the only constantly warm place in the house. Gay, according to her doctors, had suffered a stroke or been affected by polio just before birth. Apart from her tiny size, she had one leg almost an inch shorter than the other. Her troubles took a lot of Mother's time and were to cause much worry over the coming 10 years.

Father and Mother lived in a small house, Lynton Cottage, high on a bank above Hoe Lane, in the tiny hamlet of Flansham. The lane, under a tunnel of elm trees that tower from the high banks on either side, runs from the main coastal road between Littlehampton and Bognor, away past the cottage and eventually fades into farmland a mile to the west.

A 'No Through Road' sign at the main road deters all but local traffic and in the 1940s, the only things we were likely to see passing the cottage were horses and carts, a very occasional tractor or motor car, the odd village dog or cat, a farm labourer on foot or a herd of cows, munching the verges as they moved in or out, four times a day, from the milking shed, situated in our old barn a hundred yards up the lane.

Father's family had farmed in Flansham since the mid-1830s, increasing their acreage and moving from being tenants to landowners progressively as the years rolled by. Before moving to Flansham they had lived and farmed nearby, at Rookery Farm, Pagham, since sometime before 1650 but were finally driven from that low-lying part of Sussex by severe flooding in the 1860s, when some two hundred acres were reclaimed by the sea and my great-grandfather, Alfred Adames, moved to Flansham to join his uncle, Ephraim in farming portions of the surrounding land.

Alfred himself took more interest in trading, and as soon as his eldest son, Owen, was old enough, he left the farming to him, concentrating his own efforts to his butchery and hostelry businesses in nearby Bognor. Owen, my grandfather, moved into the farmhouse, then known as Flansham Cottage, near Weller's Corner at the southeastern entrance to the settlement on his marriage to Ada Kimbell from Fishbourne in September 1904.

Mixing farming with his duties in the Sussex Yeomanry and a passion for hunting, in various forms, kept grandfather busy, although farming appears to have taken second place in his priorities. Most of the land grassland, as indeed it is today, although sheep, cows and horses were kept then, whereas today it is just cattle.

Owen involved himself in some rather casual early 'share farming' of sheep with a city-dwelling friend and, as with so many well-meaning joint ventures, they finished up in the High Court in London, fighting a long and expensive case which was never quite resolved. From my reading records of the case almost a century later, it appears to be an instance of over-enthusiasm and under-funding and when things became difficult the friendship faltered.

He also ran a fairly successful livery yard and horse-breeding operation which centred on hunters, and the then fashionable high-stepping 'hackneys' used for carriage work. We have many early photographs of these horses in family albums, but the most notable is of the stallion 'Admiral Togo', which Owen shipped to Japan to the Imperial Emperor's Palace in about 1908.

My grandfather Owen Adames, haymaking in Weller's field at Flansham c.1908.

*My great grandfather, Alfred Adames (left) outside his
butcher's shop in Bognor High Street c.1893.*

Hunting, however, was Owen's real passion and his reputation lived on for many years, particularly among a number of the 'side saddle' riders of the County, apparently, and especially those of the Goodwood and Charlton Hounds.

This then was the scene in which my Father grew up in the years around the Great War. 'Jack' (Owen Dennis) was born in 1906 at Flansham Cottage. A large and comfortable country house but one inadequately funded, and it was not long before the family moved to Chessels, a rather smaller house next door. It appears that Grandfather had realised that, with two sons (Alan followed in 1910) and a remarkably faithful wife, he had to knuckle down and earn a living before he spent it. At that time, during the dark days of the Great War, much of the local labour force had answered the call to arms and had gone off to be slaughtered in the muddy trenches of northern France, and times were hard for those left on the land. By the time Father was packed off to Steyning Grammar School, he had already learnt the rudiments of farming by hard experience and necessity, and was quite competent at hand-milking, horse-ploughing, 'stooking' corn, working a team of horses – and was an extremely competent horseman.

Indeed, all these experiences at such an early age, far from putting him off farming, made Jack excessively enthusiastic, to the extent that his schooling became the burden. By the age of sixteen both parents and masters had agreed that academia was not for the fast-growing young Jack, and he said goodbye to Steyning in 1922 just in time to save the bailiffs from moving in on the family holding since, despite his obvious charms, Owen senior had been going from one lifeline to the next, losing money as he went, and the farm was struggling to keep afloat.

Now, with all the enthusiasm of youth, Jack 'set-to' in an effort to turn things around. He became a fanatically hard worker, nothing was beyond his physical ability, and he quickly taught himself all the various aspects of farming. Already competent at horse and stockmanship, he learnt rudimentary veterinary skills and developed an extraordinary woodworking ability which was to give him much pleasure for the rest of his life.

These attributes, coupled with almost obsessive self-restraint and great perseverance, pulled the family through that crisis, and then for over 15 years of difficulties, he staved off the bailiffs and 'turned the corner' – only to be confronted by the 'depression' of the early 1930s!

The stallion 'Admiral Togo', shipped to the Emperor's Palace in Japan c.1908.

A rare family day out for Owen Adames and family, 1917.

For several hundred years Flansham had remained seemingly untouched by events. It shows on early maps, such as Will Gardener's and Thomas Yeakell's of 1778 as having some 15 dwellings and 5 groups of farm buildings, this being much on a par with the dozen or so dwellings that made up the nearby Great Bognor (which, in many people's eyes, would today be a better place had it remained thus).

The old King's reported deathbed remark "Bugger Bognor" really had some element of foresight about it, since in the past 50 years it has turned from a genteel Regency resort into something truly awful; buggered indeed! Flansham, too, has changed, but not so much that it cannot be recognised as that from which it primarily evolved; a farming settlement.

The quiet lane, forking at the village 'triangle', a small grass island, and the wandering dual routes out into the distant brooklands, passing through sunken lanes, quiet ponds and elm trees that have stood for hundreds of summers, are the same routes that our late resident local writer and historian, Gerard Young, surmised as being "trod by countless local smugglers as they ferried contraband to and from the coastal villages, to ships waiting off the coast at dark of night... As one passes these lanes (at night) you can still almost imagine you hear the muffled whispers of those adventurers of old."

The Flansham of the 1940s and of my youth, consisted of some 21 houses, only about 6 more than on the Gardner/Yeakell map, and all except two, including the wrecked 'The Retreat' that housed the local barn owls, were occupied by farm personnel. Of these, four were farm houses and the remainder farm cottages, the significance of this being that the central interest in the settlement was, purely and simply, agriculture. All the money coming into those dwellings emanated from the local farmland, and therefore the residents' loyalty and interests lay in the well-being of the village farms.

Crime and vandalism were almost unknown; apple scrumping and egg collecting from the free range fowl, being about the most serious offences committed by the local children, for which, if caught, instant justice was done, and 'felt' to be done – without recourse to 'legal action' and subsequent 'counselling' or court appearances.

The situation has altered over the years as agricultural labour needs, indeed stock farming, has dwindled; but then, in the forties, the hamlet's two working farms employed some 20 people between them. In most families, the husband,

Ada Owen at camp.

Ada, her sisters and crew after an emergency landing on the farm, 1912.

perhaps a tractor driver, carter or cowman, had his wife employed as calf-rearer or housemaid, and one or two sons as trainees, or labourers.

Our milking cows required the labours of foreman Mark Green, his son Walt and two other labourers, to tend the needs of some 30 cows. All this I knew later, but to us, as children at the time, life was very uncomplicated. Despite the lack of television until the late forties, there was never a dull moment. The farms were full of interesting things to explore, there were many village children to play with, and even then, at five to ten years old, we had many small tasks to do.

Amongst our favourite pastimes were the fish waiting to be tempted from the local waterway, the Ryebank Rife, with bent pins; a pastime that took hours of preparation; searching for a hazel rod of suitable length and flexibility to catch and hold the expected 'whopper'; for suitable cord or line, and the digging of worms as bait.

Often aided by father, my favourite spot for this was by the side of the old Weststone Bridge that crossed the Rife at the Flansham/Yapton boundary. It seems like only yesterday that we sat for hours in summer's fuzzy heat, swatting flies and aiming our hooks at some clear spot in the sea of duckweed and reeds, hoping for a catch. Actually, we never caught a fish; but what fun it was! The nearest we came to success was when scooping old jam jars in dwindling pools in an adjoining ditch and catching three or four sticklebacks and a tadpole. When I took these back to Mother and asked if she could cook them for my tea she refused; and suggested I take them back to the ditch so they could "grow into real fish" for another day.

In spring we went birds' nesting; our favourite being the Jackdaws nesting in the hollow trunks of the village's huge elm trees. The excitement of climbing into the high reaches was increased when we found a nest of eggs.

The Barn Owls in the loft of the milking shed were another objective. All through the summer strange noises would come from this huge roof space above the cows quarters, and the temptation to see the owl chicks regularly became too much. My best friend, during these formative years was a local village boy, Johnny Field, and he and I would scale the timbers into the darkness and wait until our eyes grew accustomed to the nearly pitch conditions before venturing to the back reaches of the loft. The owlets would be sitting there erect, their still weak legs thrust out before them, claws ready to impale any young hands unwise enough to reach out to touch them. As they followed

1935. As storm clouds gather overhead, Jack leads the team loading hay at Woodhill. Mark and Alan 'up'.

Foreman Mark Green and his son Walt, c.1930.

The Adames family at Chessels Farm, 1950. The Author, Gay, Betty, Jack and Peggy the Spaniel.

you with their huge black eyes, their heads would rotate up to almost 360°, and never did they blink. Meanwhile, the parent birds would be sitting quietly at the other end of the barn observing how their young would handle these silly young humans. Even as a child I thought these most stunningly beautiful birds had the intelligence of most humans, and I had far more respect for them than I think they did of us.

Johnny and I spent all our time together when school or bedtime allowed. For some five years we were inseparable as we dreamt of new adventures. Then, as the years moved on and we became strong enough to take on more regular work, Father found more than enough tasks to keep us occupied on the farm. By this time our childish innocence, and the pleasure of exploration of our surroundings and fellow creatures, was maturing, and the chance of working on machinery and, more importantly, earning a few shillings for the experience, took precedence in deciding how we spent our free time.

They were carefree years. None of the children in the village ever had a worry about strangers, neither did our parents, and we could roam as far and wide as we pleased, for as long as we liked, as long as we came home in the evening before dark. The girls too, friends of Gay, would play around the village, go out in the meadows to pick flowers, feed the calves and horses or just roam. There were always farm staff around the fields; they all knew the local children, and even if there had been any of today's strange perverted folk about, they would have had no chance of evading the sight of someone in the village. Happily of course there were none.

TOWARDS THE MIDDLE OF THE CENTURY

My Mother was born Winifred Elisabeth Goodacre at Barnham in 1912. The eldest child of Percy and Winifred Goodacre, she grew up in comfortable surroundings as the daughter of Barnham's largest employer. Grandfather was the general manager of Barnham Nurseries, a 300-acre fruit nursery, employing over 100 people at the time of the Great War, producing fruit and fruit trees for retail sale throughout Britain. Barnham Nurseries gave my mother a thorough horticultural background and a lifestyle and education few enjoyed at that time.

By the time Betty reached 20 she knew the common and botanical name for almost every plant cultivated and grown in England, indeed she always

Ploughman and wood plough.

Alan and Jack on the binder and aircraft above in a dogfight – 1940.

referred to the Latin name rather than the common name, expecting others to know it as well. After public school, business studies and a bit of journalism, she gave her skill as a tennis player a chance to bloom. In 1936 she spent the year in the USA, visiting her mother's émigré relatives, playing tennis and seeing the United States. That summer she won, amongst other things, the Montana State Ladies Singles Championship, the Mixed Doubles *and* the Ladies Doubles Championship. Fortunately for me, she narrowly avoided becoming an American bride.

On returning home that September, she became personal secretary to Lord Hardwicke at Dale Park before agreeing, in 1937, to marry a dashing local farmer, Jack Adames. The couple settled down in Flansham after their wedding in September 1938.

So it was that I was born, two weeks before the Declaration of War in August 1939, into a bleak and nervous National Emergency, which was to affect everyone's life for some six years, although to me, a tiny child living in the country, the war really meant nothing.

For country dwellers, rationing had little effect. Whilst there was not much variety, we were never hungry on the farms, a situation helped by nocturnal visits each winter by Walter Staff, the Yapton butcher. Walter came round in November each winter, in deadly secret, to kill a fat pig in time for Christmas. When distributed round the farm staff, it ensured that no family was short of meat, despite the restrictions and severe rationing in force at the time. This was done all over the countryside, although those involved knew it was a serious offence if caught. Secrecy was everything.

I was sometimes allowed to be present when Walter came round to do the deadly deed, and I remember, as a five-year-old, watching with a mixture of horror and fascination as old Mr Staff went about his bloody business, rapidly converting the luckless animal into a pile of neatly prepared joints of meat. The creature was stunned, bled and scalded, then the hairs were rubbed off the skin, leaving the body as smooth as a proverbial baby's bottom. I recall the deft way the butcher worked, and how every possible morsel was saved and used.

All the scraps were boiled down and hung in a muslin bag to set for a breakfast treat. Trotters were put aside for old Mark Green and his wife while the special cuts, the bacon and hams were set aside to be put into saltpetre for curing. Nothing would be wasted.

Within an hour or so of his arrival the whole carcase would be stacked in neat piles of prepared cuts, ready for distribution round the cottages. This was in the days before refrigerators and much speed was required to ensure that the precious meat was put in salt or into the cold rooms before it began to go 'off'.

I remember little of my first four years, but will recount a favourite family story that my mother told on many occasions. She had saved up precious, rationed ingredients to bake a cake in celebration of my first birthday. When the day finally came, several of her friends plus their infants came to the little party. We kids were playing on the lawn when, just before food was served on that August afternoon, and with the tables laid with sandwiches, jellies and the cake, the Air Raid Siren began to wail across the fields at Felpham. Another wave of German aircraft must be on its way to drop bombs in the area, something that happened regularly, since there were several RAF airfields close by.

My mother, then Betty Goodacre (third from left) before finals of ladies doubles, Great Falls Montana, 1936.

Our Mothers were well prepared. In connection with his role as Air Raid Precaution (ARP) Warden, Father had built a large air raid shelter in our front garden. Equipped with comfortable bunks and a cooking stove under two feet of concrete, it was capable of accommodating four adults.

At the sound of the siren, the Mothers carried us children hurriedly down into the shelter and made us safe by closing the heavy door, leaving the precious food remaining on the tables in the garden. I was too young to remember, but the heat, even allowing for the dampness of the earth around us, must have been stifling, and I am sure the 'all clear' would have come as a great relief. Everyone emerged sometime later into the sunlight to resume the party, to find that Peggy, Father's spaniel, had removed the birthday cake and left it half-eaten by the front door.

After all that effort to scrimp and save the precious ingredients and for the dog to be the only one to enjoy it, was too much for Mother and she burst into tears. In those times of rationing and self-denial it seemed worse to her than the air raid, since we were safely underground, and her disappointment never left her over the countless times and years she recounted this tale.

My little sister Gay was born towards the end of the war and her health problems caused Mother many visits to London hospitals from a very early age. This made life quite difficult for the family, and whilst Father worked all day at farming and nights at security work with the ARP, tensions within the family were causing some problems.

It is not easy for young children to understand such things, but clearly there was not much holding my parents together after the end of the war, except the presence of Gay and myself. Father worked and worried himself into terrible moods when, for days, he wouldn't speak to anyone and only years later did I learn that my parents' finances were very strained at the time. Although Mother had put most of her own money into the farm, bad luck usually seemed to dog Father's efforts, which was strange because when he had stepped in years earlier to save the business from his Father, he had succeeded admirably through sheer hard graft. Unfortunately, the same thing wasn't happening now and life was really a struggle.

This put increased pressure on my parents' relationship, but Mother's constantly even temper, understanding and reason was in marked contrast to Father's moodiness. The family stayed together and through those early years the only thing I later realised I had really missed was any semblance of an understanding and close relationship with my father. However, I did from the earliest days have the utmost respect for his work ethic, and his self-taught skills in so many rural subjects impressed me from a very early age.

His handcrafting was amazing to behold, and nothing in the line of machinery development and repairs was beyond him. If a tool or piece of equipment was needed to do a job in some new farming concept, as agricultural mechanisation grew after the War, he could make it. He would work as blacksmith, carpenter, electrician, plumber, bricklayer or whatever. The strangest components would be retrieved from the dark recesses of some shed and within hours would be incorporated into some fantastic device. To his credit, they almost always did the job they were designed for, and indeed one or two of the more durable items are still functional today, some fifty years later.

We alas, as father and son, always found it difficult, impossible even, to relate to any topic other than farm issues, and even this was to become increasingly hard as I later grew more aware of business matters.

It was particularly difficult for Gay and me to see how hard, mentally, he was on our Mother, never physically, but the mental drain on Mother was huge. To escape this she involved herself in many diverse interests. They came, and in time most passed, yet always she excelled until she became bored and sought something else. One of her favourite interests was flower arranging. Always talented at this, she quickly became one of the country's leading flower arranging demonstrators who, along with the likes of Constance Spry and Julia Clements, moved flower arranging to the forefront of popular art forms. Travelling with her 'props' she was away for days on end, demonstrating her craft to thousands of ladies (and sometimes amid general surprise at that time, to men) in Village Halls, Theatres and National Centres across the country.

In the early Fifties she inaugurated flower arranging competitions at the County Agriculture Show and at the same time, with her cousin Daphne Bissett, began the still thriving West Sussex and Felpham Flower Clubs.

A highlight of this period was when she orchestrated the floral arrangements at the Festival of Flowers at Chichester Cathedral, and was very proud to be introduced to Her Majesty the Queen. After such events she would come home intellectually refreshed, ready for the next dose of Father's depression, which inevitably came.

In later years, bridge, gardening and golf were to fill her time, and as I grew up and became a teenager I realised what an amazing feat she had accomplished in keeping us together as a family. I feel certain that, had she moved out of the family home, I would either have gone with her or left to make my own way in the world, but fortunately, this situation was never to arise.

My paternal grandparents lived up to this period in the house that is today my home. Grandfather built it in 1926 when he sold Chessels, the old farm house for Chessels Farm, for a reason nobody ever explained to me. Most probably, he received an offer that could not be refused or, perhaps, the house needed a lot of work done on it.

The family moved into a new house, 150 yards further up the lane, calling it 'Barncroft'. It was built at the great cost of £1,530 to Grandfather's specifications. At about the same time, his sons Jack and Alan, who between them increasingly ran the Flansham farm, also became heavily involved in a new farm, rented from Capt. James Kitson. This was Black Barn Farm at Madehurst, near Arundel, eight miles north of Flansham on the top of the South Downs.

My grandfather Owen, who had suffered from angina since the late 1930s, died in November 1946, leaving Grandmother Ada the ownership of the farms and the two brothers the responsibility of running them.

Alan had married Betty Page, a local girl, whose father had bought Chessels before the war. Betty worked on the farm as a land girl during the war before marrying Alan, who had led a pretty wild life, 'living for the day'. They moved to Black Barn Farm to run it themselves. Under trained, with regard to financial acumen, and under-financed, Alan struggled for a number of years, with too few cows, a dozen pigs and a few chickens. Unfortunately, he had allowed Betty to firstly buy, and then keep her own racehorse on the farm – a jumper named 'Battle School' which, I seem to remember, actually won one race but bankrupted the farm and soured any future relationship between my father and his sister-in-law, Betty.

The reasons for this rift were never discussed by Father, but it seems that on one cold winter's day he had gone to Madehurst to help Alan out, only to find several of the milking cows hungry and shivering outside in a snow-covered meadow, whilst 'Battle School', well rugged-up, stood in deep straw in the cows' quarters. My understanding is that Father turned the horse out and got the milking animals into the barn with the words to Alan, "Tell your wife the cows earn the money for her horse to lose!" Any other stockman in that situation would, I think, have done the same. Anyway, the horse went soon after, as did Betty and their little girl Linda, never to return. I believe Father felt a bit guilty that he may have been instrumental in the break-up, but it would surely have happened in time, with or without his involvement.

By that time, around 1950, the damage, as far as Alan and Black Barn Farm were concerned, was done. Repayments on debts incurred by Alan, couldn't be met, and Father had to step in before Captain Kitson, growing concerned at the state of the farm, threw Alan out of the tenancy. These debts had been accruing, unknown to Father, for several years and when the split came, two other major loans – major in 1950s terms at least – also came to light.

Father, despite his quiet moodiness, was honourable; he had always had a conscience and felt a responsibility for his younger brother. He therefore resolved to settle Alan's debts in exchange for his interest in their dwindling assets at the farm. With family agreement, he did this promptly, and taking out bank loans, he squared the creditors and set about making the farm earn money again. Needless to say, all this did nothing for his black moods and the air could almost be cut with a knife.

By putting more cows on the farm and engaging a Welsh foreman-cum-herdsman, Cyril Thomas, things improved again, and shortly afterwards Captain Kitson thankfully agreed to Father taking back the tenancy in his own name, so for the next few years Jack ran the two farms, whilst Alan flitted from one deal to the next. And I grew up.

With Grandfather now dead, the decision was made for Granny Ada to move into our little cottage, Lynton Cottage, and we changed places and moved into Barncroft. The operation was carried out in February 1948, the year of the snows, and I well remember the farm staff struggling to move furniture on farm trailers in both directions in driving rain which, as the day went on, turned to freezing snow. Shuttling between the two houses with open trailers, open doors and without central heating, everyone was dejected and frozen solid. Eventually, the final door shut behind the last of the belongings and Grandmother, with her niece Nancy as companion, settled in at the cottage, as did Father, Mother, Gay and I in our new home in the main house.

Mother now had an acre of garden to re-design, relations between my parents were a bit easier, and consequently life was easier for Gay and me, although, perhaps not surprisingly, Gay was never as aware of the tension as I was. The fact she was a girl, maybe, made the old man a little softer in his relationship with her and she didn't see, or was not old enough to feel any pressure.

WEANING TIME

In 1948, the time had come to get me off to another environment – Boarding School – and little did I know how my life was going to change. On that fateful September day, we all loaded ourselves into Father's old Vauxhall for the journey to Nuthurst, near Horsham, to the chosen educational establishment, Gaveston Hall. Run by the vicar of Nuthurst Dr Gibson, this Victorian pile made an instant impression on me, and it was not a good one. The food was typical, I see now, of the period, still wartime rations and badly cooked. The

Happier days. Alan 'Buckle' Adames and new wife Betty leaving Felpham church on their wedding day in 1945. The author is seated next to the groom. Gerry Young and Jack Adames stand at the back of the

regimentation rankled with an independent nine-year-old and I was not used to being bullied.

The first term was best forgotten. I hated them, they hated me and it was hell; probably for the teachers too. On my rare weekend leaves I threw tantrums and refused to go back, but always failed.

Time passed very slowly, but by the following year I had begun to learn the ropes and the bullies had laid off, which made things a little more bearable, although I was already put off 'Church going' on a regular basis for life, by the constant marching to and from either school chapel, or Sunday Service at Nuthurst church. Marching in crocodile for over a mile in all weathers didn't appeal – nor did the fact that they gave us our 'tuck' money on Saturdays on the clear understanding that it was to go into the Church collection on Sunday. I think a good many buttons finished up on the offertory plate.

Things began to look up considerably, however by Summer Term, when I was introduced to cricket for the first time. In that distant summer, when reports of Dennis Compton and Don Bradman filled every newspaper, we were being taught the rudiments of the game.

The school had a good pitch, with a well maintained square, and I suddenly realised Gaveston wasn't all bad. Every single spare moment was spent bowling and batting. Every evening when I wasn't on some petty punishment or other, I stretched my back and tried to copy Ray Lindwall. By this time I was growing fast and had already become stronger than many of my age, probably aided by helping on the farm at home. This gave me added power to hurl the ball down or throw from the outfield; how I loved it.

After that wonderful summer, school never seemed quite so awful! I had played in a few under-10 matches against other local boarding schools and, even at that age, being in the 'cricket team' meant something amongst your classmates; and helped my self-confidence quite a bit. There was also a hard tennis court and acres of woods and streams where we could play and wander almost at will, so for many hours a week school work, as such, could be cast to the back of our minds and my days passed much more easily.

I had some pretty close shaves, with many canings and slipperings, and escaped expulsion by the skin of my teeth a couple of times for pretty mild pranks. Sadly, inexperience stopped me being found in bed with Matron, although she was quite attractive, and supervised our bath time! Nor were drinks or drugs a problem in those post war years.

On one memorable occasion I was sent to see a child psychologist, since I was deemed to be such a rebel, after Doc Gibson had told Mother, "It must be a mental disorder." I well remember my parents' anguish at the news and also their mirth when the psychologists' report said he found me to be "particularly sensible and mature for my age." I must have had an off day! Many years later Mother had confided in me that it was the best school report they had ever received about me.

The whole problem, in retrospect, was probably that the teachers, at that time, looked for pupils to conform, to give themselves an easy life. Only recently has there been some acceptance that children are different personalities and that those who don't always conform should be, within reason, welcomed and encouraged. Schools in the 40s and 50s were not so enlightened, although certainly more disciplined.

Over the next three or four years I settled into boarding school life, probably no more painfully than many others at the time. I don't think the calibre of our teachers helped over-much, but once or twice, quite enlightened tutors arrived and for a term or two I quite enjoyed my education. The only two things, apart from sport, I really learned were geography and how to set out and write a letter.

The History teacher, Miss Theresa Noble – no spring chicken and with her right index finger missing – used to supervise letter-writing on Sunday afternoons. Not only did she make us write and spell properly, but she insisted on the setting up of margins and paragraphs and in giving the letter, in her words, 'form'. To round it off she read every letter, in case, presumably, we were telling tales of harsh treatment; quite blatant censorship. When we failed to come up to her standards she would stand and waggle her stumpy finger at us admonishingly. In return we were very cruel to Miss Noble, yet when one sees the standards of letter writing today, perhaps she didn't do a bad job.

Then, in the summer of 1953, the day came for Gaveston Hall, Dr Gibson and I to part company. When my parents arrived, the Head came to say his last few words to us and wished them luck.

"He's very stubborn and he's learnt nothing of much use... Except he can bowl fast," he told them, and then with evident relief he bade me farewell. Feelings were mutual that my days there were at an end. If these had indeed been the 'best days of my life', then surely I did not have much to look forward to! However, his summary of my educational achievements had depressed my parents, particularly my Mother, whose education and intelligence made her stand out in a crowd. All thoughts of any further expensive education for their only son were now forgotten.

A place was found for me at a local "crammer" run by an old friend of my grandmother, Doctor Eugene Horsfall Ertz, in nearby Felpham. Dr Ertz was a charming, rather eccentric, but highly educated man. His control over his 'hotch potch' of pupils was, however, pretty lax, and with the farm only five minutes away, my academic side was still rather neglected until, in the summer of 1956, my formal education ended. We all just had to accept that I was, educationally speaking, brain dead; fit to drive a tractor, milk a cow or trim a hedge, but beyond that a lost cause. Native cunning would have to be my salvation and, indeed, that mixed with a fair helping of inherited common sense, was all I had to show for eleven years of schooling. There was no 'gap-year' sabbatical; no 'round-the-world' reward for my 'efforts'; not even a day passed before I was on a wage at the farm, expected to work a 48-hour week plus as much overtime as might be needed.

My first day out from Gaveston Hall – a picnic with the family, 1948.

One of the very last things Johnny and I did as youngsters, before work took over full time, had been a few years earlier in the very wet winter of 1953. It had been raining for weeks and Flansham Brooks, a huge belt of some 1,000 straggly acres alongside the Rife, acting as a boundary between Flansham and villages to the north and west, flooded fast. The floods stretched for over a mile and all that showed above the lapping water were the tops of hedges and trees and the odd fence post.

Johnny and I just had to explore the possibilities, so down the old green lane we went. Not far past the Langmead's farmyard, all land ceased, and where normally the track turned down towards the brooks, the rising waters now surrounded us. Looking for adventure, we soon found an old bathtub, used as a drinking trough for cattle during the summer, which usually lay in a nearby corner. This bath was already bobbing at the waters' edge and looked, to us two young adventurers, like a galleon fit to sail the world, so after finding two lengths of timber in a nearby fence, but with no further comforts, we bravely set off.

The bathtub grounded a few times as we pushed it down the submerged lane, but within a short distance and with Wellingtons now full of water, I jumped in, allowing Johnny to get his feet wet for a bit longer. The bath floated quite well with me as ballast, so Johnny passed in the 'oars' and jumped aboard himself. Now we were on our way, kneeling, and with one of us paddling on either side we soon reached the end of the lane and passed through the open gateway into Little Brook. Here an 'open sea' awaited us. So far the 'boat' was brilliant and we pushed forward another three hundred yards northwards with the water a constant two feet beneath the 'plughole' and a clear wake following behind us. No sharks, but deeper waters lay ahead.

Within five minutes or so we were at the Rife, treacherously muddy at all times, and a danger we children had been warned of even at normal times. Should we cross it? Those parental warnings concerned us, but neither of us wanted to suggest turning back, so preparing ourselves, we pushed over the fence wires bordering the waterway, and with a good shove we were on our way. Now our punting poles touched no earth, the water beneath us a good eight feet deep. We drifted and paddled and after what seemed an age we were across the Rife and on 'foreign' soil. Our village was behind us and we pushed our 'boat' towards the distant shores of Barnham, some half a mile away.

Some time later we struck a raised bank beneath the water; the tub grounded and rocked, but with a good push we soon started moving again, and shortly afterwards made our landfall on Mr John Ellis's land at the south end of Drove Lane, Yapton. Here we rested and took stock of our progress. Then, as we again pushed on, it dawned on us that it was getting late and that we were growing weary. On top of that it was raining hard again and nobody in the whole world knew where we were!

Soon after this we both agreed it was time to abandon this great adventure – we had come in our bath almost three quarters of a mile, across fence, hedge, ditch and farmland. Home really seemed a continent away and it would be dark in less than an hour. Slightly desperate now to end our trip, we searched for the quickest way out. Should we head north and walk to a neighbouring farmhouse and ask Mrs Loveys to ring home for a lift; or head for the nearest land to the south in Flansham, not where the bath belonged but on home soil? This latter seemed the most face-saving option and crossing the Rife again, whilst dangerous, seemed better than Father knowing what we had been doing via Colin or Anne Loveys the next time they met.

As a wet afternoon turned into a blackening twilight we ran aground on Langmead's land at Hoe's Farm. We turned the bath on its side, so it wouldn't float off and then trudged, soaked, very tired, yet elated, the half mile homewards. At the farm entrance I bid Johnny "good night". As I did, Father and his neighbour Jack Langmead came down the lane.

"You boys want to get in the dry. The lane's flooding and it's going to be treacherous out tonight," said Father.

"Yes Dad," I replied innocently.

We never dared mention what we had done that day and never had time to complete our 'voyage'. The following spring, the bathtub still lay on its side in the field where we had left it and no-one but us ever knew of the adventure it had seen. Within a very short time, Johnny and I began to grow into young adults, with no time for further such escapades, but that bathtub lay in the same spot for the next 25 years and whenever I saw it lying there in the hedge, it brought back fond memories of my little adventure with Johnny Field.

My first task as a wage earner in the autumn of 1956 sticks in my memory. It involved cutting down a large boundary hedge beside a deep ditch on the southern side of the home meadow. The hedge, still there today, mainly consisted then of hawthorn, hazel, elder, ash and brambles. It was fully mature and the only tools to help us were axes, a bow saw, a large (hand-operated) crosscut saw and long-handled hooks. Anyone familiar with such tools will appreciate the effort needed to accomplish our task of felling and trimming the hedge. Having first removed all timber suitable for the farm fires, we then had to cut up the remnants before dragging them by hand to form huge bonfires. The hedge ran for some 350 yards and the work took Johnny, Percy Large and myself the whole autumn and winter to complete before we re-fenced the ditch prior to spring turnout of the livestock. In between, we did the thousand and one other routine jobs that constantly arise on a mixed farm (as it was then). Finally, when the place was tidy, all the logs were stacked on trailers and carted to the wood-yard by the farmhouse to season awhile before cutting on the circular saw for next winter's house fires.

Between times we had forty cows to clean and bed up, relief milking, thirty sows and their litters to attend to – and then there was the hill farm at Madehurst, demanding much work to tidy up after years of neglect.

The work was hard and unremitting through all seasons, but Johnny and I were both very strong and were growing fast into young men. We had already been taught what hard work was and had the work ethic well installed. Fortunately, neither we nor any of the farm hands knew of any machinery that might provide a less laborious way to accomplish our tasks; so we just got on with it. At that time they, and we, knew no better; machinery had not yet been developed to do the hard work beyond ploughing and cultivation and not knowing what was to come, made it easier to continue with the hard graft.

Had machines been available, there certainly would have been no way that workers would have continued to toil so hard. In later years, as soon as a particular job was mechanised and the new machinery was to be seen working in the neighbourhood, the word spread fast. Woe betide any farmer who didn't equip with it quickly; it would not be many weeks before he would be advertising in the *West Sussex Gazette* for new men.

Ironically, as the modern 'Agricultural Revolution' gathered momentum it was often he who benefited most by being released from his laborious tasks who was then pretty soon, in the words of a famous politician, 'on his bike'. There was to be no room for an expensive item of machinery *and* a man no longer fully employed.

Seasons changed, so it always seemed, just in time to stop jobs becoming a real chore. Just as the long winter drudge of short days, mud and cold had begun to feel like a prison sentence, the work would suddenly change. On early March days, the chain harrows would, one evening, be out on the meadows. Soon afterwards we would be setting off for long days at the chalkland farm to begin the task of drilling the spring corn.

Each morning after the animals were tended, our packed lunches would be collected from the farmhouse and we would be off by car or tractor for the eight mile trip to Madehurst. We lads would then spend countless hours bouncing along on the cold seats of the great paraffin-fuelled Fordson Majors, sitting exposed to the elements, wrapped up against the strong winds and snow flurries as the tractors chugged endlessly across the open downland. At least it was a change from the work we had suffered for the past winter months, and we loved it. In those days, March seemed, to the memory at least, to have been much colder and drier and chalk dust would cover us and our machines for days as we set about our tasks of ploughing, rolling discing and drilling. All took their turn until the farm was planted. We became competent operators in short time, having both been driving tractors and the farm jeeps for some years. We were now the 'main men'.

Some of my happiest memories are of those now distant days: of sitting half frozen, despite layers of sweaters and coats, on those old machines; of the billowing dust following us; of white puffy clouds in the sky and often brilliant sunshine promising coming spring warmth; of the peewits, wheeling and crying around us as they prepared to mate and nest out on the newly cultivated hillsides, and skylarks twittering high above us, filling the air with their song.

March hares, too, caught our eye with their early spring antics, while deer would be regularly spotted darting from the woodland if we approached too close.

The old saying, 'a peck of dust in March being worth a King's ransom' indeed made good sense. When the dry dust blew, the machinery ran clean and well, seeds could be worked into well-cultivated seed beds, firmed up with gang rollers and all tasks completed in good time.

Work went on apace from early morning until the lengthening twilight forced us to stop. Then we returned the tractors to the cart shed, turned them off, covered the radiators with sacks against the frost, and returned to Flansham to feed the pigs, perhaps farrow a sow or help Freddy the new herdsman calve a cow, before we could knock off for a welcome evening meal.

As the days lengthened, so we worked later and indeed started earlier. Apart from cultivating cereals at Madehurst, looking after the grassland at Flansham and tending the stock themselves, we grew a large acreage of roots, both fodder beet and mangolds, and these demanded hand hoeing twice. First it was necessary to 'set out' the plants, chopping out surplus to allow each root some eight inches of clear space to grow, and then some time later, to run through and 'second' them. Chopping out any doubles left by mistake and cutting out the second growth of weeds. This was before the days of monogerm seeds and herbicides and was extremely laborious work. (With 'mono' seeds, a drill can place a prepared single seed in the ground at exactly the required spacing before the sprayer runs across the land with a selective chemical to suppress all unwanted weed germination.)

Hand-hoeing was a drudge, where, bent double in lines, the gang would slowly pass up and down the rows working their way slowly across the crop. All available spare hands, often itinerant Irish travellers, would be roped in. Anyone looking to earn a few shillings, and who could stand the backache, was welcome to try!

Some of the old farm hands had, over many years, developed a routine, a steady speed of work and a deft hoe action to make the work bearable. They called regular stops for fag breaks, but there was not much chat. Neither Johnny or I smoked, and to us these breaks, whilst welcome, seemed almost as tiring as the hoeing, as we stood and contemplated yet another row across the field.

It soon became obvious to me that the only way to get the job done before the crop and the weeds overtook us was for father to agree to pay us at 'piece work' rates. A set price for an agreed area, rather than by the hour. This way there would be a real incentive for us to get on and have the work finished. With some reluctance over the next few days Father finally saw the point. At least he would now know what the cost would be and he could see that at the speed the work was going, the crop would be half useless by the time it was finished. I think the going rate was about £11 an acre (roughly some two weeks pay then) which was to us a fortune. Currently we lads were working for about £4.10/- a week plus 1/11d an hour overtime.

Suddenly we were fully motivated. We each marked out our 'pitch' so we knew exactly the area we had to hoe, and set to. To avoid the heat of the sun on our shirtless backs, already the colour of ebony from a hot late spring, we chose to hoe early and late. Starting at dawn (about 4.30am) we worked through until breakfast time at nine. Then other work filled the day until we began hoeing again after tea at about six, and carried on until we could no longer see the plants at around nine thirty. The job, in truth, was no easier; in fact was a real bitch, but now we were earning a man's rate, plus our money on the farm during the day, it made us feel a lot better. Father got his roots hoed, we got our money and the crop looked well.

When it came a week or so later to start seconding the crop, we had no trouble negotiating a fair rate, and with the help of a few local lads we completed the work in double quick time.

Now, thankfully, the season changed again, this time to high summer. Hoeing was behind us, haymaking and harvest called, both operations very tiring but at least another change. In the meantime I set out to persuade Father that the farm could do without these root crops, or that, if he must have them, it would be cheaper to purchase them in the autumn from a nearby specialist grower, who could deliver the right quality by the load to our farm for less that we could grow them ourselves. I am not sure that they would have been cheaper, but after that year we relied less on roots and grew more kale for the cattle. It was a little easier to grow and also provided excellent cover for game birds.

THE OLD HANDS LEAVE

Remember, this was the mid 1950s, machinery was slowly coming onto the farms but there were still a lot of farm workers around, old hands, whose families had been working for the village farmers for generations, who knew no other work and who were dependent on their tied cottages and the low wages they earned. A major upheaval was about to occur that would change the balance of the countryside for ever – and not, ultimately, for the better.

Every new tractor replaced a horse's work but also probably replaced a man. In 1950, my father employed some 16 hands in the course of the year. These would include some five milkers, who tended to all the needs of the cows, three carters and three tractor drivers, plus two full-time labourers, known as 'general farm workers', who also were supplemented, between November and February, with another three casual hands, operating the recently-acquired threshing drum and baler, and working as a gang on neighbouring farms.

A tractor man earned somewhere around £6 a week, less rent (if he had a house) of 5 shillings. The stockmen averaged around £4.10s and the labourers and casual men a bit less. With Father's earnings of £8 added in, the total wage bill at peak times was some £55-£65 – a sum he was constantly seeking to contain but which was keeping some 10 families in good conditions (at least by the standards of that time) and with a dry roof over their heads. Each house had a garden and each garden provided vegetables, eggs, chicken and often pork for the family.

None of the men had cars, a few wives worked in service, and nearby shops catered for their basic needs. Transport was by foot or by bicycle, but there was little need or time to travel out of the village since most of the daylight hours were spent at work.

The gardens were the main hobby for any spare evenings or Sundays, perhaps too, some ferreting or beating for the Saturday shoot during the winter months. On Saturday nights, the 'Southdowns' pub, three quarters of a mile towards Bognor, was sometimes visited. At the pub, gossip would be shared with Langmead's men and the wives would sit together discussing the latest fashions, recipes seen in 'Women's Own' or how the children were progressing at school.

Langmead's rotund foreman, Ben Welch, had an advantage over the others in as much as he earned a few extra shillings a week for his responsibilities and also owned a bike, so he was in the pub almost every evening and was something of a celebrity, locally at least, partly because of the trials he had in guiding his bike back from the Southdowns to his home after the odd extra pint of beer.

If any of the families had a holiday together, it would probably involve staying with relatives, although more likely they just spent the time at home. Many of the men in those days had never travelled beyond Littlehampton or Chichester, some 8 miles – apart from those who had served in the war in Army or Navy, but since farm workers had been needed to produce food for the beleaguered population, not that many had joined up.

My memory of those families was that, almost without exception, their children were always clean and well clothed. They went to the local school in uniform, or at least jacket and tie and clean trousers and they all looked healthy. What's more, they knew how to behave towards other people's property and, apart from a bit of local mischief, for which PC Luck would soon clip their ear, I can only ever remember one family regularly coming before the local bench. Remarkably, all this was achieved on less than £5 a week coming into the household; a little more if wife or sons were also in work.

When they retired or were displaced by machinery they moved into the towns for employment and soon resettled. To this day many of the families are still well respected locally in their new walks of life, with no obvious handicap from their hard origins. Many remain good friends with those of us still left on the land.

Land Girls hoeing mangolds by hand.

And so through the Fifties, the shedding of farm labour gathered pace. Faces I had grown up with were suddenly, one week, not there and as time went by the countryside echoed less and less with the shouts of "whoa" and "stand on" as carters worked their horses; of gangs of men chatting as they worked; of villagers talking of the latest local news as they passed in the lane at dusk; and the fields instead clattered increasingly with machinery.

So now, around the middle of the 1950s, I forgot school and settled into learning 'the trade'. We at Chessels Farm still had several staff, around five, and little machinery apart from tractors, a few converted farm carts and a new labour-saving muckspreader.

However our working lives continued to be hard, with long hours and no question in our minds that work came first, second and third. There was, and indeed still is, always something to do on the farm, as there is in a garden, and as 'the old man' could always find something for us to do there was little chance for 'idle hands' to make mischief.

SPORT STARTS IN EARNEST

I still fondly remembered the Cricket at Gaveston Hall, and as early spring turned into warmer evenings in 1955, Mother, seeing 'all work and no play' suggested that I go down to the local Sports Club at Middleton to see if I could play some cricket. This was easier said than done for a shy youth with little experience of anything other than farm staff and farm talk. How could I break in to the tight sporting circle that existed in those days? Luckily, our neighbour, Jack Langmead, had two sons and a daughter, Ian, Don and Juliet. Although a few years older than me, they had known me since birth and, being members of the club themselves, were in a position to help me.

Jack, then in his early 50s, was an accomplished sportsman, rather in the mould of the 'Corinthians'. Before sponsorship and big money prizes turned sport from fun into business, he had played for Sussex in six or seven different sports – including cricket, tennis, squash, ice hockey and golf – and with the reputation and friends he had gathered, he was a useful man to 'open doors' for a youngster.

Finding the time was actually the hard part, but Mother made things a little easier by putting in the odd word to the 'old man'. Consequently, I was able to slip off for the weekly 'nets' and to become 'known' at the Middleton

Sports Club. Before too long, I was given a game in the infamous 'A' team, which had a bigger reputation for 'apres match' activities than on the playing field, although the game was nevertheless taken very seriously while it lasted. Here my training at Gaveston came to my aid. Increasingly, I was tossed the ball as 'first change' and put in for a few quick overs with varying degrees of success. Every Sunday, when work permitted, I travelled with the 'A' team around West Sussex, mainly to little villages in the Downs, Slindon, Amberley, Pulborough, Stanstead Park, Findon, Lavant and a lot more in between.

By the following summer, 1956, I was trusted enough to open the bowling, despite disparaging comments from some of the senior members. In particular, I had to put up with constant abusive and droll repartee from Gerry Kunz (son of the famous pianist, Charlie) who teased me unmercifully. Initially this took some 'standing', but by the time three or four matches were behind us and a few wickets were in the bag, I felt confident enough to return his 'compliments' and we became firm friends, and indeed remain so some 45 years later.

Middleton was a starting point for many famous careers and was also an August venue for many high quality games with international-standard players attracted by the likes of Jack Langmead, Billy Griffiths (the ex-England wicket keeper), Peter Rushton, the Doggarts and many other senior players at County level.

Towards the end of my second season, in August 1957, we were joined in the 'A' team by a quiet young man, dark haired and studious, who was, at a guess, about 15 years old. I had just passed my driving test and, naturally keen to drive, was asked to pick up this 'youngster', at least 2 years my junior, for the match. The boy had already made quite a reputation as a bat in Public school cricket and scored many runs for Middleton during that summer month before he and his family left their seaside house and returned inland. Twenty-three years or so later he became famous as the only English Captain able to harness the talent of Ian Botham. Our young team mates' name? Michael Brearley, of course.

My, we had fun in the A team. We still meet from time to time and usually one match is discussed before all others. Findon '57. Findon, who for some reason Middleton hadn't played for years, was a new venue to most of us, so when the fixture was arranged, Findon seemed to think Middleton were going to turn out in full strength. Griffiths, Langridge, Langmead, etc. When our somewhat shambolic cavalcade began arriving at their ground above Worthing, the hosts looked questioningly; where were the stars? When they realised that what they saw was just what they were getting, in other words, no more than the A team, they were not amused.

They were impressed even less when, after being tossed the ball to open the bowling on their sloping pitch, I opened with three fast balls that whistled five yards wide and down-hill of my good friend Peter Brazier, the demon keeper. Two went for four wides. Twelve balls later the over ended, to huge amusement and comment, particularly from Kunz, but the best thing about the day was that, some five hours later, Middleton A had held one of the strongest clubs in Sussex to a draw. We never played there again, but have never forgotten that day.

On another occasion that summer we took ourselves to Wisborough Green, to their lovely pitch in the heart of the renowned and beautiful village. Another strong popular team, they often had County players making regular Sunday appearances for them; this was of course before the counties played on Sundays, and on this day we had a special thrill.

Opening the batting was a lithe, dark, handsome young man, wielding the bat with supreme skill and timing. Bowling at him, I watched in awe as he

Mechanisation comes to the Adames family farms. The author driving a Fordson tractor, drilling Barley in 1955. Jack Adames on the drill.

picked the quicker balls and despatched them to all parts before I was, thankfully, removed from the attack. The Nawab of Patandi, 'Tiger', later went on to great things, captaining his country, India, with great flair, panache and acclaim.

After all these matches our senior team members natural skill and ability at the bar came to the fore and, learning fast, I seldom remembered the drive home. In those days alcohol was something we learnt to handle rather than avoid, and we never lost a player. If stopped for some reason the Constable would just say something like "now then young man, just give the Spur (or Royal Oak) a miss and drive slowly." Today we would not be treated so leniently.

The A team taught me a lot about growing up, quite fast, how to handle a drink and even a girl, of which the Club counted many. When the Summer ended it had also made clear to 'the old man' that farming, whilst being my number one priority was going to have to share some time with sport. He was not whole-heartedly enthusiastic, but accepted it. Mother on the other hand appeared to be delighted.

THE TENNIS COURT

From time to time during the fifties I had attempted to play tennis at various venues, often on private grass courts belonging to family friends and although my enthusiasm far outreached my ability I quickly fell in love with playing on a lawn. Compared to hard courts it was a different game but sadly the opportunities to play were few since everyone else seemingly felt the same way and spare courts were hard to find.

In the winter of 1955 when I was sixteen and with the help of Peter Pratt, who with his parents had moved into the hamlet a year or two before, I had decided to build a grass court behind the farmhouse at Flansham. There had been two choices of site, the ideal one being a paddock that adjoined the farm drive to the east of the house. This paddock was about three-quarters of an acre, running north south and was both flat, and sheltered by large elms. The snag was that, apart from the junk it accumulated, Father sometimes used it as a chicken pen or for odd animals and was reluctant to give it up to such a hare-brained idea. The alternative site was in the home meadow, where a small spinney bounded the garden on its southern boundary. By siting the court east/west, close to the garden, there would be little lost ground and besides, I suppose Father thought we would probably lose interest half way through, so we were given the go ahead.

It was clearly going to be a challenge, if only because almost every aspect of the job would have to be done by hand. There was little mechanical assistance available at the time but since the meadow was grazed tight from the previous autumn we were able to run the 12 inch garden mower across the area without too much effort. So in our spare time we mowed and fenced off an area large enough to give us plenty of side and back court space and allow for fencing and hedging outside the netted area.

By mid-March the grass was mown and the site safely cattle fenced, and despite the regular, "You must be mad – I've got far more useful things for you to do," from the Old Man, Peter and I began the hard work. We had already cleared the site of all weeds and obstructions and now we had to remove the tightly mown turf before we could level the natural fall to the south. We approached Peter's father, Cliff Pratt, who we knew had a superb shiny unused turfing iron hanging in his shed up the lane. On threat of awful things if we didn't clean and oil it every evening, we borrowed it and then began removing the first of some 1,700, 3ft x 1ft slices of turf. Previously, we had squared and marked the lines to cut and as we became more skilled with the tool, the area of newly de-turfed ground grew rapidly. Every spare moment one or both of us would be bent over either cutting turves or lifting and rolling them, then stacking the rolls alongside the site for storage.

We worked relentlessly. The steel blade would be inserted at about one inch below the surface and pushed firmly forward through the moist soil. It travelled like a knife through cheese and at times it was all stacker/roller could do to keep up with the cutter, but as we moved across the site, a wheelbarrow was employed to save journeys. Within about ten days the whole site had been cleared and huge rows of rolled turf stretched along each side of the future court. On one occasion we even set up a large light, hung on a branch, so we could work on into the night, such was our enthusiasm to complete the task.

Once the site was clear I used a tractor, with a three furrow plough, and, starting on the southwestern end, began ploughing the whole area towards the south, the lowest side, loosening the top ten inches ready for levelling.

We then harrowed the soil down to a firm fine tilth before again resorting to manual labour to level the surface. Initial levelling was done with a spirit level, wooden pegs and a length of timber as 'straight edge'. We knocked in pegs to signify the final level of the soil, prior to turfing.

Somehow, by starting this levelling in the middle of the area, we had worked out that what soil was removed from the topside would be just about the right amount to fill the lower side and, amazingly, about a week later that proved a good guess.

We had effectively lowered the north side by about ten inches and raised the lower side by a similar amount. We never stopped to work out the volume of soil we had pushed around on the barrow, or raked across the surface; but by the middle of April we were ready to begin re-laying those 1,700 yellowing turves onto a smooth, flat surface.

Every turf was bedded in and banged down with a home made 'rammer', a round log nailed on a handle, and checked with the spirit level. Quite rapidly the newly-grassed area grew, whilst Peter and I began thinking of coming matches on what was already our pride and joy. It is really amazing what one is able to do with enthusiasm, a will and endless energy.

By the last week of April the final sod was pressed into place and we were able to contemplate less strenuous tasks like raking in tons of sand and endless hand rolling before, in a couple of weeks, the mower would be needed to control the early spring growth.

Whilst these lighter jobs were being done we were helped by old Fred Budd, who dug in a row of fast-growing conifers, *Lawsonii*, to act in time as a windbreak. Then, inside them we began the task of erecting an eight foot high netting fence, supported on steel posts, to contain the fearsome serves, volleys, lobs and smashes that were already, in our minds, flying across the court.

For the next few weeks the old mower was set lower and lower and the sequence of cuts increased; then more dressing and spraying of daisies and plantains until not a weed showed on the whole area. The Centre Court at Wimbeldon could barely have had more attention!

By late May we began to think about marking out the lines of the court. Mother had found us the old line marker from Grandfather's house at Barnham, that had been used on their court some thirty years before, and after an hour or two in Father's workshop, it came out like a new machine.

Armed with a bag of lime from Cliff Pratt's store, the day came for the 'marking out'. After some hours spent lining up the corners and setting strings tight between these points, we nervously began to push the old line-marker across the grass.

By nightfall the work was done. Before us lay a pristine grass tennis court, immaculate in all respects apart from the fact there was not yet a net. That was to come the following day.

Again the old garage at Barnham disgorged what we needed, both posts and net, still in good condition after years of storage, and within a short time the posts were set in firm bases and the net strung tight between them. The court was now complete and it was not long before 'trials' began.

Within just six months of the idea coming into our heads, here was a real grass court, not yet, to be honest, quite on a par with Middleton or Wimbledon, but certainly level. We would never, from now on, be unable to get a game.

Mother, was persuaded to take up a racquet again and, on an early June Sunday afternoon, after a morning spent cutting grass for silage, we had our first game. My memories of it are now vague. The result meaningless. However I do remember that the ball bounced evenly and that bad bounces were few. The netting needed some improvement, however, since we spent much time searching in the long grass for lost balls, and as the day slipped by, the evening sun become rather tiresome.

The first problem was soon corrected, but the second was a design flaw that was, with hindsight, inevitable, since, whatever we did, the sun would always set in the west! We simply played in dark glasses, or when the sun was higher in the sky or behind clouds.

By the end of that summer the court had seen a lot of pleasurable evening matches, tennis tea parties with a dozen friends playing 'round robin' competitions and many hours of friendly practise between Peter, several locals and myself. So the whole thing had been a success; not just in the creation of a playing area, although that was the primary reason but, more importantly, it had taught me that if you really want to achieve something, with sufficient energy, enthusiasm and commitment, anything is possible. We had turned a rough bit of meadow into a very acceptable tennis court within a few short months and the cost had been minimal, since the only labour involved had been our own. The satisfaction we both felt was immense and the experience taught me that if I wanted something I should just get on and do it. As the years passed, that lesson was often put into to practise.

The following summer saw the court again in use most weekends and every free evening, cricket on Sundays for Middleton being the only other major distraction. Tennis parties, with Mother's cream teas, were very popular and the place was alive with many new faces.

The main drawback, apart from the evening sun, was the physical problem of cutting the grass regularly enough to maintain a good surface. Once a week was not enough – daily was required at times – and I found it harder and harder to keep it mown when other work was pressing.

In those days mowing equipment was pretty basic and by the end of the summer the job had, to be honest, become a chore. However it had given a lot of pleasure to a good many people and had persuaded Mother to come out of 'retirement' from the game for a few months and show us her skills. That alone almost made it worthwhile.

By April the following year, 1958, the grass was again cut and the lines marked out, but we never got round to playing. Peter was doing some fairly intense courting and other interests were beginning to call.

The court was never played again, although if we had owned a better mower it is possible it would still in use today, helped by the fact that within five years the conifer hedge had grown to such an extent that the sun barely showed across the court as it began to sink in the west.

However, now Mother was left with the task of maintaining this unwanted area of flat grass on the side of her already large farmhouse garden. She didn't relish the idea of cutting it too often and before long shrubs began to appear at one end to soften the expanse of grass.

Some five years later she employed contractors to install a swimming pool across one end and with that new attraction the same people who had once enjoyed tennis, plus a good many others (who always managed to turn up at tea-time) kept the pool fully utilised.

Perhaps, in Father's words, Peter and I were a little mad, but had we not taken on that challenge we would have missed out on a lot of experience and even more satisfaction ... and it certainly proved something to the 'Old Man'.

Shortly after that experience with the tennis court I also became involved in a rather rash venture – one which did not at any stage give me the satisfaction of the tennis court.

I had convinced myself that there was money to be made out of breeding rabbits for meat production, and set about converting some disused hovels into a large breeding unit. I cannot actually remember what brought this notion on but within six months I had some 150 breeding does installed in smart home-made hutches, built with great ingenuity by Father. In long lines, three tiers high, and all equipped with automatic watering, the plan was to produce some 50 young rabbits a year per cage – and in the process make my fortune.

Well you can dream... In theory, it was not as silly as it now sounds. Apart from one main reason. It soon transpired young rabbits are even keener to roll over and die than sheep; and despite all the latest feed additives, and the most expensive concentrate pellets, I quite quickly learnt I had made a big mistake.

I had travelled far and wide across the country learning from the few established breeders, buying stock, for which in hindsight I paid too much, and grew the unit too large before the health problems became obvious. If I had built up gradually I would, perhaps, have either learnt how to overcome the setbacks, or put the whole lot in the pot before they began costing me too much money.

The enterprise cost me a lot of hard-earned and hard-saved money, plus the remains of a small legacy. Sadly, by 1960, some 18 months after I began, I sold the whole lot, rabbits, hutches and the feed system, at an auction in the paddock adjoining the farmhouse. I salvaged peanuts, but again it was a lesson, albeit hard learned: stick to what you know. My experience was of traditional farming and if there was money to be made it would in future have to come from the areas that I knew. I also resolved that if I were to 'venture abroad' again, a little more thorough research would not come amiss. There were other things now starting to take up my spare time, leaving me less time to get involved in such 'eccentricities' in future. At least not for a good few years...

MARKET DAYS

One of the most regular features of my early days with Father were the Monday or Wednesday trips to market. As a toddler it was to Barnham Market on

Mondays, when the whole local farming community would gather in the old stock market opposite the railway station. Usually we would be towing a trailer behind the jeep, with a couple of calves or a pig or two, to be unloaded in the designated area. Watched closely by all the experts and characters who always made everyone else's business their own. All the local farmers would, in those days, make an effort to attend every week since Market was the most reliable way to keep up with the news in the district.

Father sold all his stock through Stride and Sons, the auctioneers at Barnham. Calves, old cull cows, geese, chicken, guinea fowls and pigs. Pigs were his biggest earner: the breeding herd consisted of pedigree Wessex Saddlebacks and Large Whites, the progeny of which were usually sold as crossbred weaners at about twelve weeks old.

Those market days were a wonderful experience for a child. I would wander round all the pens, particularly the small cages housing the fowl and rabbits, trying to persuade father to bid for the occasional specimen. Almost always without success. Then I would sit with him on the railings of the sheep pens and listen to the learned conversations between senior farmers about the state of farming, which consisted, even then, of mainly gloom: of the latest fatstock subsidy; the new Agriculture Minister perhaps; old 'so and so's' farm sale; the state of someone else's wheat crop and a thousand other equally vital and interesting views and opinions. Needless to say I stayed silent, and just listened.

Those were the days when many cattle arrived and left the market via the railway. They would be driven across the road by drovers onto the enclosed wagons destined for rearing units across the country, or to the butchers in London. Those were also the days when railways ran both on time, and to almost every small town. Delivery by train was often cheaper and quicker than by road.

The droving process was regularly enlivened by some awkward young steer or cow that decided to break free, and regularly the drovers were to be seen chasing some terrified animal down the road past the station and out into the countryside. Fortunately there was little traffic at that time so accidents were rare.

Before we left Barnham no day was complete without a call into Alfred Pains, the ironmongers outside the station. The smell from that shop still lingers in my memory today; a mixture of 'Stockholm tar' and sheep liniment which permeated everything.

I was always fascinated by the array of shiny new tools, the spare parts, and general gadgetry that filled the shelves, and we always left with some vital purchase for Dad's workshop.

And then, on the road out of the village we would call in at John Bakers, the local miller. At that time they still operated the old mill as a commercial unit, in its full glory and I would regularly be taken up to the top to look out across the flat coastal countryside as the giant sweeps turned relentlessly in the wind.

To watch the huge bags of wheat and barley, being raised by pulleys to the top and then to stare in awe as the same grain worked its way down through the cleaning and grinding processes; until it emerged, as flour, wheat meal, rolled oats or ground barley at the bottom level. Very often to be sacked off and loaded into Fathers trailer, for feeding to the stock at home in the coming week.

The old mill still stands today. It has been partially restored at great expense but it has been without any sails since the late forties and long since ceased to be a working mill. Probably to finally end up as a domestic residence, largely unappreciated for what it once was, or the part it played in the districts agricultural history so many years ago.

Sadly Barnham Market closed its gates for the last time before I grew into my teens and most of the local farmers switched to Chichester where on Wednesdays the same auctioneers, Strides and Wyatts sold all the local livestock.

Chichester was a much bigger centre, and for a number of years the town buzzed each Wednesday as hundreds of buyers and sellers flocked in. As before Father always attended, and when I was not at school he regularly took me along.

The routine was always the same. We arrived and unloaded any stock we were selling and parked the car. First stop was to the small row of merchant's offices along the eastern side of the site. The local agricultural traders market sites were the scene of much banter and dealing. Monthly, if they were lucky, a cheque was handed over, although at times, several months passed without one. Those extended terms were known as 'Merchant Credit', and were the reason many hard pressed farmers always paid top prices and received low ones for their produce. You get 'owt for nowt' Credit has its price.

Then it was on to the pig lines where all the farmers gathered to put the world to right. There were many regulars. Many characters. Cattle dealers, horse dealers, both rogues and honest, they all came to Chichester on Wednesday morning in the search for deals and pickings.

Many sound excellent farmers too. Ben Farrow from Sidlesham, large and friendly. Reg Hague from nearby Oving (pronounced incidently with a long soft 'o' like you say ooh) an old friend of Father and an excellent farmer, but not your most cheerful soul, would be moving on to inspect the beef cattle

Edward Dallyn from Hunston south of the city, a charming man. A great game shot and a tenant of the Church Commissioners, as were so many farmers on the Chichester Plain then, and to a lesser extent today. Old Walter Langmead would usually appear, old and frail of body now, but sharp as a razor in the mind. Often he would be in earnest discussion with his two sons Walter and Leslie, both big farmers in their own rights across the whole County.

We would move from group to group, Father talking, me listening and, occasionally, being acknowledged. Then the bell would ring and John Gates the senior partner of Wyatts would jump up on the raised board walkway running over the pens and with his clerk of the day, Henry Adams (later to become senior partner) in attendance would begin the auction.

We would watch prices anxiously as the sale moved down the lines. Father would usually have a dozen or two twelve-week-old weaners for sale and although he had regular buyers they would only pay what they had to. The price of pigs was always, and still is, very volatile. The breeding cycle is so quick and a glut halves the values. A wise farmer stays with the same herd size and takes the highs and lows. The novice gets in when prices are high and has stock to sell just as the shortage turns to glut. They never did last long, nor do they today.

As the pig sale ended we would all drift across to the cattle lines. I was always fascinated by the atmosphere around the beef grading officer from the Ministry of Agriculture. In those days this man could make or break the beef fatteners, presenting finished cattle, since the grade they were given by him greatly affected the subsidy. Subsidy rates changed weekly and it was vital to sell them right and at the right time. Presentation was therefore everything.

Some of these old farmers were artists at this and even as a teenager I marvelled at how they could persuade the grader in their favour. To say they tricked him may not be strictly true, since as they always had good cattle they would rightly expect good grades. However, everything they said smacked of psychology; distracting comments, flattery, the lot, and while I am sure the grader knew the game too these men always seemed to leave satisfied.

One of their best ruses was to arrange for the drovers to present their animals immediately behind some poorer cattle, which then highlighted the quality of the ones that followed. If they had followed other prime beasts they would not stand out so much, and would sometimes be downgraded, simply because the grader would perhaps feel he was being lax if he top graded too many cattle in one run.

The markets were and still remain the best place to sell good stock. Plenty of buyers, plenty of choice and always the option to take your animal home if you are not satisfied with the day's price.

I bough my first cow in Chichester, a big fresh calved Friesian called Goldie. She cost us the huge sum of £62 back in the early sixties, and she stayed with us at Flansham for some years.

~ *Chapter Two* ~

ADDED RESPONSIBILITY

The summer of 1957 had been the first year Johnny and I had full responsibility for the harvest. I was now entrusted to drive the combine, a machine Father had nurtured so lovingly from new in 1953, whilst Johnny 'bagged off' behind me. This was towards the end of the era of sacks, before bulk handling became the norm, and the corn rattled noisily up through the intestines of the machine until it finally arrived in a rotary 'screen' behind the driver, to be graded, before dropping into the 2¼ hundredweight sacks. Two chutes ran with 'head corn', one with the 'tail' and a fourth with thistles, poppy heads, stones and all the other trash. The working conditions were terrible; everything itched from the start of the day and choking dust filled your eyes, nose, ears and mouth.

Driving the old girl was bad enough but Johnny, working behind me in the constant dust cloud, covered with flies and sweat, never flinched. He seldom spilt any grain and was always his cheerful self. As he filled and tied off each sack he 'kneed' it to the rear grain chute and pushed it down, releasing the filled sacks with a trip rope, in lines across the stubble to be collected later. Between breaks for lunch and tea we suffered, and kept going, but when we stopped we invariably went to the closest cattle water trough and 'sloshed' ourselves clean. Often if it was very hot we would actually jump in submerge ourselves.

At all times there was a shotgun on a stand by my left hand, loaded and ready. Rabbits were, as ever, a real pest and from the driving seat they could be watched as they ran in front of the cutter bar. Towards the end of the 'turn' they were likely to 'break' for the hedge and a huge number would be shot each day. As they rolled over, Johnny would jump off the sacking platform and running, pick up the body, or jump on the wounded rabbit hiding under the straw. Most were caught and dispatched and their bodies gathered till they over-filled the platform and got in his work space.

Every break we 'paunched' all those big enough to be saleable, hanging them away from the flies and kept them cool under empty sacks. In those days local butchers would buy them for 2/- or 2/6 each and it all helped to supplement our meagre wages, and just as importantly, broke the itchy, dusty tedium.

As the day went on the corn-filled sacks were usually stood on their 'heads' by a couple of local youths to be left overnight. This helped cool and dry the grain and meant that, unless rain was imminent, we could 'crack on' with cutting and pick up the harvest afterwards at our convenience. Even if it did rain, if these sacks were stood properly they shed all the water, and soon dried out in the wind and sunshine. It would take several days of wet weather to cause any significant losses.

Until 1956 all the lifting on the farm had been done by hand since we had no machines capable of the task. The sacks were lifted by two men working in tandem, holding left to right hands, the left man gripped the left bottom corner of the sack, the other the right corner and with the weight of the bag supported by their linked arms, the sack was carried to the trailer. Swinging the bottom up onto the trailer floor, and using the impetus gained, the head of the sack was pushed upright.

Then either a lad with a 'sack cart' or 'wheels' moved the bag to its stacking position on the floor of the trailer; or else we loaded a dozen or so, and then got up on the platform ourselves and again manhandled them into position. The trailer would take about 60 sacks on the base, and fully loaded another 25 laid on top, (about 8/10 tons). When full the load was carted either back to the farm, or to the merchants at Barnham, giving us about half an hour by road to cool off! And then they again had to be unloaded by hand.

The trailer we used for this task was in those days a bit special. Father had found it at one of the regular ex military sales, disposals of recently redundant war equipment, and this had been an RAF trailer built to carry long light loads, such as aircraft wings. When he bought it there were two central wheels but, on the farm this was hopeless since it became unbalanced and stuck after the lightest shower.

The following winter he converted it into a four wheeler with a fully rotating turntable and with its huge length, for those days, of 21 feet it was certainly the longest and biggest load carrying agricultural trailer in the area at that time and capable of moving weights undreamed of before.

So it was with this tool Johnny and I carted all the grain from both farms. By the end of September, with some 1,600 sacks and over 10,000 bales of straw, loaded and unloaded by hand, it became clear to me that to continue like this was a sure recipe for bad backs; and a rapid turnover of labour. However a 'front end' loader had recently been seen working on a local farm and, with a bit of persuasion I thought I might be able to encourage Father to improve things before the next years harvest.

And so this was how we gradually mechanised the farms; very, very slowly taking the worst of the intensely hard work away from manual means and came to rely more and more on hydraulic power. I realized that with money tight it was not something that could be changed overnight but every little helped. As work was made easier it became faster. The benefits were obvious and even Father became increasingly enthusiastic to mechanise. But the problem always was that of funding, and it was not a problem that would quickly go away.

OLD BILL'S DEBT

Thinking back to the early days of that big old trailer reminds me of a long standing debt which father called in with the services of the great beast. There was a farmer locally, who, well past his best days as a farmer, struggled on simply because that was all he knew. Father had known him for many years and, for a few years in the early fifties, had done all his harvesting with our new combine.

Old Bill had a nice level free draining farm, around two hundred and fifty acres and as times became harder his dairy herd dwindled and the cereal acreage grew. Father's combine spent many days harvesting his corn and at the end of the first few seasons, despite Bills promises the account was never settled in full, always there was a tidy sum left outstanding, promises but no money.

It was a running sore with Father. He needed the cash almost as much as Bill but in those days debts seemed to run on much longer than they would today and, after all, everyone knew and liked the old fellow. And he kept giving people orders, and Father work!

In '57 I had done a lot of the harvesting on Bill's farm. I particularly remember one field of oats that had gone completely flat in the winds that July. When we came to cut them the only way was to cut from the south, with the crop lying away from the cutter bar and the reel set low, to let the fingers on the pick up pull the cut straw up slowly. It was vital to avoid blocking the threshing drum at all costs. Clearing a blocked drum of oat straw was positively the worst job I have ever had to do on the farm. And I do mean *ever*.

Harvesting that field was a rotten slow job, the weather was 'shucky' and old Bill was convinced that we would not manage to get it cut, and that he would lose the lot. Certainly before the arrival of combines, the only solution would have been to use fag hooks and Irish travellers. So when I finally finished the field, some twenty acres, he was naturally delighted. I was quite pleased too; firstly that it was finished and secondly that he was happy with our work.

When the seasons contracting was finished, towards October, since there was a lot to cut apart from our own farms, the time came for the accounts to be sent out to the half dozen or so farmers for whom we had worked the combine.

This time Bill came on the phone to Father quite soon afterwards. Perhaps now, after owing us money for so long, he had a twinge of conscience?

"Jack," he said to Father, " I can't pay you all this yet, but would you like to take some pigs and a couple of loads of hay in exchange."

The last team of horses used for ploughing at Flansham, 1944.

At least, thought the Old Man, this was a start, so he agreed. Next day he and I set off with his car and trailer and selected half a dozen nice 'in pig' sows which, as they were due to farrow shortly, were worth quite a bit of money – substantially more than they would be worth now, as I write, some forty years on.

He also inspected the hay, and having seen Bill making it earlier in the summer knew it to be good quality, and he saw it had also been stored in a dry barn. He therefore agreed with Bill that, next day, we would take two loads back to Flansham.

The following day, Wednesday, was market day at Chichester, and Dad knew Bill would be off early after breakfast and, what with market, a visit to the Chichester Club and a good few drinks, the old fellow would not be home before evening.

My father, Owen 'Jack' Adames, tractor-hoeing beet in the 1940s.

Bygone days, when real horsepower was at the heart of agriculture.

Next morning after breakfast Johnny, Percy Large and I went off to Bill's barn with the big trailer in tow. We pulled alongside and very soon got a good load up, roped on and set off for home.

Now, what Bill didn't realise was that we had a long-platformed trailer. Most trailers on farms in those days were converted horse carts and suchlike, with a capacity for perhaps seventy or eighty bales, but this one, if loaded well, would take about three hundred and sixty bales each load.

Two loads, Old Bill thought, would still leave him plenty for his few cows that winter, since there were the best part of eight hundred bales in the barn. So we three spent the next hour or so unloading that first load, and then returned again after lunch to Bill's farmyard for the second time, to be again loaded and away before the old farmer returned to see what was going on.

When we pulled back into the farm drive at Flansham we stopped and saw Father. We reported that we had the two loads, and that, yes, there had been enough hay in the barn to fill them both up.

Next day Father expected to have an early call from old Bill asking him what had happened to his prized crop, and in anticipation we unloaded the lot early into the barn so that, if he wanted it back, he would have to find someone to reload it. Hay is not the nicest crop to heave about, and those were good solid bales. Neither did Bill phone.

The following summer he again asked us to cut his corn, and when the accounts went out that autumn he was the first to settle up. It seemed he had learned his lesson and was not going to get himself into a position to be stung again!

The matter of the two loads was never ever mentioned, at least not between Bill and Father. The old chap died the following year and we were rather sad. He was a terribly slow payer but he was a nice old man, and we missed his dry humour on market days.

DAYS WITH A GUN

Another sporting activity had also been featuring in my life for a few winters since 1950. Whether one likes it or not, shooting contributes in many ways to the countryside, and the need to learn the act of safe gun handling, and competent use of both shot gun and rifle is very important to a great many countrymen.

Guns have been around me all my life from first memories. Father had an arsenal during the War from sources never divulged, and encouraged me to handle them, usually empty of ammunition, from an early age. By the age of 12 I owned a single barrelled .410 which I used on rats and rabbits.

In 1953 when I was 14, Father and Jack Langmead were jointly shooting over their two farms in Flansham, since Jack had found two locals to undertake vermin control. In exchange for this they acted as keepers for the Saturday shoots and were allowed to shoot the farms each Boxing Day. This meant that instead of just a few days rough shooting they were now, with these chaps' help, able to run the shoot with standing guns and beaters. More to the point, as far as I was concerned, was the fact that Jack decided I could carry my gun for a day on the next Saturday shoot.

My excitement during the few days leading up to that first Saturday was almost unbearable. The gun was polished, cleaned and oiled almost hourly; my new Harris Tweed jacket tried on for size with the gun up to the firing position, and the new cartridge bag filled with enough ammunition for the anticipated day's sport. Finally, Saturday morning came and I was up long before normal, before first light, checking the gun again, double checking the weather of the dark morning outside, indeed anything to pass the hours till 9.30.

The meet was, as usual, in Jack's farmyard, behind their old granary at 9.45. Father, Peggy our spaniel and I were first there to greet Jack and his new 'keepers', Teddy Page and Algy Burningham. Then steadily the guns began arriving. Usually first were Frank and Hugh Robinson, said by many locals to be the best partridge shots in Sussex. Colin and Bill Loveys, Jack's cousins from the next door hamlet of Bilsham would arrive full of joviality. Doc Ferris fresh from an early emergency always turned up last in his latest sports coupe, scattering the dogs and Teddy's beaters as he skidded to a halt in the yard.

Jack and Ted went through the early drives, synchronized watches, and then Ted lead the ragbag of village youths and farm hands out of the yard and away to the east of the village. The dogs by now were going wild. Bill Loveys always had a pretty excitable Labrador and there was invariably a fierce dog fight before the off.

Now Jack was in charge, and after giving me clear instructions that I would be standing between himself and Father, we set off, unloaded guns under our arms, down the old Brook Lane. Beneath the dripping elm trees we went and across the cow pastures to Worms, to a deep, tree-lined ditch where we quietly took up our positions at the marked 'pegs'.

Within minutes, in the distance I heard a whistle, then a shout, "to your left Frank!" Like grey bullets came the first covey of partridge, screaming down the wind. Two or three birds fell from about 8 shots; I remember particularly one falling in front of Hugh Robinson, and how impressed I was at the distance he must have shot in front to have managed to land the dead bird in front of him. At the velocity they travel, only the very best shot can do that, and only once have I ever seen a pair 'right and left' fall dead in front of a gun. That was by Frank Robinson again, a few years later at nearby Shripney.

The whistles were blowing furiously as birds rose out of the undersown clover and stubble. Father got a pheasant and partridge; Jack a couple of partridge and Colin shot a hare coming through a nearby gateway. I had two shots at partridges high over my head but probably missed them by 20 feet and caused no damage.

There was much banging further down the line by the Doc and Bill and then suddenly the drive was over and guns unloaded.

Jack was ecstatic.

"Bloody good show Teddy!" he said.

"At least sixty birds came forward Sir, and two large coveys swung toward Yapton," replied Ted.

"You get over to the Rife ready for the next drive, Ted. We've got some picking up to do," Jack continued.

'Picking up' was, and still is, the most important part of the day, when the dogs are put after 'runners' (injured birds) and dead birds are collected.

"Doc says he has five birds down," said Bill, "but I only saw two!"

"We'll let the dogs work to use up some energy," said Jack.

Our bitch Peggy, and Father were looking in the Rife, now about eight feet deep and full of reeds, for his pheasant. I went to watch. A couple of minutes later Peggy emerged out of a side ditch with a cock bird that still looked full of running, and brought it right to hand. Father took it from her with a "Good Girl" and a quick pat encourage her and she was off to help elsewhere.

All except one of Doc's birds were eventually collected and within ten minutes twelve partridge, three hare and six pheasant were carted off by Jack's old (now retired) foreman, Charlie Harding to the game trailer he had driven round the meadows with an old tractor for this purpose.

Now we turn and 'line' the Rife, for the beaters to beat a huge swathe of newly sown wheat ground and stubbles back from Bilsham and, we anticipate, drive many birds over our heads.

Suddenly, without warning, there's a whoosh and two rapid shots. A pair of partridge had come between Father and me. He had seen them in time. I just saw the second fall about 60 yards behind.

"Good shooting, Jack," said Hugh.

All I thought was, 'if I had been a bit more alert I could have taken shot at them!'

This time the birds came at us steadily, at least 100 in about 12 coveys, and high. Down the line, a bird hit in the head 'towered' (flew straight upwards until it died and then fell straight to earth).

I attempt a long shot and again miss; the range of my .410 is short, and with only one barrel I don't get a second chance.

And so the day went on. Lunch was taken in Langmeads granary amongst the sacks, dogs everywhere, wet and vying for scraps. Thermos flasks get knocked over and eventually Jack orders everyone to put their dogs on leads or get them outside to "worry the beaters out of their lunches!"

In the afternoon we moved westwards onto our land. We had a big field of kale that Father had been throwing wheat onto for a week and he enthusiastically reported it 'full of birds'. The drives in kale are much smaller as beaters have to walk almost touching each other to get the birds up, while the guns are stationed both forward and behind to catch the old cock birds who have seen all this before and try to escape unseen.

After about three drives in the kale, with guns moving 'up the line' after every drive and renumbering to give everyone a fair chance of a shot or two, I managed to kill two hen pheasants. One was a low bird I should perhaps have left for another day, but the other was a mile up.

"Great shot Nick!" called Jack. "Best bird today!" I knew it wasn't, but I appreciated his encouragement.

Suddenly the darkness began creeping up. Cock pheasants were calling 'cock-up cock-up' as they made to roost and the shoot was called to an end. I had been 'blooded'. There had been no nervous moments, or dangerous shots and I think the Old Man was quite proud. The bag was in excess of 80 head: about 30 partridge, 40 pheasant, a few hare, a woodcock, two duck and a pigeon.

As we trudged into the yard, weary dogs flopped around the game lying on the cold concrete. The birds were checked, braced up, admired, and the senior guns passed round a hip flask. 'Doc' had to be off to his evening surgery, so the game was distributed before he left. Jack did this with great thought.

"Teddy, take these to Uncle John, a brace for Mr Walter Loveys senior, and a nicely shot brace of partridge for Mrs Owen Adames (my grandmother), she loves them". Then the hares went to old retainers and the rest were distributed to the guns. I received a brace of pheasants with huge pride that I still remember to this day. For a mere 14-year-old to been treated like a man by these seasoned countrymen was some privilege.

All the game was given out and welcomed. Nothing was wasted, not even the pigeon. A young beater with 5/- for his day's work, shyly asked Teddy if he could "take it for his Dad" as he loved pigeon breast.

"Of course, son," said Ted, and the lad went off happy, wet and tired.

So the day ended, and arrangements were made for the next shoot.

"...and bring your boy, John," (Jack Langmead always called Father John despite being John himself and father Owen) "but get him a man's gun!"

The beaters had now gone, Jack and Jack said their 'goodbyes' and Father, Peggy and I walked quietly back to the farmhouse.

"Rub the dog down, Nick, then clean your gun and we'll see what Mum has for tea." What a day that was, and did I sleep well that night.

Over the next 20 years, days such as this became the norm for winter Saturdays between late September and mid-January, except that the following year Father passed on to me an old family treasure, a Wild 20-bore, hammer percussion, double-barreled shotgun with 'damasc' barrels. This little gun became my almost full time companion at weekends and during any free time.

I shot my first rabbit with it after a long, crawled, 'stalk' along the thick hedge separating Cricket Field and Second Footroad one late summer evening in 1954 and carried it to the evening duck 'flight' on every dirty winter's twilight that work permitted for the next dozen years.

This gun enabled me to get to know the ways of wild creatures and the creatures themselves. Either shooting pigeons, from hides built in hedges and ditches, the birds drawn by decoys in their hundreds to kale or turnips in deepest winter cold; or waiting by rising floodwater for the whirring wings of mallard, wigeon and teal, coming inland to rest and shelter, after feeding on the coast during the day.

Going off alone, apart from Peggy at heel, I would trudge down through the damp darkening meadows, along the brook lane, and out into whichever brook the duck were known to be using. Often Teddy, Algy or I would take out a few pounds of 'tail' barley or wheat in our game bags, to throw around in shallow pools for the duck to feed on, and thus encourage their return the following night.

Standing quietly under the shelter of a hedge the dog and I would listen for the first distant quack or rasp of a mallard drake or for the whistle of the widgeon. On many occasions the only way to tell the duck were there was because of the sound of rapid wing beats whilst ones eyes strained to locate the invisible airborne missiles before they were gone. And the dog 'grizzling' with anticipation.

Many evenings we walked home empty handed but on many others a fat duck or two, retrieved from deep dark floodwater by the spaniel, were safe in the game bag over my shoulder.

There was no sport on clear moonlight evenings because the birds didn't fly so much and the clear sky made seeing them almost impossible. The worse the weather the better, and on many evenings the rain, turning to sleet and snow in the north easterly winds, would freeze on face and clothes. Sometimes, having stood motionless for 15 or 20 minutes, the whole exterior of jacket and leggings would be frozen in a film of ice, making the sudden effort to raise the gun almost impossible.

One evening I will always remember was as I walked along the flooded edge of the rife, with almost all landmarks underwater, making for a small bush to use as shelter. Suddenly the land fell away and I realized I had stepped straight into a cattle waterhole, dug in those days at regular distances along the rife before piped water became available. The wet day was turning into a freezing evening as, with difficulty, I dragged myself out, emptied my boots and decided that as I was wet I might just as well stay for half an hour more as the conditions were ideal for duck.

An hour later when I opened the back door and entered the kitchen the cold had permeated to the core. My clothes were rigid with ice, apart from where my knees bent, and removing the clothes was a supreme effort. There were however two mallard in the game bag. When eventually I lowered myself into a warm bath frostbite felt close to setting in. Half an hour later, with regular topping up from the hot tap, feeling began to return again, and I resolved to take a little more care next time I ventured off to the brooks alone in similar conditions.

The dog too was invariably soaked, frozen and 'grizzling' from her excursions across the Rife or floodwater, and from the general excitement. For all that, she never missed the line of a wounded or dead duck as it fell in the distance. The pleasure it gave her, and the satisfaction of the search, ending in the safe return of the dog with a duck in her mouth, made the whole thing trebly worthwhile. On that particular occasion I was not fit to rub Peggy down and Father did the job, however that was always the first task on returning home, to make sure the dog was dry and fed, with a warm bed.

Dogs in our family have always been English Springer Spaniel bitches. We have never been without at least one, and their names have with one exception been, alternately, Peggy and Judy. Why, I don't really know, but they are easy to remember and trip of the tongue quickly. Perhaps also they seem to retain continuity, and perhaps also bring back memories of old dogs, and long distant happy days.

At any form of game shoot the working of good dogs, particularly if one is your own, form a huge part of the days pleasure. To send ones dog, successfully, after a wounded bird, which if not picked up will die or be killed by rats or foxes before the night is out, is quite exhilarating.

The sight of a Peggy or a Judy, struggling back with a very live bird, held high in her mouth, and with barely a feather out of place, is a wonderful sight. The partnership that develops over the years with a good dog is a little like a marriage. Both parties know and respect what the other is capable of and in time words are not really needed!

Sometimes a bit of encouragement on a bad day will 'gee up' a young dog but, as they get more experienced, they know exactly what is going on. The sadness is when they begin to lose their sight or, to a lesser extent, their hearing. When by the end of the day the little bitch is past the state of exhaustion and can barely make it home.

Her will is still there but you know that just one more hard retrieval will virtually stop her. At this stage the truth will have dawned that the good days are almost over. When she looks up from her bed by the back door in the morning, sees you with the gun, ready to go, and just wags her tail and still lays there, she tells you everything. "Enjoy yourself but I'm going to stay here today" she seems to say, and you, and perhaps she, know it's time to begin thinking about a new pup.

Sometimes, seeing this coming, we would have found another bitch puppy in time to introduce her to the job before the old girl was worn out. Usually it was more trouble than it was worth with either the old dog getting the youngster into the wrong habits, or sulking, or both.

The best way was to introduce the new pup alone, after plenty of hours in private with a rabbit skin for retrieving practice, so as to be able to give her your full attention. Spaniels are very headstrong, very stubborn and extremely enthusiastic; when they are trained the pleasure they give is unbelievable but on a bad day they can be desperate. And indeed, a total embarrassment

Over the years, since I was a child, I have been involved with some 9 or 10 spaniels – Father's and my own – and allowing for a couple of useless ones that became household pets and time-wasters, there is no doubt that involvement with gundogs has given me some of my most memorable sporting days. To shoot, apart perhaps from formal driven days, without a dog, is akin to kissing your sister – not that much of a thrill!

However, back in 1954 much of this was still to come and both dogs and myself were on an exciting learning curve. Winters meant much hard work,

Shooting party: Jack and Nick Adames, Jack Langmead and Dick Burton-Gyles, 1961.

cold wet days and long dark evenings, with always the dog and the gun to keep me company when time and weather permitted. I absolutely loved the season and the worse the weather the better.

THE VET COMES TO OLD SPLASH

My life at this time in the mid-fifties revolved almost totally around the farms. Work itself was getting no easier, indeed with the enlargement of the dairy and pig herds, perhaps even more arduous. Father, as always lead by his own example of hard work and his deeply ingrained art of stockmanship, which was already also becoming the code to which I naturally worked.

The fact that our animals came first was never in doubt, never questioned. Winter, summer, day, night, in sickness and health, ours and theirs, our own convenience came an easy second to their needs. I had learnt from a toddler that the family never breakfasted till the animals were fed; nor had time for evening meal until every animal's needs were met. "You can help yourself. They can't," Father would say. Neither could they call for a vet of their own volition, so a thorough inspection of every animal would take place at least once a day. Every sow, piglet, calf, horse and beef animal would automatically be checked. Eyes, feet, noses, and udders would, and still do, reflect the wellbeing of an animal in an instant. The milking cows would be milked twice a day and any change of condition instantly recognised by lack of appetite or milk yield; animals in various states of pregnancy watched for abnormal behaviour; like standing alone, lying apart, unexpected vulval discharge or just instinct. On countless occasions I recall Father, sensing, for no reasons that were obvious, that he should go to the buildings late at night, or walk to the far brooks on a misty summer's dawn and invariably seem to find something amiss.

Living with this 'sixth sense' soon begins to rub off. It is not an exact science, nor something that 'risk assessment' or books can teach, but it is an uncanny knack that only a real 'feel' for your stock or long experience can teach. Education has no bearing on stockmanship and could well act against it. Simply knowing your animals, sensing their requirements, almost before they do, is something that may well be masked by learning, since learning may likely train the mind to higher things, whilst missing the 'vibrations' at base level. Growing up with this attitude permeating one's every living day, means you don't even realise you are learning about stockmanship. It becomes the normal way to behave and the rhythm one works to.

It is pretty basic logic really, lots of ways describe it:

"Look after the stock and they will look after you";

"Do them well and they will return it"; or

"A poor animal is a money loser."

All say the same obvious thing. Obvious and true, but to this day a fact too many people, farmers and, in different context but to a much larger extent, pet owners, too regularly fail to absorb.

Keeping or owning an animal, any animal, is a huge responsibility, and whether it is a budgerigar, a cat or three hundred cows, the principle is just the same. Is the person who allows a budgie, or a cat, to go without food or water when they go on holiday, or leaves a dog to die in a sealed car on a sunny day, any less guilty than a farmer who neglects to treat a sick cow?

Much is made in the media of odd acts of cruelty or neglect but by and large the farming community has a good record in Britain, and the general well-being of the country's farm livestock reflects this.

So Father educated me in the ways of animals, helped along by various herdsmen and stockmen and women, and a succession of vets from the practice in nearby Arundel who have attended our stock for three generations of the family, from Grandfather Owen, to this day.

All these people taught me different things, and yet not all were good stockmen. However, one can learn almost as much from people who did a poor job as from the ones with this 'sympatico' and one mistake, if not repeated, is often a lesson well learned.

"Anyone can make a mistake ... only a bloody fool makes the same mistake twice" is a truism some find hard put into practice.

I learnt never to neglect checking every animal at least once a day, preferably in the morning. That way, you can get them in for the Vet by daylight if need be. Left till the evening, in failing light, any examination is made harder and you might miss something important. Simple things, but worth consideration.

Very often one hears the plea that the business "couldn't afford the vet's fees" in mitigation of a case of animal neglect. That has always been a weak argument, since the cost of losing stock, or having animals unfit to send to market, far outweighs any medical fee.

Many years ago, as a thirty-year-old, I recall telling our Vet, Ian Hutchinson, when we met socially somewhere one evening, that his services were the best value 'input' on the farm. He looked somewhat shocked that a client could say such a thing and said, half jokingly, that he would increase them at once! That didn't materialise (but I did notice over the next few years significant increases!). Yet just imagine calling your Doctor at 1.30 am and expecting a personal visit before the morning! Our Vets though, phoned at any time of the night, 365 days a year, will without fail arrive within perhaps 20 minutes, in good humour, and treat any ailment or emergency that confronts them.

My first recollection of such a visit was one winter's night, back in the early fifties, at about 11pm. Father and the cowman had tried but failed to calve old Splash in the large flint barn in the lower farmyard, known as Mark's Barn, because Mark Green milked his herd there and lived in the adjacent cottage for the last 50+ years of his life.

Ringing Mike Ashton, the senior partner, Father then decided I should learn from the experience so he roused me from my warm bed. Filling buckets with warm water, finding an electric lead light that worked, and settling the animal down, we were amazed to see Mike the Vet arrive within 10 minutes. Within another five, after an internal examination and a few grunts (from Mike not the cow) his face was serious.

"We won't get it out, Jack, so there are three options..."

Father looked worried.

Mike continued, "Firstly, the calf's still alive and the cow's healthy. She could go to Clay's [the local slaughterhouse] first thing. That way she will be worth £30 but the calf will be lost.

Secondly, I could cut the calf up inside with wires and pull it out in bits, but the mother may die of shock ... And thirdly, we could risk losing her but maybe save the calf by doing a Caesarean."

Father thought for a bit. He'd never seen a 'Caesar', but it was going to cost half what the cow was worth. If she died, the loss would be huge. Slaughter seemed favourite, but then he remembered I was there and guessed correctly that I was hoping he would try and save old Splash, so he held back.

"What are her chances, Mike, in these conditions?"

"Well, a cleaner barn and better lighting would make it easier, but I reckon to lose about two in five..."

Within ten minutes of his arrival the decision had been made and preliminaries were under way. Thorough cleaning and sterilising of the area, equipment, personnel and Splash took another 10 minutes or so and Mike also decided that, despite the hour, past midnight, his junior vet should also be present for the experience. I was sent to break the news by phone and ask him to hurry. To his credit he did, and by the time the scalpel had opened the muscle wall behind her rib cage, and Mike was readying to open the womb, his assistant pulled into the yard.

Now we had five of us; Wally the cowman, Father, two vets and myself, by this time wondering if I would faint at the sight of all this blood and gore.

Making an incision some 12 inches long, Mike now probed inside the open womb. Within seconds he pulled a leg through the cut, then another. Working by himself, he struggled to hold the feet whilst searching for the head of the motionless calf. Were we too late? As the head came into the light he grasped the calf around its own rib cage and heaved it out through the small opening, lying it on the straw beside us.

"Its gone" said Father.

"No, I think its OK," said Mike, "Open its mouth and blow into its throat or tickle its nostril with some straw."

Suddenly the calf coughed; it took its first unaided breath, and then another.

"He's going to make it," said Father, having quickly checked to see the calf was a male and worth a bit more at Chichester Market. "Now lets see if we can save his mum."

The work the vets did astounded me. The extraction of the calf was not even a fifth of the job. Firstly antibiotic powder was put in the wound to arrest infection, and then all sterile hands were brought to bear to hold the two sides of the incision, whilst Mike forced a huge curved needle repeatedly through the wound. Each stitch had to be tied off and cut.

By now the pressure of holding the womb high enough for stitching, to avoid it disappearing into the depths of her body cavity, was causing cramp to set in to tired muscles. We took it in turns to grasp the womb as the gap was gradually closed; which thankfully finally it was.

Mike had taken a short break to prepare the next series of stitching and now he again took over. Just as the first wall of muscle was being gathered ready for joining, the calf summoned the energy to call for its mother.

Immediately the plaintive bleat roused old Splash, who had been standing quietly whilst all this was in progress. She tensed and heaved and at once the first stitches in the wall tore out. "Take the little bugger away!" said Mike. "She's got enough to worry about without him upsetting her for the next hour or so."

At that Splash collapsed in a heap, tired, bruised, cut and stressed.

"I'd rather she stood, but if she won't, let's make sure she stays down," said Mike. I was delegated to sit on her neck, "and at all costs, Nick, stop her rising."

For the next 40 minutes little was said; a few dry comments between Father and Mike about the vet's needlework, otherwise tired hands gripping cut muscle as the big needle works relentlessly, gradually closing the cavity.

The cow meanwhile was also showing signs of exhaustion and shock. Time was of the essence and finally, with no further setbacks, the last suture went in just before 2.30am.

"I can't do any more now, Jack. It's up to her tonight, and you chaps for the next few days," said the tired but satisfied vet, then, giving her the contents of another two huge syringes of liquid, the job was done.

Cleaning up and scrubbing down bloodied overalls and boots outside the dairy took another 15 minutes and by 3.00am the vets left, having refused a warm toddy just in case there was another emergency waiting when they get home.

I rose late next morning, about 7.30am, and went, a bit apprehensively, straight down to Mark's Barn. Quietly opening the big sliding door I was greeted by the sight of Splash standing quietly by the stall, deep clean straw around, hay at her head and a big bull calf gently playing its nose around her udder, searching for milk. Father had already been in and gone to other work, satisfied that everything was well; that his decision at midnight, under pressure, had so far turned out well, and that the worst was probably over for the old cow.

He phoned the Vet's office at 9.00 am to give him an update and arranged to meet Mike at midday for a post-operative check. Both were equally delighted as were Wally and myself. It was a great experience of then 'modern' veterinary skills and medicine, coupled with the natural resilience of a healthy animal to overcome such trauma.

Splash recovered steadily and within three days was back in the herd; although she did not conceive again, which we anticipated, the rest of her days were trouble free and the whole experience worked to all parties' advantage.

Experiences such as that were happily rare over the years. However without fail the practice/partnership unfailingly responded to all emergencies with the same speed, skill and good humour, day and night, whilst the same cannot always be said of the doctors we humans all have to rely on as much.

Mike Ashton moved on several years later, the Practice in the equally good and safe hands of Ian Hutchinson and, more recently Paul Crossman, still serves the local stockmen into the 21st Century. Mike then became a highly respected equine vet specialising in thoroughbred racing animals. With a number of highly successful training establishments in the district he was in part responsible for the well being of several Classic winners, and contenders, and helped two local trainers become champion trainer.

I still see him at the races and he often recalls events such as that night spent with Splash, or the various meetings and camaraderie shared on the farm almost half a century ago.

THE MEANING OF WORK

Physical work these days, despite what stressed young men may believe, is far less tiring and 'on-going' than it was up to the mid-fifties. Employment protection laws and machinery have seen to that, for which everyone gives some thanks, however, in those days there was no option but hard work and no respite until that work had been done. It was unquestioned by the workforce since it had always been thus. There was no other way. There was little spare cash in the industry, which had been structured for so many years around the availability of a large rural labour pool, and indeed even had the money been available, there was very little machinery to spend it on. All we had in the mid-fifties by way of a change from my Grandfather's day, was a combine harvester (that saved stooking, carting and threshing corn, but still created plenty of hard labour), three tractors that could pull ploughs, thus saving horse ploughing, and trailers that carried a bit more than horse drawn carts. Just arrived within the year was a 'pick-up baler', which actually made straw and hay carting a far harder job than handling the loose material with pitchforks, since pitchforks were all we had for handling the heavy bales with. In the dairy the milking cows were by now being milked through a small four-stall vacuum plant, which reduced the labour requirement for milking from four persons to one.

Unfortunately, the rest of the jobs were done by hand, and these machines, because they worked faster, demanded that we too worked faster. Keeping up with a horse and cart plodding across a stubble to those old calls of "Stand on Duke" or "Whoa Bessie" was much easier task, although slower, than heaving 2,000 straw bales or 1,000 hay bales, from the ground onto an ever moving tractor-drawn trailer, particularly a trailer the size of three old Sussex wagons put together.

It was much harder pitching by fork, at some 350 bales an hour, each one 40 pounds, up into the heights of the tin covered dutch barns, where the roof was often hot enough to fry an egg and inside temperatures, mixed with dust, caused men to pass out in ten minutes if not conditioned to it. There were many late summer evenings, when the sun had dropped a little in the sky, that Johnny and I would go out and load two large trailer loads of bales. 320 bales were stacked 10 high, Johnny pitching and me stacking the loads; then roping, hauling, unloading without help into the stack and then reloading both trailers, for unloading first thing next morning. Close to 1,000 bales moved and stacked in three to four hours. Some 50-55 bales per ton, each bale handled at least four times between the field and the stack. Some effort, but then we knew no different. The job had to be done, and fast, to beat the weather and we were ever faster growing into strong youths!

'Mucking out', one of the hardest jobs of all, was eased somewhat when Father purchased two new Warwick tipping trailers, 4-tonners which, he said, would revolutionize the farm, since until that time we had been using flat non-tippers, converted wagons and the like.

In Johnny's view and mine, the job needed revolutionizing. Just the year before, one of the Fordsons had been fitted with a hydraulic front end loader and this had unbalanced the work. It was easy now to load up mechanically with great lumps of overwintered, well trodden muck, but these had to be teased loose by hand forks and unloaded manually, and it was soul-destroying work. So the spiral of mechanization had begun and although at times it moved slowly it was happily to become unstoppable.

However there was no way to speed this slow progress, since the whole agricultural machinery industry was in its infancy. For centuries horse carts, wheelbarrows, spades, forks and shovels had been almost the full extent of our industry's needs. Now suddenly new ideas, on the back of Harry Fergusons invention of tractor hydraulics, were creating demands for tackle that simply didn't exist and it was going to take a little time for these ideas to become reality.

Until this time, silage making (done since the late 40s in tandem with haymaking, where we had front mounted hay 'sweeps', to push the grass across the meadows in huge piles for hand forking) was carried out with rear mounted 'buck rakes' – huge tined forks which were reversed along the rows of cut grass, forcing the crop into huge knotted piles, before being raised on the tractor hydraulics and carted back to the sunken, earth-banked, silage pits.

That was a slow job with the 'short straw' being drawn by the men who spent the day in the pits, 'teasing out' each load and levelling it in layers to be consolidated by tractor wheels between each load. The job was made worse by the fashion of spreading black treacle, molasses, on every layer to aid fermentation. This job was a sticky hell. At the end of the day we and our clothes would be covered from head to foot with tacky sweet smelling syrup. No amount of 'kidology' would encourage village youngsters to last more than a day or two at this task and several men walked off the farm never to return when faced with another hot day on the 'clamp'. Even after the grass was clamped, the material needed sealing and this was still several years before the arrival of plastic sheeting. The solution then was to cover the pits with lime or cows muck, or both, the idea being that when the seal was removed it could be spread back on the land as a nutrient. Waste not, want not, but yet another rotten, labour-intensive task for us 'peasants'.

The Ministry of Agriculture even encouraged farmers in this by paying a hefty subsidy for lime coverings on pits, so naturally it was used regularly. The loads would arrive by lorry, tipped at the end of the pit and 'barrowed' or 'trailered' across the pit and spread about 3-4 inches thick to form an air seal over the whole surface of the grass. Even as I write I feel tired at the thought of it! We just got on with it because we knew no better and the job was there to be done.

Now, suddenly though, with the arrival of tipping trailers, we could move on a little and perhaps things really would get better.

To compliment the system, the next machine we acquired was a new Martin Markham forage harvester, a flail cutter that cleared a 40" swathe of fresh grass, and then blew it into the trailer running alongside, or towed behind, the harvester.

Father modified the trailers the following winter, with steel and corrugated iron sides and a hood, with a large swinging tailboard and very effective they were too; although putting these sides on, and then taking them off at the end of each silage season, was a major task for three men, requiring half a day. The effect however was excellent and now the trailers were able to bring in the chopped grass, grass which although still needing spreading, was at least manageable. The snag arose when the clamp grew higher and consolidation became poor, as it always did as the grass heated up beneath. Tractor and trailer would invariably become stuck half way over the clamp, regularly needing a tractor with a chain to pull the unit over and discharge the load. Several times trailers tipped over and tractors slipped off the high sides of the clamps. Luckily, all this was years before the arrival of Health and Safety Inspectors but nevertheless, quite alarming as young drivers jumped from the stricken machines before they toppled. Luckily all the damage could usually be repaired with the farm welder, and the only things lost were time and sometimes tempers; usually Father's.

It did not take too long before his cousin, 'Bogie' Sadler of local engineers Goodrowes, suggested to Father and fortunately in my hearing, that "We've got a new small, back-mounted silage fork. If you tip the grass on a concrete pad you can fork it up by tractor and it hardly needs any spreading."

Next year this arrived too.

NOT ALL WORK

Between the seasonal pressure points of Spring sowing on the hill farm, silage and harvest I began, by the mid to late fifties, to feel the need to do more with my time. I had my A team cricket in the summer but it was increasingly important that I had other outside interests. My relationship with Father was, to say the least, strained. His black moods had not improved and a depression usually hung like a cloud over the farm house.

I considered alternatives. A friend with a farm in Suffolk offered me a break, but Father vetoed this since it would mean finding another hand, a full wage! The Police Force had appealed to me for a while but things drifted, and the routine remained largely unbroken.

Between haymaking and harvest back in 1954 it was suggested by Ray Millam, a farmer cum horse dealer from Arundel and an old acquaintance of

Father's, that we night have room for a couple of ponies, well one pony well past its youth, and a large cob. Both hard used and in need of some gentle work and kindness.

Gay thought this was a wonderful idea since she was by now 10 years old and, beginning to recover from various operations to lengthen her leg, was gaining confidence. A quiet pony to feed and groom and walk her around the farm would suit well.

Within a day the pair arrived. Pinto and Punch were quickly put in the paddock beside the farmhouse, and Gay and I told to look after them. That evening the remnants of fathers riding kit was searched through. Bits, bridles and saddles were repaired and cleaned. Gay and Pinto became inseparable within days, and the horse proved a grand therapy for my fragile little sister. Punch the cob meanwhile grazed quietly in the paddock putting on weight and idling the summer away.

Next door but one, in the family's long-sold farmhouse, Chessels, lived the Penfold family, very old friends of my parents, and with all the trappings of success. A grand Bentley Continental car, three children, one a baby, and a small paddock with two ponies which Pam aged 15 and Judy aged 10 rode at all the local pony shows and gymkhanas. As the summer went on Gay's horse brought the families closer together. Judy and she were as inseparable as each from their horses. Judy and Skylark and Gay and Pinto were constantly blocking the lane for the farm traffic as they trotted to and from trips to the beach, pony club days or just a walk around the fields.

I also noticed Pam a little more and it was suggested I might like to 'saddle up' Punch and ride with her and a friend to a Gymkhana at Pagham on Saturday.

I could actually ride fairly competently, having been on and off Father's big horse Tiger over several years, so this seemed a good idea. Even more so when our new companion arrived that Saturday. Angela Beales was the eldest daughter of a local butcher, from nearby Fontwell. A tall, dark, vivacious girl who immediately made me realise that horses were actually a rather good idea!

That summer went in a flash. Work seemed like nothing, just short interludes between local shows, rides along the Downs: days with the girls and the horses. We won rosettes for jumping, at which Pam and Angela were the experts; Punch and I won some novelty events, and by September we had even gained the confidence to arrange and run the first 'Flansham Horse Show and Gymkhana' in the Home Meadow behind the farm house.

On the day, over 40 friends arrived with horses, parents and horse boxes. Jumps, freshly built by Father, were erected, as was a small marquee and stands made of bales. A roped arena, encircled by cars, formed the show ring. Graham Penfold, Father and Dick Burton-Gyles were the Judges and Stewards and our mothers, always enthusiastic, made huge plates of sandwiches, cakes and sausage rolls.

The day was a wonderful success. Happy faces carried off home-made rosettes and plates were emptied by hungry riders and grateful parents. Gay and Pinto won a special prize for "best behaved pony" and by the time the day turned to dusk, plans were well advanced for the 2nd Annual Flansham show the following September.

Angela, her young sister Sue and I had become good friends and life was beginning to seem better. At least now I could see there was something beyond constant hard work which, despite the fact that I loved the countryside and farm life, did become at times almost unbearably wearing and repetitive.

Winter too, with its regular Saturday shooting parties and duck, and pigeon shooting, also passed faster.

I hunted that winter, on Boxing Day at Midhurst. The first and only time, since Punch went lame after a couple of hours and had to be lead back to the horsebox on foot. The girls too were back, on tired horses, before long and we were boxed back to clean our horses, put old Punch in a warm box, and then to tea at Chessels.

I never hunted again, but I could see that with a fit, fresh horse it could provide a high level of exhilaration. It was also clear that the foxes were more likely to survive than some of the senior riders and despite today's 'politically correct' attitude, I feel it does far more good than harm to the general environment. Unlike controlling foxes by shooting and snaring, the element of suffering is minimal with hounds. The fox, at the end of the day is either very dead or very alive, albeit tired, and can fight another day.

As many foxes hunted with shotguns drag themselves off to die slowly of gangrene or blood loss as are killed outright. 'Live and let live' may not be quite apt, but too often nowadays people oppose things simply because they don't understand them. Perhaps 'each to his own'? Long may hunting continue.

The following Spring, Ray Millam arrived with another horse for me to try. A fine, big fellow, but as Father pointed out, "four white socks" [or fetlocks]. In his language this meant a dud, and despite his looks he never jumped at a show or appeared at a gymkhana. In fact, although I attended all the main local shows and again helped run our own Flansham event, I never rode competitively again.

The girls still rode a bit, particularly Judy, Gay and Sue, but Pam, Angela and I were beginning to adjust our sights. We remained good friends, but the horses were giving way to parties, squash and tennis at Middleton and on the court at the farm. Days out in the company of new friends and, before many months, newly acquired driving licenses gave us a freedom that a year earlier had been unimagined.

Over the next two years, as independence grew, most of our spare time was spent in each others houses and with new friends. In 1956 I passed my driving test and would drive up to Fontwell one, two or three evenings a week to chat, have a meal, or take Angela or Sue out. It mattered not which one, since we were 'just good friends'! A trip to the cinema, to the Sports Club, or a meal. It was a lovely gentle way to get to know girls and, unlike today, pressures were non-existent. Drugs consisted of, for the girls perhaps a cigarette; for the males a pint.

Old Splash, some time after her difficulties.

In the Fifties, sex was not the well-promoted monster it is today. One grew aware that there were 'feelings', but there was no pressure to form deep relationships from an early stage. Living together was quite unheard of for youngsters and mothers would usually be at the front door to see their girls delivered home. "Don't dally in the driveway" was the order of the day!

All these things were to come, but in our mid and late teens we just had fun with good friends of both sexes and sex was something that, in most cases, waited a little longer.

My 'wheels' at the start of my new driving career, consisted of a Morris Eight, open-topped and bright red, lent to me by Jack Langmead. It had been his daughter Juliet's car, but she had moved on to better things and it had languished in a cart shed, gathering chicken muck and cobwebs. My first job was to give it a full 'valet service', probably the only time in 40 odd years I was to do this, but then it was exciting. It was a little gem, in good tidy order, except the hood leaked a bit. Yet who needed a hood? That car propelled me around Sussex during the whole of 1957. Filled with cricket teams and equipment we 'flew' off each Sunday to all the Downland venues. If a shower fell we either pulled into a pub or I drove faster and the car seldom let me down. My, that was living! Then during the week, after work and a bath, I would go up to Fontwell, collect Angela or Sue and off to Middleton, the cinema in Worthing or Bognor, or just out for a drive.

Angela was driving now too, being only a month younger than me we passed within six weeks of each other, so I let her take a turn at the wheel from time to time. Sue, just 15, had to sit as passenger, but either way it was exhilarating. A lovely girl, hair blowing in the wind, an open sports car. Neither Stirling Moss nor Mike Hawthorn, I felt, had it any better.

The only time that little Morris ever let me down was one evening that September. I had just dropped Angela off at Fontwell and had reached Bilsham, a mile and a half from Flansham, when the engine, without warning, died. Damn. An open car, hood at home in the garage, and rain threatening. I had no doubt what to do. The car had to be got home. There was no torch and repair was out of the question, since electrics were not a strong suite with me then, nor are they today. So setting out by The Lamb, and with no lights, I started pushing. She went along quite easily and with the window down, guidance was no problem.

We had reached 'White Rails', Langmeads northern boundary when I heard a car coming in the distance. Not wanting to be seen in this situation I jumped in, stopped the car and slid down in the seat, well hidden from sight. The car rattled past, I recognised it as belonging to a member of the sports club, perhaps he could have towed me!

Peace settled again. It was after midnight and not many cars were out at that time. Pushing again with increased energy I reached the Littlehampton road and onwards to Comet Cottage, and past PC Luck's house. Not wishing to rouse our local 'copper', I went very slowly by, and then turned off towards Flansham Corner, down the narrow hedge lined road, which in those days passed for the main Littlehampton–Bognor road.

Suddenly another car was coming, this time from Bognor. I stopped and jumped through the hedge into Jack's stubble field. The car flashed past and I returned to the road. Only another half mile now and I would be home. As I passed Keen's smallholding a dog started yapping. A light came on and I pushed even harder.

A few minutes later the car came to a halt on the grass outside the farm entrance. I couldn't push it up there without help, and anyway we were home now. I found a sheet to put over the open seats and then walked up the farm drive, up the back path and turned the back door handle on the farm house

Johnny Field coming down off another big load of hay in the farm drive.

which was always unlocked, to be greeted by old Peggy and the young puppy Judy. Shushing them up, I crept upstairs. Father heard me.

"You're late. Don't oversleep in the morning."

"Night Dad."

By the time he was up next day the car was in its garage. I had gone out to attempt to get it home before any villagers woke and started asking pointed questions. Just in case, I put the key in and turned it. She started like a bird! That day after work I drove her down to Mr Barnett's Empire Garage for a check. His mechanic, Ron Middleton, could find nothing wrong and in the few more months during which she was on loan to me, there was never another hitch.

THE HOCKEY TOUR

At the back end of 1957, along with one or two members of the Club 'A' Team of cricketers, I joined the Hockey section to fill in the odd Sundays through the Winter. We had by now become a close gang. A particular friend from the cricket was the opening bat and wicket keeper, Peter Brazier, from Worthing. A big, amiable chap, Peter always had a new sports car, and a pretty girl in tow, and we got along easily together. I think he took me, as the 'raw farm boy', under his guidance and he was open, easy to relate to, and we got on fine.

After a couple of games of hockey Peter suggested I should join the team trip to the Bournemouth Seven-a-Side weekend, and so, with no shooting on that particular Saturday I readily agreed. It was my first weekend away from home without the family, apart from Gaveston, and would make a change, even if I didn't get to play.

Peter had yet another new car – he was in the motor trade – an AC Cobra I believe, and the journey to Bournemouth was a thrill. On arrival we all met at our hotel and prepared for a night on the town. Well on Bournemouth! A meal, followed by an endless search for the hot spots and, what was then referred to as crumpet, turned into a foot slogging pub crawl before we realised there were no hotspots. Nor little crumpet

Several of the team had taken girl friends down for the weekend and, for some reason, they seemed to be the first to feel the pace and go back to the hotel. One girl in particular, an Anglo-Asian, had been attracting the attention of almost every man who crossed our paths that evening, our party included.

This girl, Diana, was a friend of David Wright, one of our spin bowlers and was absolutely stunning. When she retired, the whole group strangely seemed suddenly to have lost the need to continue partying and so by around 2am we slipped off to our beds.

Next morning Peter and I were down at around 9am for breakfast and were surprised not to see anyone else. Hockey began at 10.30, and they had planned practice, exercises, etc before that. Gradually they appeared in ones and twos, until by 9.30 most of the team was there. They looked absolutely awful. One sent a message to say he couldn't make it and we presumed 'practice exercises' had already taken place overnight; although his girlfriend was at breakfast, looking fresh and happy.

Diana was also there, still affecting everyone in the same way as the night before, although her David looked particularly peaky.

So this was what these ace players had been bragging about and looking forward to for months. Certainly it wasn't the hockey, as the two games they played saw them comprehensively out of both the main event and the 'plate' in double quick time. Afterwards they flopped around like limp rags, mere shadows of 24-hours earlier.

Peter and I decided to leave for the journey back to Middleton early, he offered Diana a lift back to Sussex but, to our great distress, she was going back to London on the train as soon as she could find David, who had been taken poorly again and disappeared. We never met her again; I never played hockey again, since it appeared the pre-training was too strenuous. Although the weekend had its moments.

When we arrived back at the Club to be greeted by Hutch, the eternal Steward and confidante, he didn't seem too concerned about the result. He and others around the bar were far more interested in the various sleeping arrangements and how everyone involved had emerged next morning! They too all asked about Diana.

SAD TIMES IN THE FAMILY

That winter of 1957 was a hard one on the farm. Father had not been too well of late and had spent a lot of time in bed with bronchitis. Eventually he had some tests done and the Doctor, rather hastily, told him the results almost certainly pointed to lung cancer.

His mother, my Grandmother, had also the same problem at the same time and, with his depressive moods, the last thing he needed to know was what he was told that day. The mood around the farm darkened. Poor Father, worried enough about Gran, didn't need this on his mind as well and rather lost interest in everything; almost resigning himself to an early grave. A month later another test told him that the earlier diagnosis was incorrect, he had a shadow on one lung but it was not cancerous or life-threatening.

Now, the Old Man was never happier than when he was being miserable. He had convinced himself that he had cancer and was 'on his way out'. Most of his friends knew the earlier report and he spent the next five years giving them the impression of disappointment that, perhaps, he was going to pull through after all!

All this gloom made him even harder to live with. A family friend who knew him well and saw these moody interludes, presented him with a little framed ditty, to hang above his chair at the end of the kitchen table, it read:

Why be so difficult
When with a little more care
You could be bloody impossible!

Naturally he thought that this was great fun, and with no effort at all did his constant best to live up to it. To be fair, things were not helped when the following February his mother, and our dear gran, died. She had lived the past 10 years in the little cottage I had been born in, had always made everyone so welcome and seemed so bright and cheerful.

When she died Father was naturally distraught, even though she had been progressively frail and we all knew it was coming. She had been the cushion protecting him from the harsh treatment which his Father, with his somewhat dubious Victorian values had dished out. There was always a sympathetic ear and a soothing word. Now she was gone and he had not really developed the same close understanding with our Mother. She was his wife and mother of his children, but they could not discuss things to any extent, certainly not to the same degree he was able to with his mother.

After Grandmother was buried, alongside Grandfather, deep in the Madehurst chalk at St Mary's Church, Madehurst, right next to the family's lovely farm, Father went into his shell even more. That year he spent more time in his workshop than on the farm. Johnny and I now did almost everything. I was 19, almost 6ft 5ins tall and as strong as Father had been. We also rather relished the opportunity to show what we could do. Johnny wouldn't take decisions or want responsibility but had a huge capacity for work and we worked together like hand and glove. That spring and summer we did everything on both farms apart from full-time milking, although one or other of us would do the relief milking, but the cowman Wally, despite problems with too many women in his life, kept the herd going.

Often I would go to the workshop, or see Father at meal times, and ask for advice: this he gave as best he could but he had really lost interest and we argued, too often, because I felt all he ever did was criticize just for the sake of it. He may have been right at times, but it doesn't help a youngster's confidence, and if he didn't like what we were doing he could put it right by pulling himself together and helping out.

By Autumn, with Harvest safely in and everything on the farm up together he slowly began to come out of the shell. Mother and he decided that it would probably be the last time we were likely to have a family holiday together, so in late September we drove to the Lakes and Scotland. Mother had, as always, been behind such positive thoughts and Gay and I agreed it could be fun. We had done the trip to the Lakes several times in the fifties, spending many happy hours on and around Windermere, Coniston, Shap Fell and at Grassmere, and loved these high, wild, and beautiful places.

A few days later, after a gruelling thirteen-hour journey on those awful largely unimproved post war roads, behind caravans and 'British Road Services' lorries, we arrived at the Old England Hotel, Bowness, tired but happy. We had been there several times before and loved it.

Over the next two weeks we boated, walked the fells and then moved on to Scotland where a couple of years earlier we had stayed over night at the Lochearnhead Hotel above Stirling and liked it so much we decided to go back.

The owner, Ewen Cameron, was a giant of a man, well over six feet tall and big with it, and more impressive still to us southerners since he usually wore his kilt. He offered Father and I the freedom of his high moorland, either side of Glen Lyon, which runs north west from the Hotel at the top end of Loch Earn.

The 'old man' now began to come out of his long 'gloom'. We walked and walked. We shot a number of grouse and followed herds of Red Deer across peaty gullies and from tumbling mountain streams we quenched our thirst from the icy water, and soaked up the views.

It was the first time I had ever spent so much time with Father and we almost began to understand each other. Really the problem was that we were both as bloody mindedly stubborn as each other; but he had had far more time to practise.

One day Ewen's assistant, Hamish, a wild looking, moustachio'd Highlander, took me up alone to even higher terrain to stalk deer. Using .303 rifles we crept and crawled for what seemed hours until suddenly Hamish pointed out what appeared to be a lone stag. Resting the rifle on a large rock, my own heart pounding and my lungs almost bursting, he whispered "Aim behind its front leg, straight at the heart". I squeezed the trigger and the stag fell stone dead to the shot. To this day I have always thought he was pretty unlucky. A second later Hamish too had dropped another to the left and we ran across the rough mountain side.

Both were stone dead. "Good shot laddie"; "You too" I replied. At once Hamish had his knife out and had 'bled' both animals. "Now sling your gun over your shoulder and take hold of the horns." He lifted the beast up over my shoulder and I took hold. "This is the hard bit", he said. "Start walking and keep going 'til you get to yon track half way down the Glen".

Jack Adames and Dick Burton-Gyles judging the Flansham Gymkhana, September 1955.

I cannot understand how I made it. We stumbled on for some twenty minutes, which seemed two hours, never putting the two deer down. Hamish lead the way, my muscles and hands were aching, my arms nearly falling off, but we kept going.

Eventually I saw the mountain track. As we reached it we both dropped the deer and sat down. "Have a bit of this laddie" says Hamish passing me an old hip flask. Never having tasted whisky I took a mouthful, and almost choked. "We can leave them here for now, lets get home and I will send someone up with a horse to bring them back".

Late that evening he came into the lounge bar where we sat round a table after dinner. Again he brought some drinks. "Compliments of the House" he said. The venison is in the game room and we are well stocked. Ewen sends you this with his thanks" Again it was whisky. Father looked at me, and Mother looked concerned. I didn't drink. "Go on Nick", said Dad, "but drink it slowly". That night I slept very well.

Two days later we were on our way back via Stirling, Carlisle, Manchester. Those roads were again hell, all those same British Road Services lorries and caravans going nose to tail in the other direction. Father allowed me to drive a little since I always felt car sick in the back seat, and it broke the journey. As we too did in the Midlands, before arriving home the following day.

Father was a different person after that. The trip did him good and he even found time to be pleasant to Mother. It probably wouldn't last but at least home life was a bit easier and work on the farm became less traumatic too.

THE LINKS BECKON

The spring of 1958 also saw my involvement in another sport that was progressively to take my spare time and make me friends across the world. Through Jack Langmead I had one day been introduced to Tony Mote, a member of our local golf club, Bognor Regis, which almost adjoined the boundaries of the home farm. Tony was a year or two older but we hit it of at once.

Tony rang me next morning. "Nick can you play tonight, there's three of us and you make four."

"But I've not played..." I protested.

"No problem," says Tony, "you will have a good partner. Just come and enjoy yourself."

That evening at 5.30, fresh from a day on the tractor, I arrived at the clubhouse; Tony is already waiting at the entrance. We changed shoes, me into borrowed ones, and he introduced me to two youths of our own age. "This is David Yallop" he said, "and this is your partner, Martin – Martin Christmas."

As we made the first tee a small crowd gathered. The Club Pro, Harry Riseborough; the Secretary, Mr Charles Sayers, who had waived my green fee, "seeing as who you are with," and three or four others. I knew not why they were so interested, and they made me more even more nervous.

"Off you go partner," says Martin and full of fear but having hit a few practice shots in anticipation, I take a huge swing and moved the ball about 120 yards mainly along the ground. "Its in play", and, "if you're going to miss it, miss it straight" echoed round the spectators. Then up steps Martin and with no practise swing hits it 'out of sight' down the middle of the fairway. Even I knew that was good.

Tony and David follow, both with good shots, but not quite as good as my partner and thankfully the gallery then retreated back to the bar, offering wagers among themselves as to the result. I managed to hit a few shots in the air and finished several holes close to 'bogey', the standard before the days of par.

Every time my partner hit the ball it went down the middle, landed on a green, or finished close to or in the hole. Tony and David played almost as well, but with no thanks to me, Martin and I won somewhere before the eighteenth green.

Already I was smitten. This game was down to personal effort, no team to fall back on, and the company was different somehow. After play that evening we went back into the old club house, where everyone was very friendly. Jack Langmead was there, offering drinks all round, and all the assembled members seemed so interested in how our game had gone. We four lads had a couple of drinks and then had various reasons to leave. I think I had a sow farrowing, they may have had girlfriends to meet but we agreed to play another game that weekend.

In between I practised a bit. I borrowed some old Slazenger clubs, on trial from Harry Riseborough, and he gave me a few tips. I couldn't wait for Saturday.

This time they gave me a handicap, rather than a stroke a hole as before, and things went a bit better. As before, the others played very steadily and my partner was again brilliant. The game of golf was all so new to me, and its history and its great names meant little yet. I had read in the papers about Arnold Palmer, Bobby Locke, Sam Snead and Co, but they didn't really register yet. Were they better than these amateurs?

Those games went on through that summer. So keen was I now becoming that only once more did I play cricket for the A team at the Sports Club, and soon I'm sure they found another fast bowler to bowl wides at equally great speed!

Jack Langmead and Tony proposed me for membership of Bognor that summer, and so keen were the Club to find young members that they accepted me at once, and gave me 6 months free use of the Club. There was no Entrance Fee in those far off days and the subscription stood around £7.50 a year.

Between work, and after work, I played all hours. Practice, practice, play, play. A couple more youngsters, local butchers son Barry Targett who I knew from cricket, and Chris Martin, also joined the games regularly, and our small group grew very close.

Martin seemed to be away a lot and often people would be discussing him but so important was our own game that little else mattered at that stage.

By the end of the summer the Secretary had given me a handicap of 12, the first official one I had, and it meant I could play in competitions within the Club. Twelve seemed very high to me because most of the fellows I was playing with were at worst in low single figures, so I always received strokes.

By the spring of 1959 excitement was rising in the Clubhouse. There was a suggestion that Martin, my old partner, was about to be selected to play for Great Britain in a major international golf event. However in those days the "Walker Cup" didn't mean a lot to me.

That early summer he was away even more. He won several big events and was runner up in the 'Brabazon Trophy' (British amateur stroke play championship) and the English Amateur championship. Sport and particularly golf were not quite the popular pastimes they are today but suddenly, across the national sports pages were headlines and Martin's name and photos, on a weekly basis.

And indeed Martin Christmas did get selected for the Walker Cup. That summer he flew off to Seattle to play against a strong American team containing a certain Jack Nicklaus. And, what was more, in a huge defeat, with the UK only winning one game, Martin returned to Britain as the only winner. He had won his singles match, scoring that one lone point, with the United States the 11-1 victors.

Two weeks later he was back playing with us at Bognor, just as if nothing had happened since the last time we played. At that time we didn't really appreciate it but in our midst was probably, the best potential golfing talent Britain had seen for 20 years, and was to see for another ten, until golf became more popular with the advent of television. And then a host of strong young talent entered the game.

That small group was to form the basis of my closest friends from that day to this and we still regularly play and meet socially. Tony Mote was also to be instrumental in directing my future in other ways over the coming years, but more of that a little later on.

The effect of all this activity was that by the time autumn '59 arrived, I had decided that it was time to concentrate my sporting efforts on golf. And it was clear that the only way to do this, with any success, was by constant practise. Consequently, there was not to be much spare time between March and November, excepting the demands of work and golf, for the next twenty five years.

POINT THEM DOWNHILL

By now things were really starting to buzz socially, and even more excitement was around the corner as we approached Christmas of '59. For Peter Brazier had been delegated to arrange the regular skiing trip from the Sports Club to the Alps.

Since before the War, indeed as far back as 1926, one local family, the Fuentes, had been travelling out to a small Swiss village on an annual basis, broken only by the Second World War. After that, in about 1947, they again made plans and gradually brought together a group of young people who, never having skied before, quickly became addicted, and the club ski trips had became locally famous.

Our trip in 59 was to be to Kitzbuhel, in Austria, and immediately I was invited I began scraping together the princely sum of £100 needed for the trip; and we all excitedly looked forward to the end of January.

I was to travel out with three others by car, across Germany, whilst about another 16 went by train. My companions were Ian Langmead, whose car we used, Bill Stuart a great friend of the Langmeads and John Gillingham, a farmer friend from Billingshurst.

The journey was an experience on its own: two days across a still pretty devastated Europe, passing towns and cities we had only heard of as targets for the '1,000 bomber' raids. Our arrival at Kitzbuhel was almost an anti-climax, but never the less it was not many hours before we were all kitted out with skis, boots and sticks, and arrangements made for enrolment in ski classes. At least for us beginners.

The next two days were very tiring: we spent most of the time getting back on to our feet, or standing in long lines watching the teacher, before making fools of ourselves. It seemed I would never learn to 'lean out from the mountain' or 'let the skis run', and I wondered if this was really such a good idea.

Out of the blue, next day, arrived Barry Targett - my golfing buddy. Having skied before he knew the basics and so suggested that we went out alone that afternoon, after ski school, and 'give it a go'. That was Barry's formula for life. Within an hour, and following his instructions to "Point them downhill", albeit virtually uncontrolled, things began to click into place.

What the instructor had said made more sense at thirty mph, than it did stuck in a class at 3 mph. Turns became simple, if ragged, and stopping and 'sideslipping' a doddle. There and then I decided ski school was over for this trip; now lets get some practical experience!

Two days later Barry and I were hurtling down the fearsome last drop of the famous Streif run on the dreaded Hannenkahm. A run where still, today, the World Cup races of that name are run each year. Admittedly we were on our faces as often as on our skis, but we were learning a bit of control as well.

As the holiday progressed the other senior members began inviting us to join their trips and we explored all the regions in the area; then after skiing, all the night spots. We met European girls, American and South African girls, and even had the cheek to invite them to ski with us. That was almost always a mistake because these girls were invariably expert skiers and made us look silly.

We concluded the answer was to watch the pretty girls in ski school who were struggling, as we had been, and then ask them to join us. This was a much better and more successful idea.

When the time came to leave, plans had already been made for the next year's trip and the days counted off. All we needed now was to hone our alpine 'techniques', and not just on skis. And to start saving the money, which whilst it may not seem much today was indeed a small fortune at that time.

And so now, at the start of 1960, just short of my 21st Birthday, the world had really opened up. There was an ever widening circle of friends, in an enlarging range of interests. Shooting, skiing, golf and socializing; although my friends have never accused me of being a social animal. Even in work my contacts were growing, and life, which twelve months previously had seemed not to hold too much variety, or indeed expectations, was really in danger of becoming quite interesting.

Lunch rest during harvest.

~ *Chapter Three* ~

FAMILIARITY BREEDS COMPLACENCY...

Mechanisation on the farm continued steadily along in the early sixties. One of the machines we acquired was a vacuum tanker for cleaning slurry from the dairy drain pits, and being the only one in the village it got called into service regularly, also by the Langmeads, whenever a drain blocked. Basically it was a vacuum pump, driven by the tractor's power take off (PTO), sucking air from a 500 gallon pressure tank on wheels.

The slurry was sucked up through a flexible pipe, and when loaded the unit was driven out to a meadow and the load discharged via a spinning plate at the rear. The speed of flow was controlled by a lever on top, which in turn regulated the bung in the valve above the spinning disc below the discharge point.

The tool was used daily in the winter and I had sole responsibility for it, since at this time Johnny was away on National Service. The novelty had worn off after about one winter, since blockages regularly caused a huge pressure build up which, when cleared with a bar up the back valve frequently covered me and anyone close by in cold smelly slurry.

When Johnny returned that year from the Army he was quite happy to take the tool over and I didn't argue. I knew its quirks.

One day not long after he was spreading slurry down the brooks and about midday Mother heard the tractor pull up in the farm drive and, after a bit, noticed Johnny signing to her.

When she got to the tractor she realised something was very wrong because Johnny was white as a sheet. Looking closely she noticed blood all over the foot plate and that he was losing blood from a bad wound in his foot. She made him stay on the seat whilst she got the car out and called Father from the workshop.

They helped poor Johnny down into the car and off to hospital in Chichester where next day the surgeons had to remove several of his toes. I went in to see him as soon as I could and to find out what had happened. It was only then I understood how lucky he was to still be alive. What he told me was this.

"When I went to open the back up, to spread, the valve had jammed and wouldn't move. The spinner was already in gear and as I was in a hurry I jumped up onto the guard to free the control rod with my big Stilsons."

He went on. "As the valve began to move, my footing gave way, and suddenly my foot was on the spinner and I was on the ground beside unable to free my foot which was being constantly cut by the plates on the spinning disc. The only way to free myself seemed to be to put my other foot on the bottom of the tank and force myself free before my whole foot was cut off."

This he managed to do and then found himself with all the top of his foot shredded, toes hanging nearly off, covered in slurry and half a mile from any help. Somehow he got onto the tractor, put it in gear and drove home, despite the fact that he was slowly losing consciousness. Had he not been so fit and had Mother not seen him, he could well have been found dead in the farm drive.

Gangrene set in and amputation of the toes was the only solution, such was the infection caused by the slurry in the open fleshy wound. Johnny was in hospital for some time and off work for many weeks. When he came back, life was very difficult, since he was unable to wear Wellington boots, the standard farm footwear in winter.

He gave it his best, as he always had, but the next year the job became unbearable and it was with great sadness that Johnny and his young wife moved out of his cottage, Oak Bay and he left farming to become a painter and decorator.

We had been good friends for many years, grown into men together, and it really was very sad. It solved nothing for Johnny to admit it was his own fault and that he should have turned the spinners off before climbing above it; but it did act in making us all aware of the dangers of PTO driven machinery. Many hundreds of farm workers have since been killed or seriously maimed by similar incidents of momentary thoughtlessness. Familiarity breeds complacency.

In a year or two Johnny made a fairly good recovery but never again could he play his beloved football and much fun went out of his life. Another sadness was that compensation and injury insurance was almost unheard of then. In today's litigious climate there would have been a large claim, which despite his admitted carelessness would have been met to a considerable extent from our compulsory employment insurance scheme.

TROUBLE WITH BOYS

It took us some time to get used to the fact that Johnny was no longer with us after so long. We had worked so well together and it was obvious that he was going to be sorely missed. There were a couple of local boys, the Reillys, who were always hanging around the village and helping us at busy times, so I suggested to the eldest, Michael, that now he had finished school he might like a job and a regular wage.

He filled the bill quite adequately for a while and then his brother Nolan, a bit of a tearaway, asked for a job as well. I was already at that age aware of a saying Father would regularly use about too many lads on the farm. Something like this. "One boy is a boy, two boys is half a boy and three boys is no boy at all." A reflection of the mischief lads will get up too in groups. Dad was initially reluctant but needs be and in the end we took him on.

For the next couple of years there were again enough hands and the fact that they were younger than me made it easier for me to control them. This was not always the case with older men, who just saw the 'boss's son' as an inconvenience and did not usually accept any instructions, unless it suited them. With the two Reillys I was now able to have some input as to how the work was done and began bringing in some new ideas.

Nolan was a little devil and had a real sparkle. I well remember one cold wet day when we were hand cutting marrowstem kale for the cows up in Chessels Six. This was an awful job, even in good weather, and we were having to stop regularly to warm our hands on the exhaust pipe of the tractor. During one break Nolan reached into his pocket.

"Ere, see these... Found 'em in me old man's bedroom, but don't know what they's for." He presented a packet of what looked like strange little balloons. "Lets put one on the top of the stack pipe and see what 'appens."

Next thing he'd unrolled one of these things and forced it over, and round, the exhaust pipe and started the tractor up. Immediately it expanded to about eighteen inches and took off over the kale and out of sight. He then did the same with the others and they both exploded, so the fun was over, soon forgotten and we went back to work. Next morning Nolan was in on time, at 7 am but had a fairly red face and looked a bit down in the dumps.

"What's up with you today" I said.

"Me old man went mad with me this morning. You know those things we blew up on the exhaust pipe yesterday?" I nodded. "Well 'e couldn't find what 'e called 'is 'Johnnys' last night and at breakfast went on at Mike and me until I told 'im where they were."

Better to have kept quiet, perhaps.

The quick backhander he had received from his father had caused the wheal on his face. We didn't play that game again and to be honest didn't really know what all the fuss was about, 'til putting two and two together a few years later. I was very innocent in those distant days, however I am not so sure that young Nolan was. I suppose with that hindsight one was better able to see why old Mr Reilly was so annoyed that night.

At this time I was still relief milking the herd, managing the pig herd at Madehurst, doing almost all the tractor work and filling in on every aspect of the two farms. The next step was to persuade Father that the rollercoaster of pig prices coupled with poor litter sizes was ample reason to sell the pigs. This we did in 1963, and at the same time found a relief herdsman-cum-general farm worker, which gave me more time to concentrate on the overall farm without the tie of the pig herd.

THE VERY CONFIDENTIAL SECRETARY

Although I was by now taking more and more of a hand in running the farms, the financial side was a mystery to me, quite simply because I knew about little more than the practical requirements; the financial aspects of running a business were yet to come.

About this time Father had engaged, on a part time basis, shared with another local farmer, Reg Hague, the services of a lady secretary. Mrs Kirby was the ultimate Private Secretary, for whom, for the following thirty years, during the time she worked for Father and then for me, confidentiality was the name of the game. The Hague family had been friends of ours for many years yet never did Mrs Kirby, as she was always addressed, discuss one iota of their business or report gossip picked up elsewhere. Similarly, we knew our business was kept equally private and that anything she learned would be left in the office as she went home.

When she began in the position, Father's moods were at, or approaching, their worst. He upset everyone by 'barking' at them or sulking. Everyone that was, except Mrs Kirby. To her he was sweetness and light, always polite and reasonable. Everything she did he thanked her for. Unusual in itself! She was a lady of good breeding who had obviously found herself on harder times. Looking a little older than she probably was, she and her husband, a self-employed insurance advisor, had a young son upon whom she doted. Peter was the apple of her eye, quite naturally, and no day in the farmhouse began without full details of her son's schooling. Her book-keeping was faultless, she took shorthand at speed, and typed likewise.

The only problem with having such efficient records was that now they quickly highlighted the fact that the farms were losing money at an unsustainable rate and it did not take long for even me to realise that things were very difficult in the business.

Father banked at that time with Barclays in Bognor whose manager, John Reynolds, was a close friend, since the two Reynolds children, Jenny and David, were keen on horses and spent their free time here with us during the mid fifties.

Father had somehow managed to keep John happy at their various official bank meetings, and whilst the overdraft increased annually, there was always a good reason to continue the overdraft facility as prospects "were looking better next year".

During this time Father negotiated the sale of a 14-acre field near the back of Felpham. Even at that time I felt there were better ways of raising cash without selling one of the 'crown jewels', but suggestions of a mortgage through the Agricultural Mortgage Corp, at around 6% over 40 years, fell on stony ground.

To many of Father's generation, borrowing money was unheard of and although the Agricultural Mortgage Corporation was brought into being for the specific purpose of lending long-term to farmers, many still feared handing over the deeds to their land.

Land at that time was worth about £130 - £150 an acre and the offer of a £1,000 an acre down and another £1,000 an acre on the granting of planning consent, surely only a few years ahead, was too good to pass by.

So the field was sold, and then leased back to us for a peppercorn rent, and for a while the overdraft 'red' turned to 'black' and everyone was happy.

Mrs Kirby, however, could see with her book keeping experience that nothing had changed: that the money had solved the overdraft in the short term but that the business was on a downward spiral.

When I sat in the office she would sometimes start pointing out the problem areas: static milk yields, poor crops of cereals and inexorably rising overheads. This was as clear as daylight, even to my untrained eye, but Father either couldn't or didn't wish to see it. Every year since 1950 the accounts had shown a loss, and every year it was according to Father, 'going to be all right', once 'so-and-so happens'. Mother had put most of her private funds in and received nothing back; even, it appeared, barely any thanks, except that she, Gay and I had a roof and food.

The crunch really came in the mid 60s, but the light began to dawn on Father when John Reynolds was moved by the bank to Jersey and Henry Trump took over as his bank manager. Henry was also tolerant. He saw the value of the land and the houses, and continued the arrangement. The bank's price was to take the deeds of everything Father owned, 80 acres and 5 houses while continuing lending to him at an expensive rate of interest.

All the farm's foodstuffs were supplied through Sadlers in Chichester; who were then, naturally, the first at the door once harvest began, buying the entire crop at rock bottom prices to square the accrued debts. Very sensible too, but it didn't help our business; it was called Merchant Credit and whilst it was convenient, and accepted by farmers across the country, it was not cheap. And so our troubles continued to grow.

Mrs Kirby worried, and made me worry too, yet Father was still hoping things would work out, whilst doing nothing positive to help. Finally Mrs Kirby spoke to him. I never knew quite what she said, but in 1963 Father announced that since I was now old enough and taking such an interest, he was going to form a Limited Company and give me almost half the shares.

I quickly reasoned that half the shares meant responsibility for half the debts, however, accountants and solicitors were instructed to draw up the terms and the debts of 'O.E. Adames (decd) and Sons' became Adames (Flansham) Ltd. Outwardly little else changed, but things were already being considered to get the company on an upward track again.

The first area I looked at was the milking herd, 60 mixed Ayrshires and Friesians whose output, instead of rising, had dropped steadily for five years since the Madehurst herd had been incorporated.

That farm now only grew cereals, whilst, until recently, we still had the sows running on some scrubby hillsides, neither enterprise being particularly profitable, since the sows had developed a nasty habit of eating their own piglets or those born to other sows and grain prices were no higher than 10 years earlier at around £16-£18 per ton.

The farm had also been increasingly overrun with couch grass, which at that time still had no effective herbicide control, and this smothered the crops every summer, affecting yields severely.

So the milkers seemed to be our salvation. Chessels was ideally suited to cattle, consisting as it still does, of small fields with good shelter belts in the form of hedges. The buildings were not ideal by today's standards but capable of housing 70 cows through the winter. Slurry and muck was a constant problem though, and the buildings, set in the lowest site on the farm, were very prone to flooding.

In those days, these things didn't matter too much, since we didn't have the pollution laws of the 1990s, and if slurry entered the ditches or silage effluent flowed alongside the lane, apart from the smell upsetting the neighbours, farming went on.

Wally, our herdsman, had given up trying to keep all his women 'satisfied at the same time' and had suddenly taken up with a new girlfriend, leaving us at a week's notice, which in those days was not unusual, but still an inconvenience.

Father found another man, Bill Pile, from a nearby village, who kept good time but to whom hygiene was an alien word. His parlour and dairy were definitely not the cleanest and how we never lost our license I didn't understand.

My concerns grew but, being quite young, I found it difficult to get across to Bill his shortcomings. He was a pleasant, laid-back, fellow whose main interest was a daily visit to the bookmakers in Yapton. Eventually I lost my patience when yet another year's figures, with more purchased cows and good grass, finished lower than the last. I told him that he could have a job as a stockman but his days as cowman were over. I gave him four weeks to decide what he wanted to do and advertised in the *Farmers Weekly* for a new man.

Shortly after this, I engaged the first man I had ever personally interviewed and selected. Jim Jays had worked for Tom Parker at Droxford. Mr Parker was one of the county's leading dairy farmers and ran several herds and a large milk round in the Fareham are. His reputation was high and since Jim had been there some years and was leaving for genuine reasons, I considered that he would be ideal.

Four weeks later he moved in to our old Lynton Cottage, which, since Gran had died had been let, and the following Monday he started work. His wage for a 6-day 55-hour week was £18 10s plus a rent-free house.

Bill, meanwhile, decided he had had enough of animals, and left, which was for the best because his interest in farming had gone.

That was the turning point in our fortunes and although the climb back would be slow, at least, from that stage, with some small hiccups, things began to improve. It became clear within days that what had gone on before would not be good enough for Jim's high standards, and I soon saw that if we didn't agree to a few improvements he would be gone as quickly as he had arrived. It was also clear that he had, to twist the old expression, 'forgotten more about cows than I ever knew' and it was pointless trying to kid him. I accepted this and although he doubtless thought I was a push-over, we rubbed along well enough and I set about picking up some tips from him.

I spent a lot of time around the dairy helping him and improving working conditions within the constraints of the funds available. New cows were purchased and the herd pushed up to 75, the limit for the buildings. When Jim's blue eyes flashed, I knew something was irking him and to look out for fireworks. He was 100% reliable and a very competent herd manager as opposed to the cowmen we had previously employed. In the four years he was with us he taught me more about feeding and milking cows than anyone before or after.

So now we again had an improving and regular income from the Home Farm and I began to look to see what I could do at Madehurst. This was harder and contained the added problem of Father's brother, Alan, who still lived in the farmhouse and 'helped', loosely speaking, on the farm. This 'help' was very limited and sadly showed little likelihood of improvement. His marriage had folded years before and he continued to spend his money long before he had earned it. Sadly, his input into the farm business was merely a hindrance, such was his lack of interest.

Father knew this, the men too, but Father had a conscience about Alan, his young brother, and could never bring himself to do anything about the situation. It was clear that Madehurst was going to be a tough problem to crack because of these family complications.

Yet I knew that growing barley was not the way forward. Before the days of the CAP and 'set-aside', UK 'Deficiency Payments' were 'pennies', and with yields of about 21 cwt an acre, perhaps 30 from wheat, giving a gross return of under £25 an acre, a dunce could have reached the same conclusion. Rent was only £3.00 an acre at that time, but the trends were rising fast.

Without major surgery I realised we could yet have to accept defeat and give up the tenancy of that lovely farm. It was quite a serious situation and the only solution to it was the thing I presently lacked most: money.

During these years, the first half of the sixties, many other peripheral, but momentous things, were happening to my life yet one of my steadiest guiding lights was Mrs Kirby and I owed her a bigger debt as the years rolled on.

UP WITH THE GODS

Back in 1960 we embarked on our second Sports Club ski trip. The same personnel formed the main party but several new faces, mainly females from the Sports Club, were encouraged to join us. The venue this time was an old Swiss resort that the Fuentes and Langmeads knew well. They told us beginners gripping tales of the steep 'black' runs, sheer rock faces and huge mountains towering skywards all around.

Again we drove out, this time Peter Brazier and his latest girlfriend, another stunning blonde, Ingrid. Crossing the Channel on the evening boat from Dover we travelled all night through rain and then snow. The route, through Arras, Bethune and down Route National 7 with cobbles in the streets and poorly marked roads, was quite exciting. Peter drove on into the Juras where, with a fresh covering of snow, we put chains on and pressed on south east through the night and early morning darkness.

Through Neuchatel the sky began to lighten and by Berne, excitement rose as we saw distant mountains covered in snow and hazy morning sunshine. Around midday we nosed into the tiny alpine village of Lauterbrunnen, with snow falling from leaden skies. Parking the car, we transferred to the cable railcar to Grutschalp and then to a two carriage, wooden-clad and wooden-seated rail coach that was to take us the last short, five-mile journey to the village.

After about two minutes of twisting and turning over bridges and round cliffs, the cloud to the south began lifting, patchily, but we were able to catch faint sight through the breaks, of sunshine and huge snowfields in the far distance. Suddenly we were in that sunshine ourselves, blinding, brilliant and hot, as we rattled along through the snow clad landscape.

Across the deep valley below us, perhaps 3 miles wide and covered by a blanket of puffy and apparently bottomless cloud, stood the most breathtaking sight I had ever seen. I had been told about the views, but nothing had really prepared me for this. The whole far side of the valley consisted of high peaks, white, blue and grey/black, snow, ice and rock. Three main mountains, which I was later to come to know as well as my own home, stood towering above.

To the left, with puffy smudges of cloud hanging to its walls, was the Eiger, showing its dreaded north face. Then the Monch, with the high observatory gleaming in the sun close to its peak and to the right, partly hidden by its lower ramparts was the Jungfrau.

Cameras clicked, newcomers stood, as every day before and since, in awe, and very soon after, with a quick stop at Winteregg, for carriages to pass at crossing points, we pulled into the station.

This was my first sight of Murren. Once seen, never forgotten.

The village was tiny, not a car had ever run on its roads, horses pulled sleighs for luggage, farm work and supplies and it was silent except for happy laughter, bells and distant music.

Murren stands on a high ledge, with the vertical rock face below falling over 1,000 feet into the hidden pastures of the Lauterbrunnen Valley. Above us, on the opposite side to the Jungfrau colossus, skiing areas, either developed or found only by half a day's climb, reached up to 10,000 feet. Beyond all that was a deep blue sky.

I fell in love with Murren on the first day of that visit. It was, and to this day retains, a magic to which mere words cannot do justice. That first trip was to shape my life and the holiday was full of excitement and discovery.

A ski instructor-cum-local butcher's son, Hans Feuz, free of ski classes for the period, offered to teach three of us to handle the boards; his price was to be a (very) regular drink. How regular we had yet to discover.

John Gillingham, Tim Lane and I began next day with Hans, and our adventures with him during those two weeks with 20 friends would make another book. The end result was that by the time we came to leave we could ski, be it piste, through trees, deep powder, or crusty and variable crud, we feared nothing. Black runs became routine, but the best bits were the variations down steep hidden gulleys and the quiet banks where the martens, chamois and capercaillie lived.

I broke three sets of skis in those two weeks and, despite the wreckage, by the end of our stay Frau Ruth Stager, in the ski shop, was treating us like her own family. As we left that far off January day, she loaded us with some 20 bars of fine Swiss chocolate and kissed us each farewell.

"See you next year," she said, and that she did, and almost every year after that until she died some 15 years later.

Many friendships were made that year. Two engagements were announced within weeks of our return and one or two more were expected but never bloomed. I was still in the early stages of that particular 'learning curve' – and there was much to be learned! I made a start in Murren, but work and sport were to take up most of my energies for several years to come. The difference between the sexes seemed to be something to enjoy without being rushed into anything. After all, my 21st Birthday was still half a year away, and in those days there were few pressures for early betrothal. Nor did most of us, of either sex, have any obvious wish to give up our new-found liberation. This was, after all, the start of the 'swinging sixties'. There was much to do, much to see and much to learn. And quite a lot of swinging to do!

My romance was now with Murren itself. The thought of that village, its hospitable natives and the freedom of its mountains had me counting the weeks and saving my wages to ensure that I would be back again next year. As I write some 40 winters later, that romance is still with me and the village has altered very little. Many old friends have left the slopes for ever but their memory is vivid.

WORK AND PLAY

That break in the Alpine snows, the only holiday of my year, invigorated me for the coming months. On the chalk downland we began sowing spring barley early in February, weather permitting, and as the days began to lengthen, work became endless.

Ploughing, cultivation and sowing; harrowing and rolling meadows, fertilising and spraying went on well into April, since as soon as Madehurst was sown, we moved all the tackle back to the home farm at Flansham, usually wetter ground, to complete there. Cleaning stockyards would then take us through to mid-May, when silage making began in earnest.

With the forage harvester and trailers the job was easier, but it still took ages – three or four weeks from start to finish for a job that today the contractors will do in a couple of days at most.

We knew no better, however, because farm mechanisation was in its infancy, so we just kept going, thankful for whatever equipment we had available.

Despite the slow work rate we were able to make time to get away from the farm and on a good many evenings the golf course beckoned. Either the course or the practice ground became our home until well after sundown and Tony, Chris, Barry, and I were never far away from it. Martin though, had early succumbed to the charms of his fiancee Pam, and we saw less and less of him.

Usually after golf we would have a drink at the Club with the regulars, who treated us with great generosity and friendliness. Probably since we were the only juniors in the Club, and to have youngsters who played as well as Tony, Chris and, particularly, Martin gave the senior members great pleasure. The encouragement we received from the likes of Jack Langmead, Ron Aris, Reg Martin, Dal Dalglish and Mac Pettie was stimulating and drove us to work at our game and improve. By this time I too was down to 7 handicap, and on the fringes of selection for the Clubs senior side.

Any one who plays sport will know the advantages of being able to play or practise with better players and this was an advantage I luckily had from the start of my golfing 'career'. The standard my friends played to set a target for others who played with them, and one learned little 'tricks' of the trade, which helped make the game easier. Of those tricks the most certain one was the truism that 'the more, and the harder, you practised the better you became'

From the Club, on many of those evenings, we would usually move back to one or other's houses where our Mothers would churn out plates of food, at all hours, for however many arrived on the door step.

Alternatively we made our way to the Sports Club or the Spur at Slindon where Ieun Roderick kept whatever hours his customers wanted, and often gave the local constable a beer at the back door too, when he came calling to see we were not still using the bar's facilities. "Of course not, Constable, and while you're here there's a horse of Fred Clay's, or Fred Pontin's, running at Newbury tomorrow that is expected to 'go in'. Which was most likely the reason the 'law' had looked in, and what the Constable really wanted to know!

The Spur was to become an increasingly regular port of call over the coming years.

A GIRL IN MY LIFE

At about this time Tony had stopped 'playing the field' with the Bognor and district girls, much, so he would tell us, to their dismay and had become extremely affected by a very pretty brunette from close to the Sports Club in Middleton.

Suddenly Sue was always close at hand. Most weekends she would appear at the Golf or Sports Club and it became more likely that Tony would slip off early. He was clearly smitten and with good reason.

One evening that July 1961, he had agreed to meet Sue at the Sports Club after we had played golf, and since I was at a loose end, I arranged to go along and join the two of them before making my way home. We arrived at the Club just as a cricket match was finishing and watched a few overs as the home side attempted to knock off the runs.

Suddenly Sue appeared behind us with a pretty, dark-haired girl I had seen once before but did not know. They came over and introductions were made.

"Nick, this is Mary Darrington," said Sue, and we shook hands.

Cricket was soon forgotten and we moved to the bar where Hutch, more interested in 'his' cricket team, hurried the drinks and left us four to it. Immediately we were at ease; Tony and Sue, always lively company, Mary, a striking younger version of Jackie Kennedy, and myself. We chatted easily for an hour. A meal was suggested but Tony and Sue had other arrangements so Mary and I decided to walk onto the sands at the end of Sea Lane. We struck up an encouraging relationship very quickly. Mary's parents lived in a house called 'Overbridge', immediately opposite the Club entrance, which was also convenient. Our parents knew each other socially and we soon found we had many things in common.

Mary was working on a modelling job for Ford, who were launching their new Cortina car and she shared a flat in London with other girls, coming down at weekends when other dates allowed. Sue and she were long-standing friends.

Over the next few weekends we usually found a reason to meet each other as a two or as a quartet, with Tony and Sue, and it soon became clear that maybe this was 'something' with a future.

Over the next couple of years the friendship was on and ... not quite on ... not off exactly, but 'on hold'. Mary had other friends and I had too, and golf and work were also pretty important.

The group we were in grew and changed steadily. Usually it was the girls who changed but Mary, who had by now been around for some time, was accepted as everyone's friend, but mostly mine, although already some of my golf mates were doing their best to prise her away from me. Half-jokingly they implied that a girl like that needed a chap with a bit more in the way of experience of the ways of the world and knowledge of the way to treat a girl ... a bloody nerve! ... but possibly correct at the time.

Despite all this, we stayed friendly and grew quite close. We played some golf, ate out and at each other's houses, saw the big city and some shows. It was the start of something, but many felt it wouldn't last.

The harvest of 1961 was by then in full swing and girls, however special, had to take a back seat, so to speak. We pressed on as hard as possible to beat a variable patch of weather. It was important to me to be finished by September, because every weekend of that month always involved a golf event somewhere in Sussex or Hampshire and I had a good chance now of getting selected to play for the club team.

At that time the club still had a number of very good players to choose from and, although I was perhaps only reserve, I usually travelled on the off chance of a game, or just to carry one of the other fellows clubs. It was a good way to learn the game at that level, and made for good team spirit and friendship.

One of the players keeping me out of the team was a new member, recently introduced into the club by Barry Targett. The first time I had met him he and

Barry turned up in the Club car park in a cloud of dust at the head of a convoy of huge estate cars emblazoned with the name 'PICCADILLY'.

"Nick," says Barry, "this is George Hammond."

George, six feet tall, hair receding and with a smile that could charm even a stone-hearted parking attendant, worked for the cigarette company Rothmans. He had just been promoted in charge of a team of reps to promote the brand around the golf clubs of England and, knowing something of the game, and with an extraordinary confident line of chat, he was clearly making his mark. He was a couple of years older than me with a handicap of 3; and an expense account that opened the eyes of us country boys.

Very soon he, his wife Ginny and their young son had found a flat to rent and moved into the nearby village of Felpham. Immediately he joined the Golf Club and Barry, George and I became a very close gang of three, within the group we already had.

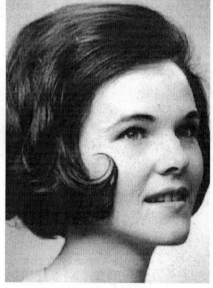

Mary Darrington in the 1960s.

(above) Portrait taken in 1962 by Charles Sayers, secretary of Bognor Golf Club.

Rothmans were just entering the world of golf promotions, sponsoring professional tournaments, and this was the first and, as yet, closest contact Bognor Golf Club and I had seen of this exciting new world.

What made it even more exciting was that since we had formed this close and easy friendship with George, it was almost unsaid that if he was involved in a big event, then so were we. Whether it was recording scores, controlling spectators, or in later years partying with the stars and their wives, for the next quarter of a century, wherever the action was, we were there too. Thus a friendship that began in the car park at Bognor golf club was soon to take several of us around almost all the main golf events and to many famous golfing venues in the UK, opening many doors and creating hundreds of new friends in the process.

That winter I eased off on the golf because I had hurt my back on the farm, although I managed to get it right in time for the January trip to Murren. This time Tony and Sue came with the party and before many days had elapsed Tony had tried his best to strain their relationship. Almost as soon as we arrived in Murren he spotted a pretty Swiss girl who smiled at him, fatal thing for a pretty girl to do, and effectively challenged him for a date.

Sue and he were not then engaged, so he fell for the challenge and promptly arranged to meet her that evening in a nearby hotel bar. To his horror, when he arrived there as arranged she was with a large Swiss Frau whom he had spotted close to her earlier, and who, it was now clear, was her mother, by his description "a daunting woman". Unable to split them, Tony quickly decided to 'cut and run' and an hour later turned up in the bar of the Palace Hotel where we all met in the evening.

In his usual confident way he breezed in and announced his bad luck, to great mirth all round, before sidling up to a slightly frosty Sue, who was clearly and unsurprisingly not over-amused at his evening's work and promptly left for bed. The atmosphere next day was cool between them; Tony was a bit chastened, for him anyway, and Sue would not talk to him. The only way they communicated for the next two days was via intermediaries or by notes passed along the party's big meal table.

It was clear by the second day that Sue was actually 'milking' the situation to the maximum, really making him pay for his ... well it wasn't actually pleasure, rather his folly. However within another day she relented and everything was back to normal. He may, naturally, have noticed other young

Swiss maids that trip but there were no more adventures along those lines during the stay.

Again, the skiing was excellent and with Hans Feuz tied up in ski school most of the time we improved on the previous year's techniques and stayed a little more sober. The only occasion we got involved with Feuz was one tea time in a nearby hotel bar where he introduced us to schnaps which was, of course, taken in tandem with a Swiss beer.

This nonsense went on for a good two hours. When we finally decided to move, I staggered to my feet, still clad in ski boots, and managed to tip the whole table over and broke something in excess of 60 stem glasses. All empty, so it wasn't a total disaster, but the noise and subsequent mess were quite memorable. It had been the result of Hans offering us one small Schnaps, reciprocated too many times. The management, knowing Hans well, smiled as we tottered out. I think had he not been there a similar group of foreigners would have been presented with a significant bill for damages.

On the way home Tim Lane climbed a lamp post in the street for a lark and on sliding down filled both of his inner thighs with huge splinters, which he then asked one of the girls to help extract, in our joint bedroom. That didn't concern me since, feeling the need of a bath before dinner, I left them to it. Feeling pretty poorly at this stage, I almost passed out in the bath before somehow managing to pull out the plug to avoid drowning. Then I went to sleep in the empty tub.

When I awoke, Tim's splinters were mainly out, at least where decency had allowed his friend to operate – the rest were down to him alone to remove.

We reached the dinner table as the last diners were leaving, and the fact that we were too late for anything other than cheese and biscuits was actually a great relief. An early night was called for, but for different reasons we didn't sleep that well.

FRED BUDD

As with any small community in those days, everyone in Flansham knew each other. Stopping to chat over garden fences was a good way to relax after work or at spare times and, being keen on the ways of the countryside, I became involved with some interesting characters who lived in the hamlet.

One such was Fred 'Jinny' Budd. Fred was Johnny Field's uncle. He lodged with George Stoner and his wife Dodie in Yew Tree Cottage, just across from our farm entrance and next to one of our big barns.

Fred worked hard. His day job was with Bognor District Council on the dustbins. Then they were called dustmen but no doubt today he would be a 'waste disposal officer' or suchlike. He was to be seen all around the area, covered with a dirty jacket in winter and stripped and bronzed in summer, hurling refuse into the old rounded dustcarts, part of a gang of cheery men who actually appeared to enjoy their work.

In late February each year, as the evenings lengthened and after Fred got home and had his high tea, I remember Mother used to seem a little nervous as she looked out to see if Jinny was in the kitchen garden.

There was never any formal agreement, nothing was said beforehand, but like the return of the swallows in spring, so would Fred appear... One evening there would be a sound in the kitchen garden of steel striking stone, of a spade turning and breaking down the soil.

'Jinny's here!' someone would say, and we knew that Spring was surely now almost here and that the garden would be tidied and planted.

Muck was barrowed in from the farmyard and dug in under each 'spit' he dug. Left rough over winter after the previous crop, and similarly dunged each year, the soil broke like fen soil and soon Fred had an area the size of a tennis court turned and ready. He worked at a prodigious speed and, as early evening turned to twilight in those late winter days, sparks could actually be seen flying as the spade hit stones in the soil, as indeed they can from a plough working late.

Later into March through into early May, Jinny would prepare and plant celery, beans, peas, potatoes and lettuce. He would weed the asparagus bed, prune the gooseberries and currant trees and sow the seeds for the bedding plants It was amazing to see what, in the odd hour each fine evening, he could accomplish.

Fred had done this in the farmhouse garden since before we moved there in 1948, doing it for Grandfather and then transferring to Father. He said little and just kept working; March and April were his main months and he left much of the weeding for others, but digging and sowing he loved and it was an art form in which he took great pride.

Between times he helped George Stoner dig a similar area at Yew Tree Cottage and at other seasons he did other things around the hamlet. Some Sunday afternoons in Spring he would wander round the deep ditches adjoining the Rife. He always carried a long stick with a tablespoon lashed to one end and as a child this always fascinated me.

Soon I found out what the sport was. Jinny liked moorhen eggs. Finding a nest out on the water he would reach out with the stick and work the spoon under an egg. When he brought it carefully back he got his pocket knife out and cut a hole in the shell, just large enough to 'draw' or suck the yolk through. After testing it was not 'setty', part incubated and already showing development of a chick, he would simply put it to his lips, suck the contents out and swallow them. The whole nest would go the same way except one egg, but if they were set he would leave them to hatch.

For weeks Jinny would go his rounds. The one egg left previously would have encouraged the hen to continue laying and the following visit invariably produced another meal.

In early summer time he hoed mangolds and beet, stacked bales or just chatted over Stoner's gate of an evening, passing on local gossip. George Stoner, though, was something of a loner, keeping himself to himself, with no obvious social life or friends beyond his wife. This could well have been the result of his experiences in the trenches during the 1914-18 War, which changed the lives of so many men for ever.

George was a strongly built man with dark, bushy eyebrows and a glimpse of dark hair which was usually kept firmly under his brown trilby. Strongly built and erect, in shirt and tie, with a dark waistcoat under a dark brown jacket and trousers and heavy studded work boots, George made little concession to summer heat. In winter too his only additional garb was a heavy trench coat and, in later years, a scarf. The only time he would be seen in conversation, always in quiet confidential tones, was over his little front gate by Yew Tree Cottage as evenings drew close. With Dodie standing alongside, he would offer passers-by little snippets of local gossip, doubtless getting theirs in return.

Between them they tended their collection of chicken, ducks and geese during the day and somehow busied themselves on their overgrown acre. That, with Fred Budd's weekly rent, and George's War pension, seemed to satisfy their simple needs. They had no children, no bicycle or car and made few trips outside the community. His only relative appeared to be a brother, who looked like his twin and lived in Flansham Lane, but who, strangely enough, I never saw in the hamlet.

Once a week, Dodie would walk to Flansham Corner, catch the 31 bus into Bognor and later could be seen tottering back from the bus stop with two large bags of stores. Apart from that I never saw either of them beyond the end of the lane.

Fred Budd, on the other hand, was quite extrovert by comparison. Around 5ft 8, receding sandy hair under his 'Andy Capp' hat, well built but without an ounce of fat, Fred looked every bit a local poacher. He always wore the same design trousers when working, tied with string round the ankles, presumably to double as cycle clips for his trips to the 'Southdown' pub.

Winter time was when I kept Jinny company. He and George kept a couple of hutches of ferrets in the back yard of the cottage and such characters didn't keep animals as pets. They had to work.

During winter Sundays, after work was done, they put the best ferret in a sack, gathered their handbill, spade and nets and set off for their sport. Catching rabbits with ferrets was, and still is, an art form, not just a matter of netting and catching, but of knowing how the rabbits live, think, and react. Fred and George would work their way slowly round the village ditches and banks as winter wore on, clearing, netting, catching and filling holes. Unhurried, they would light a fag, trace out and identify every single hole in the 'run', peg down the fine nets over each hole. When all the holes were covered, George would kneel or stand at one end and Fred the other, ferret squirming in his fist. Deftly he would raise the net, thrust the creature in and then smartly drop the net again. The two men would keep quite still, watching intently for signs of life. There would be a thumping of earth, perhaps a squeal and then a rabbit would suddenly appear and crash violently into one of the nets. George or Fred would grab it, pull the net off, break the rabbit's neck with a quick, flat-handed karate chop and fix the net back. Perhaps half a dozen more would be taken in the same way before the ferret appeared, blinking in the daylight to be returned to its sack.

On occasions, nothing would happen for half an hour. The men would silently kneel with their ear pressed to a net, listening for sounds of life. It was critical to the success of the operation that it was done outside the breeding season, since a nest of baby rabbits would soon sate the ferrets appetite and he would then curl up and sleep for hours. On such occasions if there was no sound, all Jinny and George could do was wait. Sometimes darkness would fall and they would go home and return the following day to retrieve their small co-worker. On other occasions they would try to locate the creature and dig him out, but hours were often wasted if the digging was in the wrong place. As often as not, the ferret would turn up eventually of its own accord.

An alternative was to put the ferret in the hole with a collar and a length of line, but that was often dangerous, since a root in the run could easily snag the lead and unless they knew where to dig, the ferret would die before it would be reached.

I once saw Jinny listening for action, with his ear pressed to the net, when a rabbit bolted out and knocked him sideways, followed hard on its heels by the ferret.

I joined Jinny and George on many such adventures. Never were they unsuccessful; sometimes they caught two or three, sometimes two dozen. They needed enough to feed the ferrets for the coming week and the rest would be 'paunched' and sold amongst the locals in exchange for some beer money for Jinny, who walked to the Southdowns pub every night of the week. Stoner, however, saved his proceeds. He never visited the pub and the story round the village was that the Stoners kept a hoard of money under their bed. True or false, we never knew.

One winter's night in early 1962 I heard a frantic knocking at the back door below my bedroom window. After several minutes I heard Father answer the call. It was George Stoner.

"What's up George?"

"Jinnys been in the lav since 11 o'clock". It was now 2.30 "He aint answering, can you come and help?"

Father pulled some clothes on and the two men left in the darkness. Fred was an old friend and had been looking a bit peaky for several weeks. Half an hour later Father was back. As he returned upstairs I opened the bedroom door and enquired what had happened.

"Poor old Fred's gone. Stone dead in the outside lav. Had to lever the door off to get him out." He went to bed.

Next morning he told us that Fred had had a heart attack and collapsed against the door. When they eventually got him out they took him indoors and laid him out, only calling the doctor when normal folk start work in the morning.

"Poor old Fred was dead. No need to spoil another man's sleep for something that could wait until daylight."

For years afterwards at tea time in early Spring, we used to remark "Old Fred will be round any day now...". If only. Our kitchen garden was not to be looked after so well again for over twenty years.

People such as Jinny were irreplaceable. They contributed to village life because they got pleasure from their involvement. They earned pocket money, yes, but they didn't make a big issue of the pay. The ferreting, gardening and poaching were their hobbies and they enjoyed being part of the village scene.

LAST OF THE SUMMER WINE

Yet another character moved into Flansham in the fifties, fresh from a broken marriage. London-born and with no knowledge of the countryside, over the next 45 years Ron Middleton was to become an indispensable part of our community. Ron's first job in the area was working as a car mechanic at Mr Barnett's Empire Garage, opposite the Southdowns Pub. One day, after he had been there a while and had got to know Father, Ron asked him if he had anywhere he could park a caravan. Since he was such a cheerful soul, and as Father would have seen the benefit of having a mechanic living close by, he offered Ron a site up behind George Stoner's house at the back of the old stockyard. The terms of the arrangement were that Ron paid no rent for his site but would help out with any small maintenance jobs in his spare time. It was an arrangement that was to last for almost half a century.

Shortly afterwards, Ron and his caravan arrived, and within a few months, with his cheery manner making many friends, he was filling in his free time doing odd electrical or mechanical jobs on the farm and for other villagers.

In about 1962, Father was on the point of selling the yard and barn to a London businessman, Gordon Summerfield, to build a house. Ron would have to move. The only site away from the prying eyes of the planning officers was up Hoe Lane, past Gerry Young's cottage on the left, in the now defunct brickfield.

A hive of industry between the Wars, the area of the brickyard, about four acres, had fallen into complete disrepair when World War II came along and was completely overgrown by the 1960s. Father reasoned that Ron could hide his caravan up there and be safe from snoopers from the planning office, so one weekend he moved, did a deal with Dick Puttick in the next door cottage to allow him a power supply and settled in.

The years went by and Ron left Barnett's and worked as an electrician for a large factory in Bognor. All the while he would never refuse his help to anyone wanting a job done on an engine, an electrical appliance, wiring a house, mending a fuse, or even, once, driving a group of us in a ancient minibus to London to a function.

The word in the Hamlet in any crisis was "Send for Ron" and day or night, Christmas Day or Easter Sunday, Ron would drift in with his toolbox and more likely than not, after a lot of chatter, much improvisation and a few cups of coffee, the magic would have worked.

When the road past his home needed repairing, since it was, and still is unadopted, Ron was always the one who spent hours with barrow and shovel, levelling the odd loads of rubble dropped close by for that purpose. The other residents looked on whilst Ron worked.

Ron and old Joe Wilkins, one of Langmead's retired farm workers who lived opposite in Rose Cottage, became great buddies and in later years, after Ron's retirement, Joe's wife Molly took him under her wing and often fed him in exchange for the good company and comradeship he offered old Joe.

One of the funniest situations occurred more recently with Ron over his transport. He had acquired two cars, both blue Ford estates but different models. One, incidentally, given him by George Hammond who had nowhere to dump it and who knew that Ron could never turn down a bargain, particularly a free one. Both cars were basically worthless, having failed their MOT, but Ron was not deterred. He got one restored in his garage and persuaded a mate in a local garage to pass it and then set about restoring the other car into a similar condition.

Over the next ten years he would present whichever car was in the best condition for the annual MOT; and every year he had a blue Ford Estate car with a valid certificate. But, I hear you asking, how could this plan not be foiled by the obvious differences between the cars and their number plates? Well, amazingly, quite easily. The cars were both Fords, both were blue, and both were Estates. The little matter of number plates was overcome by the simple fact that he had only one set, and they were transferred to whichever car was presented. Once he had the MOT again, the disc and plates went on whichever vehicle was thought to be in the best working order.

When I suggested to Ron the risks of getting caught he laughed, "I'm 86 now", he said, "I can't afford another car. I won't be driving much longer and if they lock me up I won't have to look after myself."

Pretty sensible, so I left it there...

Earlier days in Flansham. The author's grandparents with young Jack and a cousin, New Year 1909. The old smithy and farm cottages behind.

~ *Chapter Four* ~

THE GRAIN DRIER

We were, by this time, involved constantly in building works, new barns, removing expensive and poorly maintained thatched roofs, concreting previously muddy yards and trying to make conditions more suitable for machinery to operate. Now, having changed our old combine for a bulk model I had the idea of complementing it with a 'continuous flow' grain drying plant with bulk storage bins attached.

The site of this drier was to be where we had the range of pig sties, about 30 in all on an area the size of two tennis courts. In the late winter of 64 I began the task of demolishing these sties and clearing the site. All the brickwork was broken up with sledge hammers and the site cleared; by hand and wheel barrows.

Once it was clear I laid out the footings for the drier plant, hand dug the grain pit and laid the access for trailers, finally allocating the position of the new grain bins which were to be situated in Marks barn, immediately next door.

By early that March, when I had to go and help the Reillys complete spring sowings at Madehurst, the new building was half way to eaves high, and Father was busy finding enough good second-hand timber around the district to fabricate the roof trusses. These were required to be some 40 feet long and he constructed the five trusses with his usual ingenuity; he was in his element.

By the time silaging came around in mid May the roof was timbered and ready for sheeting. The new Alvan Blanch drier had been delivered and the floor concreted to accept it.

After silage, which went well that year, I had eight weeks before harvest, when the grain would start flowing and the grain bins, four of them fourteen feet high and reinforced, still had to be built. I was my own bricklayer and

(opposite page): The Author cutting barley under a stormy sky in the Glebe field at Madehurst, with spaniel Judy in the foreground. July 1972.

labourer, mixing cement and sand, carrying it to site, and moving and laying the heavy 9" x 18" hollow blocks, each weighing about 50 lbs. This was hard work and the higher the walls rose the harder it got. When that task was completed the interior had to be rendered and the floors water proofed.

All the while Father was fabricating sliding doors, additional round galvanised grain bins and most vitally, overhead in the rafters high in the top of Marks barn, the important continuous chain and flight elevator to deliver the grain to the new bins.

Goodrowes installed the drier, the grain augers, oil burner system and the numerous electric motors, wiring and fuse boxes. All that now remained, as the first barley approached full ripeness at Madehurst, was to fill the grain pit and pray. It had been six very hard months' work.

I was away cutting the corn on the hills and so was not present as the first load went in but messages relayed back, via Buckle or Mike Reilly as they returned from the 16-mile round trip between drier and combine, with empty grain trailers, were encouraging.

By that evening Father, who was to be in charge of the plant for the next dozen years, had the whole thing under control. The surprise was that the system really worked a treat, the only modifications being needed concerned the transfer of grain from the old Penny/Porter cleaner/grader, to the overhead chain and flight elevator in the roof of Mark's Barn. Father called in Ron Middleton, and between them modifications were effected which largely lasted the life of the drier, which was to end 23 years later on the night of the great storm of 16/17 October 1987.

I returned from the hills that first night and heard the humming drier and saw the golden dried grain cascading down into the distant new bins, every aspect exactly as I had planned it and as Father and I had built it. The satisfaction was immense. The only part of the system that caused concern and much dusty work over the following years was the emptying of the big bins into lorries at point of sale, during the winter and spring.

Ideally we would have transferred the crop to an overhead bin, with enough capacity to fill a lorry, augering the grain up before the vehicles arrived. As it was, the lorry had to stand whilst the auger lifted the grain from floor level and at times the buyers and drivers became impatient, with some justification. However, that didn't become obvious in the first harvest and with the end of sack carting, and humping, the task had become infinitely more bearable. And one less back-breaking bottleneck.

In fact the only really hard slog left on the farms then, hard physically that is, was the handling of bales; and at that time, in 1964, there were still to be another 10 years of hand lifting between 20,000 and 25,000 bales a year, from stubble to trailers, from trailers to stack. Luckily I didn't' know that then! That job was to take a heavy toll on my long back and cause much sweat to run! It also broke the hearts of some of the labourers who, after a day or two, would fail to come in. In all honesty, there were some hot days when I could have given up too, but then I had a bit more at stake than mere wages and also had the thought of the coming autumn's golf events to keep me going.

NEW HORIZONS

The autumn of 1964 was to be special. I now an automatic selection for the golf club scratch team, helped by the fact that Tony and Martin had left the club as marriage and other commitments took them away from Bognor. It was special also because George Hammond had, that Spring, landed a 'plum' commission, a job that was to give his close friends, many years of very special sporting memories.

George's employers, Rothmans, had been sponsoring golf promotions for a few years, nothing too grand, and George as a keen golfer of ability and, it must be said, an exceptional line in smooth talk, had become increasingly involved. In the spring of 1964 it was announced that, in conjunction with a successful American golf promoter, Mark Macormack, Rothmans were going to sponsor an exclusive event in Surrey the following October. It was to carry the largest prize money ever offered and feature the best players in the world.

There was a great buzz around Bognor Golf Club. Already George had lined up a number of his mates to help with the event in different capacities, although almost every member tried to get in on the act or to get free tickets! The event was called the "Piccadilly World Match Play Championship" and featured eight of the world's best players, among them several British Open Champions like Peter Thomson, Gary Player and Arnold Palmer.

George had arranged for one of us to accompany each player during every 36-hole match, starting with eight players on the Wednesday and down to the final two on Saturday in the first week of October. Sunday golf was not, in those days, acceptable. Happily agreeing to 'help' for the whole event, I was guaranteed a job, walking with the players and caddies on each day.

When the tournament began, Barry and I travelled to and from Bognor to Wentworth each day, leaving by 6 am and home by 10.30pm. Mary found time to come for two days.

On the course, I was responsible for passing information, gleaned from my own eyes, the caddie or perhaps the player, as to which club had been used, for the TV and subsequently the film makers to include in the commentaries. These films became extremely popular around the country's Golf Clubs each winter and largely helped justify the expense of the promotion as the Piccadilly brand became increasingly synonymous with golf.

That week was a dream, and a world removed from heaving bales, cleaning cow yards or building grain driers. With George's help, our group was quickly accepted everywhere by officials, caterers (where we had priority for food and drinks, so vital was our task!), caddies and even some of the players. If we were really lucky, even with the smart 'Piccadilly Girls' working with George's crew promoting the brand!

The week ended with a tremendous final between Arnold Palmer, already the first modern superstar of golf and Neil Coles, a particularly non-flamboyant but doughty performer at that time. Palmer won on the 34th hole, watched by a crowd of enthusiasts the like of which I never witnessed again at any event in the country.

Sometimes thirty deep, they lined fairways and careered down narrow paths behind the players. Crowd control was not yet developed or ready for such scenes and it was a miracle nobody was trampled to death, the players included, so enthusiastic did the galleries become.

Palmer made a wonderfully eloquent speech at the prize giving and we all congratulated ourselves on how well we had run the event! Or survived it.

George was suddenly thrust into the limelight, TV and the national press featured him regularly and his star was on the up, but to his credit he was never anything but the same person we saw at home and he continued to treat everyone the same.

A few days later at the Club he suggested that Mary and I – at that time enjoying a quite steady period in our friendship – join him and his wife Ginny for ten days in Malta. He wanted to buy or rent a house there and sought to make a holiday of it.

Despite work demands Father agreed, and a couple of weeks later, in late October, we flew off in a foursome from Heathrow. My first flight, and my first time beyond mainland Europe.

Paradise Bay, at the extreme west tip of Malta, was then quite unspoilt, with one hotel, where we stayed, and nothing else but sea and rocks and sunshine. Mary and I, who of course had single rooms, had a ball – we hired our own car and funded it by nightly visits to the Dragonara Casino where we played roulette 'til the early hours.

George found a small house at St Paul's Bay and the sun and the warm sea completed the stay. We also visited museums and saw the sights, returning in early November to mud and grey skies.

SHOOTING OFF TARGET

Altogether 1964 had been a busy and fulfilling year, but now with winter again upon us, routine filled the weekdays, and thoughts turned to the coming Saturdays when we would be shooting on the various farms belonging to our growing little 'syndicate' of neighbours.

Seven different landowners and between four to five thousand acres of land were involved. Each week we met at a different farm and shot over a portion, trying not to overshoot what was still a natural habitat with only wild birds. Some land held partridges, some pheasant, but because only two villages still had dairy herds, Flansham and Barnham (where John Forse farmed), only these spots still retained cover suitable for both birds.

We also had literally hundreds of hare and these were a big feature of several days shooting. Teddy was still involved with the beating and keepering, although Algy had moved away after he and his wife fell out. Langmead's head cowman, Percy (Pat) Morris, also helped. We always tried to have at least eight guns each day and often this involved inviting non-farming guests. Some became regulars, though others, whose safety and gun-handling was to prove a bit doubtful, came but once.

'Doc' Ferris still came at times, but he was in the throes of retirement and preparing to move north to Banchory, and we saw less and less of him. Another memorable medical guest who came just a few times was Doctor 'Budge' Pain, the same man who a dozen years earlier had told Father he had lung cancer and had a lot to answer for! But life is too short to hold things like that against someone, and he was invited too.

I can remember to this day a drive we did that winter, the first 'stand' of the day down in Jack's brooks. We stood, backs to the Rife, waiting on a cold morning for the beaters to bring in Worms Field stubbles. Teddy had promised some good coveys of English Partridge and we waited keenly. The odd birds, pigeon, starlings, etc flew overhead. Pigeons usually attracted a shot or two from guns, getting their eye in, but most flew on. 'Budge' stood two guns to my left, Father was in between. Nothing was imminent and I talked quietly to Bill Loveys on my right.

Suddenly there was a 'bang ... bang!'

Surely we hadn't missed the first covey?

Looking across, Pain ejected two shells from his gun. As guns on both sides watched in amusement two starlings flew off to the north over his head. Nothing was said.

Still we waited. Again, suddenly, a muffled 'bang', again from Doc's direction. Fiddling with his gun he had inadvertently caught the trigger and discharged it into the ground between his feet. From where I stood he appeared as white as a ghost. Then father called across for all to hear.

"Get him Doc?"

The good Doctor looked particularly sheepish. It was an occasion, and a remark, that those of us still around remember to this day. It was also the last time Budge came shooting with us.

In the early to mid sixties the farming system was changing. A rapid switch from under-sown stubbles and root crops to early autumn drilling of wheat, meant 'game cover' was reducing. In a very short period the only land worth shooting, but being shot too much, was Flansham, where Langmeads and we still had our dairy herds. We had acres of kale and fodder beet for 'cover' with a similar situation at Shripney, where Langmeads grew acres of cabbage, sprouts and broccoli for the local wholesale greengrocery trade.

Too often, after a barren morning's sport at Ford or Barnham and needing some sort of 'bag' to distribute at the end of the day, someone would suggest "lets go to Shripney or Flansham". This always produced the birds, but the extra pressure diminished the subsequent bags and also the number of wild birds going into the next breeding season. Foxes too were an increasing menace and few weeks passed when one or two were not killed.

Six or eight years previously, we had been shooting perhaps 15 brace of partridges and 50 wild pheasant a day and now it was down to perhaps 25 pheasants and a brace of partridge. One day over our lunch in a cold hay barn at Ford, Bill Loveys, now the MP for Chichester and living in my family's old house in Flansham, questioned how we could keep things going, since without action our shoot was certainly going to fail. Bill and I agreed the answer may be for us to rear and release perhaps 500 birds in the best locality, Flansham.

But where to rear them; and who could do it?

We had an old Victorian granary, by now thankfully disused, so I offered it for the job. The other guns, when approached later, agreed to this and also to pay about £100 each for the costs of chicks and food for the first year. Pat Morris agreed to look after the birds, since Teddy was increasingly tied up in national sea-fishing competitions and having great success, so was rather losing his interest in shooting.

The following year, Pat Morris and Alan Woolven (John Forse's manager from Barnham Court) converted the building, built a large outside release pen in a quiet corner of our field Marlhole, to the north of the village, close to the centre of the best shooting, and took delivery of the day-old chicks.

The results that next season were encouraging and the year after that we shot significantly more pheasant, although the partridges declined steadily. Whilst the other farms were less and less worth visiting on shoot days, at least we could get good and regular sport at Flansham and the land close by, and so, for a while, the shoot continued quite successfully.

THE HIGH LIFE CONTINUES

The year following the inaugural World Matchplay, George and Jinny had rented our old (Lynton) cottage for a while since they were in the process of having a house built to accommodate their growing family. George and I were playing a lot of golf together around the South and as well as his golf interests Rothmans were involving him in sponsorship of horse racing.

Mary and I enjoyed my first ever day's racing at Lingfield that May for Rothmans hosting of the Derby Trials, and a group of us golfers were incorporated into the massive hospitality complex for an exciting day's sport.

This really was living ... country boy meets Society! Dennis Compton and Keith Miller sat at the next table, Prince Karim, later to become the Aga Khan, who I had actually seen the winter before at a prizegiving in our hotel in Murren, had a horse running and many famous names flitted in and out. George, as always, knew them all and never had any hesitation in introducing his personal friends. Needless to say we had a ball.

The second Piccadilly tournament came that October and again Barry and I were in full attendance. That year Jack Nicklaus played, as did Gary Player, and our list of friends and contacts grew.

Already a particularly easy rapport was struck up between Gus Payne, the main caterer for that and many other sporting events, and Mary and I, presumably, as everyone suggested, because he liked Mary – but then everyone did...

Because we were always around and George was by now such an integral part of the golfing scene, Gus always involved us in his private gatherings. He ran his complex of private hospitality marquees for various companies and had his own private marquee, squeezed in out of sight of the general public, where he always found time to entertain friends at about 10.30 - 12.00, before the thousands of paying guests began pouring off the golf course looking for refreshment.

In the early years, we 'workers' were too busy enjoying the spectacle of these great events, but as time went on, Mary and I received much kindness from Gus. He was in the mould of Mr Pickwick, on the stocky side with a huge set of side whiskers and a cheery extrovert personality. His career had begun in a stall next to Jack Cohen, later of Tesco fame, in Covent Garden. Those he didn't know in the City were, perhaps, not worth knowing.

Gus ran his staff like a benevolent dictator and relied on his manager Alan Cox to sort out all the minute to minute problems, so quickly Alan too became our good friend for many years.

By the time the 'World Matchplay' had been running for three or four years, the week had become something of an institution for golf fans in Southern England. People who didn't see each other for the rest of the year would agree to meet as usual, 'by the 8th Green' or 'the 11th tee' or wherever they had first made each other's acquaintance at an earlier event.

The first day, Thursday, was always the most crowded, because all the players were on parade. After that, although huge crowds continued to come, many, after having been for a day, would watch the rest of the event on TV where in those days it received full and comprehensive coverage.

My parents, only just getting interested in golf, would watch avidly for signs of Barry, Tony, Chris or me, as we passed by in sight of the cameras at some vital stage of a match. By this time in the mid-late 1960s, I had moved on to being 'crowd marshal', supervising the stewarding and crowd control for a match and on many occasions found myself in conversation with the players.

It was always a matter of timing as to how those conversations went. Severiano Ballesteros, in the later years of the event, was a charmer when winning and like a heavy thunder cloud when not. An inspirational golfer, he used to appear to grow a foot in stature when his game was really alight. The most easy ones to communicate with were the likes of Tony Lema and Tom Watson, who were always totally courteous. Peter Thomson was to be avoided at all times and in the early years Jack Nicklaus and Gary Player were in their own cocoon of concentration, and all communication was through their caddies, Jimmy Dickinson and Willie Aitcheson. Another hugely communicative man was Lee Trevino, the extrovert Texan, who would talk to anyone and later took over Willie as his caddie, from Gary Player.

At the same period George's promotional work took him around the world most years, contracting players for Wentworth. Augusta in April, the Far East, the US Open, and the British Open. In 1966 he suggested that Mary and I might like to go to Muirfield, East Lothian, for the event. To make it 'above board', my trip was, however, to be earned by me having to spend the four days of the event on high photo towers, 20ft above the crowds, naming the players for the film crew. The cameramen knew nothing about golf, certainly not the players, and as by that time I knew almost every player on the tour by sight it was a vital but often a very cold job as those northern breezes whirled around the course. All this again was for the benefit of the subsequent film to be shown during the coming winter around the nation's golf clubs.

As you can imagine this was the sort of working holiday that most golfers would die for, with free accommodation, the best restaurants every evening (the Open Arms at Dirleton being our favourite in 1966) and above all the chance to meet the world's top players socially.

1966 was also a quite momentous year at home, since Father, then aged 60, announced to my great surprise that he was going to step back and leave me to run the farms. Quite against his character, and to my great relief, he intended to spend his time, apart from when I needed him, fishing with a local friend, Mr Baker, and golfing with Jack Langmead.

Everyone found this quite hard to believe, because farmers are notoriously unable to hand over the reins to sons until either death or bankruptcy force events. Father, being such a hard taskmaster and so Victorian in his outlook and actions was thought by all to be one of the most unlikely of men to take a back seat. However, I was 27 and had begun to mould the farms in a more progressive way, and that clearly counted in the decision. Also, although it was never said, he was probably greatly influenced in this, firstly by Mother, who knew more than anyone the strain of two strong-willed men under the same roof, and secondly by Jack Langmead.

I am certain that he decided the best thing for Father was to learn to relax. Fish, golf, meet new faces and get away from the farm. Jack himself had handed over to Don, his younger son, some five years earlier, since his brother Ian was not very keen on farming and was keeping chicken in a quiet corner of the hamlet.

Jack found things went surprisingly well and felt the same would happen with us. He was indeed correct and although we still had our difficult moments, they were much less frequent and the men on the farm now knew I was 'boss'. Two bosses make for impossible situations, as one often countermands the other's orders with the result that both look fools in front of the staff.

Another factor that doubtless influenced his decision was that it was becoming increasingly likely that Mary and I would eventually (it was five years since we had met!) become engaged and probably married. His son would need room in the same way he had 28 years before.

Not that Mary and I let on to any one, in fact everyone else seemed to be more concerned about our relaxed situation than we ourselves. Several friends had married around that time. Tony and Sue had moved to a house west of London and he was now with a large firm of surveyors and commercial property agents. Chris had married Margaret, an old sparring partner of my sister Gay, he becoming a partner in his Father's legal firm in Bognor.

Barry had married Heather, daughter of Bognor's then controversial vicar Dr Sinclair Snow and sister of John Snow, later a cricketer of repute. Barry and his father ran a chain of four butcher shops in the area and, in those pre-supermarket days, this business ensured a good life.

Martin had married his 'Lancashire lass' and moved to East Sussex, his prime golfing days behind him, since he had no interest in becoming a professional golfer; although for the next twenty years he remained as competent a player as any, professionals included, in the British Isles. His friends regretted his decision to forego golfing fame more than he ever did. His decision, in retrospect, was probably right because whilst his ability was unquestioned, his dedication was, shall we say, somehow diminished when the game was over and a few drinks, a game of poker, or the greyhounds at Brighton were suggested. These, and Pam, and fun, were his scene and a great talent was probably largely unfulfilled, with few obvious regrets by the man himself.

All these betrothals made our situation more vulnerable, but despite that, those years were fun and socially very carefree. Eventually however, in early December, Mary accepted the challenge so many doubted she could handle and I obtained permission from her father, George Darrington, one evening before we went to the Red Cross Ball at Arundel Castle. Her parents and her two sisters, still at home, were clearly delighted at the prospect of an imminent celebration, particularly as they, Jane and Peta, were to be bridesmaids.

We later arrived at the Ball, saying nothing of the event, and it was a good hour before a local 'matron' noticed a shining new ring on Mary's finger. As the word went round our fellow dancers they mostly expressed a feeling of relief that we had finally conformed. I jokingly said it had taken so long because I needed to teach Mary both to ski and play golf, and to enjoy both, since the prospect of a marriage without strong common outside sporting interests would, to my thinking, have been a dull liaison and unlikely to last. The date was set for 30th September the following year, 1967, and consequently the Christmas celebrations that year went with an extra zing.

PREPARATIONS FOR THE BIG DAY

And so 1967 went like a flash. The biggest problem we had was in finding alternative housing for Jim Jays and his large family who were still living in Lynton Cottage as we struggled to gain permission for their new farm cottage. With the influence of Bill Loveys, our MP, we eventually, just in the nick of time, obtained consent for a new bungalow and hurried its completion by late Spring. Mary and I, with the kind help of Peter Pratt, spent every spare moment painting the house, supervising re-wiring, which Ron Middleton did himself, and installing central heating which was to be our special luxury.

At Mary's suggestion we renamed the house 'Flansham Cottage' that name now free since our original house of that name was renamed when the Loveys moved in some years before. Then, hardly before we realised it, harvest had come and gone, and the day was almost on us.

For some time Mary had been living back at Overbridge, working with her Mother in the chain of fashion shops her parents were building up. By this time some seven shops and this took a huge amount of the Darrington family's time. Consequently she worked six days a week, right up to the weekend of the event.

The wedding was set for 30th September at Yapton Church under the guidance of the Rev Herbert Hamnett who, as an ex-Army Padre and member of the Golf Club, was the human side of the Church and had become a firm family friend. He had already married Mary's brother Michael to his wife Paula, and was anticipating some considerable business from the family in the next few years!

The evening before the wedding, somewhat foolhardily but the fashion in those lawless days, I set off with a large group of friends for an evening at the Spur; the pub run by the Roderick family where we had spent so much time in recent years. Herbert Hamnett, also a Spur local, was in attendance and clearly intent on enjoying himself, so we all ensured his tankard was full.

Long after closing time we all moved to the Well House in Slindon where our friends, Peter and Viv Brown handed out food, drinks and friendship to all, and the house heaved with noise. Peter Brown warned everyone that his aged mother, living upstairs would be kept awake and cross, but we ignored him and partied till the early hours.

Herbert was one of the first to break ranks needing, he said, to prepare for the Service on the Altar step. The most pressing concern we shared was of his condition to drive home, but someone concluded, "He has God on his side" and off he tottered. As he stepped out of the front door there was a gasp, a splash and a shout from above. Herbert turned around, soaked. Peter's Mother had prepared carefully and the contents of a jug of cold water had hit the first one to leave the rowdy party. It was a memorable sight to close a memorable evening.

Next morning a group of us played golf at Bognor, but our heads were too cloudy to concentrate and after a 'hair of the dog' we slipped off home to dress.

Yapton Church was a picture, Mother had supervised the flowers with Jessie Hague, every pew was packed and when Mary arrived, not too late, I turned to greet her in the aisle. We smiled broadly at each other and the whole congregation seemed to smile with us.

Tim Lane was my Best Man and didn't forget the ring. Our sisters, Jane, Peta and Gay were lovely bridesmaids, George and Ginny's boys, Charlton and Russell were page boys and Herbert struggled with difficulty to get the words right. This caused some considerable amusement amongst all present who were mainly aware of his antics the previous evening.

After much snapping of cameras, chatting and laughter in the sunshine outside the old church we all removed ourselves to the Richmond Arms Hotel at Goodwood for an amazing buffet reception in a huge marquee in the grounds. Here we were joined by yet more friends who, unable to fit into the old church just came for the reception.

The time flashed past. Suddenly it was time for speeches; from Bill Loveys, Tim and the groom. George Darrington too felt the need to say a few well chosen words about his daughter and then, with very little further delay we changed into 'civvies', piled into my old Land Rover, tied with the obligatory junk, and drove off to our new life together.

On the way out of the car park, a very tipsy Graeme Penfold, camera in hand, walked straight into the car and fell in a heap. Fortunately there was no damage to the car and as he picked his camera up we sped away with the waves and wishes of the gathering behind us.

After briefly stopping at Middleton to change cars and clothes at Overbridge, within a short while we were on the road north... and since honeymoons are meant to be private affairs, so was this one.

Suffice it to say that having enjoyed ten days travelling around Scotland, we managed to time our return south to coincide with the opening day of the '67 Piccadilly at Wentworth where, for a change, instead of working for George we were spoilt by Gus Payne and wined and dined around the event.

When we arrived home on Saturday evening all we wanted to do was rest, such had been the effort of enjoying ourselves. Within another two days we were both back at work, almost as if nothing had occurred!

Life now seemed very comfortable and instead of going to each other's houses we enjoyed our own. Here was privacy we both enjoyed and at the same time our families were near at hand.

Mary and her mother Kay were very close and worked well as a team. They talked ten to the dozen about their buying trips to London, what fashions their clients would be wearing next 'season', about staff, recipes, and their business and so largely I got on with my farming and golf when there was time.

Mary would leave home by 8.30, six mornings a week, my lunch left ready prepared in fridge or oven and drive to her shop in Brighton some 24 miles east. At the end of the day she would arrive home at about 6.30 and do the housework. Unsurprisingly, this was hard work and before long we came to the conclusion that there were two things we needed in our new home. Shortly afterwards we found a local 'daily' lady to come in for three mornings a week and this helped Mary enormously. It gave her a little time to unwind when she came home each evening and freed the weekends a little too.

One Sunday about six weeks later, I was playing golf at West Sussex GC with a good friend, Ian Tuson. When we had finished and had the customary drinks in the club I asked Ian if he would drive home via West Chiltington because I wanted to visit someone.

At Mr Steele's farm, some five minutes later, we were lead to an old stable where, when throwing back the door, the farmer revealed a Springer bitch in the straw with a huge litter of puppies fighting for her milk.

Luckily I had heard of this litter early and was the first to come calling, and so had the choice of the bunch. As we entered, the little bundles of brown and white fluff left their feeding and came bounding across to clamber over our feet. As all dog owners will know, pups at this age are irresistible and these were no exception.

I looked at them all as Mr Steele pointed out their already developing personalities, but I was only interested in a bitch so this cut the choice almost in half. But which was it to be? I handled them all as they scrabbled for attention. Ian fancied one particular one and tried to influence me. Then I noticed the 'runt' of the litter, sitting minding her own business in the corner where they now lay, having quickly tired of socialising. She was small but strong for her age and as I went to lift her she rolled over on her side and eyed me cautiously.

I lifted her and looked her into the eyes and as she looked confidently back I knew this was the one for me. With no doubt now in my mind I paid Mr Steele the princely sum of £10 (he asked £12 but I argued she was very small). As we got into the car and drove off she promptly piddled on me and then dozed off in my lap.

When we arrived home I bundled her up inside my golf clothes and Ian and I went into the kitchen where Mary had lunch ready.

"Sorry we're late, got a bit delayed," I said. A regular golfer's excuse which, already, my bride knew only too well.

"What on earth is that under your arm?" said Mary, and with that I looked down to see a little short stub of a tail wagging gently. I unwrapped the sweaters and, a little nervously, revealed the tiny mite.

Thus the second thing we needed to make our house a home had arrived. The last family dog had been a Peggy, so 'Judy' was immediately christened and ten minutes later lay asleep in a small seedbox by the kitchen radiator.

Ian, Mary and I finished our lunch, which included a good bottle of wine to celebrate the new arrival. It had been a well spent half hour, Mary was seemingly as delighted, and not once over the following 16 years did I ever have cause to regret my choice of canine companion.

TROUBLE WITH BANK MANAGERS

Despite these 'diversions', my priority was still that of securing our financial base. Just as it had been for my Father, so it was for me and would continue to be for the following thirty years. Improvements in the dairy continued apace, but early in 1968 Jim Jays, looking for an easier life, opted to move his family to Bognor, where he had the offer of a secure house, and gave in his notice. This was a setback for us, especially when a replacement man, found by a recruitment agency, proved to be an expensive disaster. He had all the right qualifications but no experience, common sense or work ethic and was totally incompetent. He lasted just over three years, cost us a lot of money in vets fees and herd health, disturbed the fragile cash flow recovery and was finally given instant notice for yet another disaster. It was a relief to see the back of him.

This period without an efficient herdsman had affected our income quite substantially and the new bank manager at Barclays, who had taken over after the retirement of Henry Trump, became nervous. This man clearly had no experience of agriculture and gave me a hard time from 'day one'.

It was not long before I received a phone call advising me that Barclays would honour no more company cheques unless by specific agreement. I immediately protested, pointing out that, as everything, including the weekly staff wages, was paid by cheque, I would need to be constantly on the phone to comply with his wishes.

At that time we had an overdraft limit of around £15,000, which I have to admit, was almost always stretched . I was regularly spending money on building up the herd numbers, since this increased cash flow, but it was taking a lot of cash. This was before leasing and HP arrangements had become common practise and an overdraft was the simplest way to fund such investments.

The company owned some 110 acres of good land in Flansham, adjoining the coastal strip of development. We also owned four good houses and the working assets. Not, admittedly, worth a fortune, but anyone other than a bank manager would probably have seen some potential.

Sadly this man didn't, so now I had to move fast. During my travels around the golf courses of the county, I had already made many friends who were to help me tremendously, in many ways, over the years. One such was a Goodwood member, Tom Chadbon, a very pleasant man, a good golfer and also a bank manager for the National Westminster in Chichester.

On receipt of Barclays ultimatum, I phoned Tom in his office and he made time to see me that day. I explained my problem in some detail and he then requested information on certain aspects of our business, took the accounts I offered and finally gave me some fearful-looking budget forecast sheets and cash flow identifiers, which he asked me to fill in over the next few days.

Then, promising to speak to his head office at once, we said our farewells and, much cheered, I returned home. That evening I began struggling with the cash flow projections.

Fortunately, Tom had given me several blank sheets and by using a pencil rather than a pen, I had, after several long evenings and with much head-scratching and rubbing out (since I had no calculator) managed to complete the form. There is no doubt that filling in such forms serves two purposes. They give you a projection, which if done on a 'worst-case scenario' basis, rather than on the assumption that everything will work perfectly, sets a realistic target.

They also made an inexperienced farmer, as I was then, aware of the effects on the timing of vital purchases, particularly larger ones, on the overall financial picture. I learned a lot about the business that I had not even considered before. Father had routinely used the back of envelopes for his calculations but I quickly realised that those days were gone for ever!

A week later Tom called me from his office and a meeting was set for the following day. This was a great relief, since Barclays had been on the phone every day that past week giving me a lot of aggravation. When I arrived, Tom welcomed me into his office and we sat and talked of golf handicaps, the week's other news, and almost everything but finance.

Then suddenly he said, "I've got this chequebook for you. When do you want to open your account?"

Just like that.

"Tomorrow will suit me fine," I said, "But what about the overdraft?"

"You can have £20,000 now and we will keep it under review for a year. Just do your best and if you have any problems come back to me. We won't stop any of your cheques, so don't worry."

Life was suddenly much sweeter as I walked back to my car. Now I could repay Barclays in full.

Mrs Kirby was in the office when I returned home and we immediately discussed things in detail.

"Write to Barclays," I said, "instructing them to transfer every single item they hold, the account and any documents to Nat West, as from today. Close the account and say no more."

I really did enjoy signing that letter.

The pressure was now released and I could get on with farming without the constant worry of money. Mary and I had a small drink that evening and went to bed light-headed. We had both been under pressure that we could have done without. The most immediate effect was that I woke up around midnight with the most intense stomach cramps; awful, debilitating surging pain, so bad that I poured with sweat and almost cried out as it increased in intensity before ebbing again. This went on for some three hours.

Mary wanted to call the doctor but I refused and she fretted whilst the attacks continued. At about 4 o'clock the intensity of the cramps began to diminish and by the time *Farming Today* came on air at 6.10, I was as right as rain.

Clearly this was some kind of reaction to the recent traumas and their even more recent solution. The pains did not return although from time to time, under pressure I was prone to similar, lesser attacks, although I became accustomed to them and almost knew when to expect them. However, they never again matched the intensity of that night.

The matter was concluded the following Monday when the manager from Barclays called me on the phone. He was beside himself.

"I didn't realise…" he spluttered, "I don't want to lose such an old customer…"

"Too late," I told him. "You've had your chance and blown it."

It was very satisfying. I heard soon afterwards that he had also lost several other old local farming accounts at the same time, and within a few more months he was gone. Not wishing to be small minded, I kept my personal account at the bank and over the next 20 years a succession of managers, several of whom I got to know personally, kept striving to regain our farm business, but to no avail.

The way was now clear for me to begin putting the next stage of the recovery plan into action and during the coming summer, I got to work.

STARTING THE NEW HERD

Seeing the benefits of a dairy income as opposed to cereals, I decided to turn the farm at Madehurst into a milking unit. The one at Flansham was progressing steadily and I wanted another to complement it.

This time the plan was to start a herd of hardy Ayrshire cattle, which we would calve early in the new year and keep outside the whole time, relying mainly on grass. It was to be the simplest system possible, calve the cows in a close 'time pattern' between January and the end of March, graze them all through spring, summer and into late autumn to be 'dried off' and kept out until they began to calve again the following January.

The type of open-air system had been developed some years before on the Hampshire Downs by a pioneering farmer called Rex Patterson. He had milked a number of herds using 'milking bails' (movable outside parlours) and his low cost production methods had been very successful.

He had farmed on the same sort of dry, well-drained chalk-land that existed at Madehurst, which seldom cut up in wet weather and grew good grass and I resolved to 'give it a go'. It had the added attraction that, with the cows out all year, there was no need for more than a few emergency loose boxes to handle sick animals and no need either for straw for bedding. The other bonus was that with the herd dry for two months in and around Christmas, the herdsman could have a good break from the grind of early morning milking and just become a stockman.

During that summer of 1968 the farm was alive with activity. We built a new small abreast parlour in the old cowshed, just four milking units on a raised step, to save the herdsman's back as he put on and removed the milking clusters.

Goodrowes installed a new bulk tank and all the ancillary equipment. We dug a slurry pit in the chalk and laid out and concreted a collecting yard and access tracks. Out on the farm we put up miles of electric fences and laid water pipes.

During that summer I spent many hours visiting distant farms, inspecting and collecting bunches of Ayrshire heifers, which by the autumn were gradually delivered to the farm to settle in prior to calving. With a shortage of these hardy cattle in the south, I finally had to purchase about thirty from Scotland and these arrived just before Christmas, making up an initial herd of eighty animals. They were all turned out in two groups and spent that Christmas settling in to the fresh cold air of the South Downs

I had appointed a new herdsman, Robin Jackson and over the next few weeks, before milking was due to start, he and his wife moved into one of the empty farm cottages up near the church, where he settled in and got to know the farm.

By the end of the year the whole operation was complete. We had built the dairy and parlour, installed a refrigerated vat and collected a herd of 80 strong, young, in-calf Ayrshire heifers, for a figure that worked out at £92 a head, inclusive of everything. Even by the standards of the day that was a remarkably low figure and gave the unit a fair chance of success.

Captain Kitson's new agent, recently co-opted to look after the old man's interests, was reluctant to offer any thing towards the improvements at that time, and so as we had to find the whole lot from the overdraft it was imperative to keep costs down. In a few years time, however, when he had seen the results on the farm, his attitude changed, and he was prepared to help with some future capital costs.

We still continued to grow grain and this soon became more profitable, since a new chemical, glysophate, a grass control spray, was just being released. Suddenly that bane of our lives, couch grass, was controllable and we could grow grain without it becoming smothered by couch in early summer and consequently yields almost doubled.

So too did the prices when, three years later the UK entered into the Common Market and Common Agricultural Policy (CAP) influences almost trebled our grain prices.

Additionally, fertility began improving dramatically as muck was put back into the soil, and a rotation was reintroduced to the land. We grew kale, grass and cereals around the farm and each benefited in turn.

By the late spring of 1969 we had the whole herd calved and production followed the graphs predicted in my bank budget. Suddenly, we had a monthly income with the milk cheque, which maintained our cash flow through the months when the herd at Flansham was drying off.

With one herd calving in the New Year and the other from June until October, the flow of milk was consistent and we knew that on the 20th of every month the cheque from the Milk Marketing Board would be in the bank – a very reassuring and comforting feeling.

Five years earlier, when I took over control of the farms, our largest milk cheque had been £520 and the total milk income for the year £5,270. Now, with two herds contributing, we were 'flying' and in the first full year, income from milk was £21,000.

Should modern dairy farmers gasp at what would now perhaps be only an average monthly milk cheque, I should remind them that we received only about 4 old pence per litre (about 1.6 new pence).

It took a lot of milk to earn that level of income.

BEHIND ENEMY LINES

Although Father and Jack Langmead had been almost lifelong friends there had, during the late forties, been a distinctly cool period during which they barely saw each other or spoke.

It was only many years later, in the mid sixties, that anyone was reminded of, or indeed became aware of, the reason for that coolness, by which time it had ceased to be of any importance anyway. However it is worth repeating if only for its historical value. Let me tell you the story.

Back in the dark early days of the 39/45 War, all local communities became involved in doing their own bit for the war effort and, for the menfolk that usually meant joining the Home Guard, since it could fit in quite easily with their routine jobs.

Jack Langmead did this as did Father's brother Alan and several other residents of Flansham and nearby Bilsham. However it soon became clear that Jack was going to become the local senior officer, and with this awareness Father became uneasy.

The two were great friends but they were also equally as independent and at times as bloody minded as each other. The prospect therefore of Father having to take orders from his neighbour decided him that, whilst he wanted to help, there had to be another way.

Making enquiries Father found out that there were a few spaces in each locality being reserved for men to act as Observers. They were to spend nights outside with the particular task of watching the skies for enemy aircraft, and would be known as Air Raid Precautions wardens. ARP for short.

Despite the fact that Father was working very long hours on the farm this task immediately appealed to him, certainly far better than taking orders from Jack! And with little further ado he applied and was accepted for the job. It was a task that he was to share for the duration of the war with local butchers van driver Dick Puttick and old George Stoner.

This solved the potential clash of interests and for a while, apart from incidents such as those portrayed in *Dads Army* on television, the 'sensitive feelings' amongst the two neighbours remained unruffled.

About a year into the war, Father received a phone call from someone purporting to "come from the Army". He wanted to visit Father urgently. "And," he added, "Not a word to anyone, not even your wife."

A day or so later, the meeting took place. It transpired, years later, that Father had been selected to be responsible for the protection of and, if the need ever arose, deployment of, a cache of explosives, to be used to delay the Hun offensive should they land on our southern beaches.

The arrangements were made, although father was apparently quite reluctant to become too involved and a day or two later, well into the small hours when the residents were asleep, an officer arrived with a loaded Army truck and some soldiers. The plan was that these explosives would be hidden away from the houses and prying eyes, out on the farmland. Father chose a spot in his field 'Crooked Twelve', which had a deep dry ditch north of the lane and on the boundary between the Langmeads' land and our own.

Father led the way and guided the lorry across the dark meadows to the site where, half an hour or so later, after a lot of spadework by the troops, the booty was interred. Instructions were given as to its deployment, and again the clear orders were given that this matter was top secret. Father was briefed that the targets for destruction would be the railway lines to Bognor, the pier, the gasometer and then a list of secondary targets likely to delay the invasion or make the going more difficult for the enemy. He was promised further instructions in a few days time.

So that was it. The soldiers departed and Father got on with his own war effort, between milking cows, cutting crops, tending sheep and the hundreds of other routine jobs. The war kept him up for many nights through those following years. In the early days, the Army also secretly built a deep fortified bomb shelter in the cottage garden which Dick, George and Father would repair to when air raid sirens went off and which was designed to provide accommodation for the three of them in 'dire emergencies', of which, happily, there were none (apart from when my first birthday party was spoiled and the dog ate the cake). Neither was there any need for Father to put his demolition plan into effect, as the invasion risks faded after about 1941 and, some four years later, the war finally passed into history.

Peace returned to the little hamlet. The Home Guard and the ARP were stood down. Father and Jack had run their own shows and everything had been pretty friendly. The farm work, as always, took over Father's time and he quickly forgot about the Army and his hidden cache of explosives. The Army, for their part, seemed also to have forgotten about him, and nothing further came of the matter until some two years after the war had ended.

One day the phone rang.

"We have a note here that you have some of our ordnance in your care Mr Adames." Father quickly put two and two together and said the caller had better come round to discuss the matter. The same day, an officer and a couple of men arrived in an army truck in broad daylight – no secrecy now. Having confirmed their *bona fides*, Father jumped into the truck and off they all went up to Crooked Twelve. Across the other side of the hedge Langmead's men were working down a field ready for sowing a spring crop and they looked with interest at the action.

Half an hour later when the cache was on the lorry, the truck moved off and Father sighed a relieved sigh. All had turned out well and his own secret war was now finally over.

Back on Langmead's land, Charlie Harding the foreman, grew increasingly puzzled at what the military could be up to, but not wishing to seem nosey, he kept away until they had gone. After work was finished and he had seen all he could, he returned to the farm and, knowing his boss was likely to be home from his day's golf, decided to call in and report the matter.

Jack too was intrigued and within minutes was on his motorbike and driving up the slope to Lynton Cottage to see what was, or had been, going on. Father invited his friend in and, relieved of his vow of secrecy, was now happy to tell Jack the whole tale.

As he was finishing he noticed Jack, as he sometimes did, going a bit red in the face. Suddenly his neighbour exploded.

"Why did you keep this from me? You should have bloody well told me!" and made to leave.

Father was really taken aback. "Well Jack, I couldn't say a word, they had sworn me to secrecy. I didn't even tell Betty."

Yet nothing placated his old friend. "He was in the Home Guard... The local Major... He should have been told..." and with that jumped on the old bike and stormed off. Months of silence followed, with barely a wave of greeting as they passed in the lane. There was no shooting in the hamlet that autumn and no socialising. It seemed nothing would ease Jack's anger.

In those days the whole community, adults and children, were invited to the Langmead's house, Flansham House on Christmas Day for drinks at lunchtime. It was a sure recipe for marital disaster and burned lunches, since huge amounts of liquor flowed. To his surprise, that next Christmas Father, Mother and us kids received an invitation and everything was back to normal. Jack greeted Father like a long-lost friend and nothing was said of the Army matter. Relations returned to where they were before the war and the following year the shoot carried on as if nothing had happened.

Nothing more would probably ever have been heard of the issue of the arms dump. After all, only Father and Jack and perhaps Charlie knew of it, so why should they talk about what was clearly a bit of an embarrassment after so long? The thing that finally opened it up was another Christmas party at Jack and Margaret's some twenty years later, when the usual flow of drink had loosened tongues and made them relax. Suddenly the story came out. They even half-laughed as they relived it to a few of us around. Don and I were amongst the listeners. The only thing that was still a mystery was why Jack had become so upset. In the end Father picked up the courage to ask him, risking reopening the sore. The reason still makes Don and I laugh to this day. It seems Jack was simply furious that Father put the stuff in a ditch that was partly his land and the boundary between our two farms.

It was nothing to do, so he still swore, about the Home Guard being kept in the dark, nor that Father had kept his word to the Army and remained silent about it all that time. Just that the boundary ditch was shared property and Jack felt the secret should have been shared too.

A silly little story really.

DAYS IN THE CHAMPAGNE TENT

My confidence was increasing considerably as the seventies got under way, both in running the business and also that the business was on the right track. I also had a wife who encouraged me and whose own upbringing, surrounded by nice things, naturally lead her to want the same things for our own home.

One quickly grows to like good clothes, nice furnishings, a reasonable car and good food. These things and more we enjoyed, although much of the funds came from Mary's income from the shops, but it was money she gave freely and happily as we built up our home.

The one thing we did miss for a few years was our skiing holiday and apart from the occasional trips away with George to golf events, we were unable to afford to go to the Alps from 1967 until 1971.

However, those trips to Scotland and the Piccadilly made up for a lot. By that time, we had taken to sharing the rent of a private house close to the event, as this was much cheaper than hotel accommodation and there was much more flexibility, since we could keep whatever hours we liked and invite many friends back.

We usually shared with Gus Payne and a great friend of George's, Pat Heneghan, a slightly mad Irishman who ran the old Irish Open Golf Championship for his employers, Carrolls, who were the main sponsors.

Pat and George travelled the world each year following the golf tour, living on seemingly limitless expense accounts. On their travels they made a huge number of friends who, when the Open came around, would be in and out of our house day and night.

These people, as friends of George and Pat, became friends of ours and for years every Open, and indeed the Piccadilly too, became a continuous round of socialising and pleasure.

Those days went by too fast. We spent many evenings in the company of golf personalities and superstars of the period with Mary and treated I basically as equals. This somewhat took our breath away initially, but within a short time we became accustomed to socialising with many of the top players or celebrities from other spheres. After all, they were only human and we were together because of our common interest in golf.

There were times when we would spend a whole tournament without seeing a golf shot apart from on a TV screen. Despite the fact that these great players were performing on some of the world's finest links courses, only yards from us, we saw nothing, such was the flow of friends dropping in to share our Bollinger and then producing one of their own in return. A ten thirty glass of 'bubbly' with Mary, George and Pat suddenly became a question of where to meet for dinner! The golf would have finished and another day's sport was completed.

Those days were truly memorable. Regulars of the world press corps were the first to join us since, whatever the readers of their columns may believe, most golf reporting was done then between drinks in the press tent – to be quickly cross-checked and filed before they continued with the socialising.

Very few of these fellows ever walked the course and watched the play. The two exceptions I came across were Peter Dobriener and Michael Williams, both serious and dedicated journalists and both sadly now departed. As to a slightly lesser extent was the famous *Daily Mail* writer Jack Wood. Jack became a good friend and was hoping to rent a cottage from me on the farm in Flansham when he was tragically struck by cancer.

These chaps could drink though, and with the help of Dudley Doust, Ben Wright, by then working more and more in the USA, and an Aussie writer

Tom Ramsay we passed many happy hours. This probably sounds extravagant, since it was always Bollinger champagne, but it really wasn't. What was perhaps extravagant was the fact that we had travelled huge distances, some round the world, to sit partying, whilst these great sporting events took place alongside us. At times, the players probably heard more of us than we ever saw of them.

THE CHANGING FACE OF THE HAMLET

Meanwhile agriculture, unchanged for centuries, moved up a gear as education and technology made possible things that even ten years before were not dreamed of. Farming and its labour requirements had moulded these Islands, founded and framed many of its traditions. It created villages and supported village life since for centuries village life had been the farms.

The farms were the village too, and in the late sixties as motor cars and post war affluence gave towns people mobility, change had began to stir. To many farmers this was a window of opportunity, but I was personally unhappy about the way the countryside was going even then. Now my fears of thirty years ago are sadly confirmed. It is a fact that outside money, and urban migration to these rural settlements has steadily destroyed so much of traditional country living, fellowship and standards.

One can only speak from personal experience, as I really only know two such settlements closely, Flansham and Bilsham. Both hamlets, since neither has a pub, a shop or a church although we do have a post box. In the late 1940s the Loveys family at Bilsham had their old farmhouse, set in amongst the high trees with its large walled pond and lovingly clipped bay tree. Down the lane, as it ran westwards below high banks until it petered out in farmland near Diamonds Mead, were four more buildings. One the old disused Chapel was Loveys' farm store; the other three were cottages tied in to the farm and occupied by Loveys' employees. There was also a large granary.

Behind the pretty old farmhouse, with its Virginia creeper veneer, stood a range of single storey flint and slate roofed cart sheds, forming three sides of a square. The buildings were surrounded by fenced paddocks nearly always full of prime Devon cattle, tidy stockyards and constant activity from the large gang of farm staff employed to grow and tend some 500 acres of sugar beet, wheat, oats, barley and leys. The whole farmstead was surrounded by huge elm trees and, atop them, the most enormous rookery with a constant cacophony of noise.

South of Bilsham stood Flansham, my home. The two were separated by the Ryebank Rife, cut hundreds of years ago as the main drainage channel for the flood plain, and joining the Aldingbourne Rife before finding its way into the sea between Felpham and Bognor.

Flansham was larger than its twin, but its roots identical. Farming was its life and almost the sole reason for its existence. The little place left civilisation at Flansham Corner. A locally famous bus stop in those days. 'Single to Flansham Corner please'.

Famous at least for those travelling on the green Southdown double decker No 31 bus between Bognor and points east to Brighton. Flansham Corner, where the Littlehampton / Bognor coast road turned sharply round the line of Langmead's farm cottages and the entrance to Flansham was marked simply by two white rails guarding the deep ditch right by the side of the main road.

Four pairs of sturdy Victorian villas with their large tidy gardens lined Flansham Lane, running south into a long line of council houses. Flansham ran westwards from here for about a mile before reaching Hoe Farm, but before that another little lane split off at a small green, our 'triangle', before it too wandered off past Langmeads farm into another sunken track.

Lined with huge elms which totally enclosed the damp lane beneath and with deep ditches and ponds on either side this secret little track lead out to the brooklands that we shared with Bilsham along the rife to the north.

Back in the lane the first house on the left was the home of Bill Loveys and his family. It had been my grandfather's house at the start of the century when it was called Flansham Cottage but the Loveys renamed it Bonhams after their last house in nearby Yapton.

Then came Chessels with its large garden and orchard. The two houses were separated by 'Lovers Lane', an elm canopied footpath that had earned its reputation. Chessels backed onto our farm but since my grandfather Owen sold that in 1926 a flint wall cut off the old entrance to the farmstead.

Then came Fieldings, set in an acre paddock and built by Mr Kane, of 'Kango Hammer' fame, as a retirement home, a lovely proportioned and well-kept non-farming property. Next to this was the new Chessels Farm House, known as Barncroft to save postal confusion, but known as Chessels Farm to most. This was, and still is our main house, and a long drive leads round our paddock with its huge elm trees and the inevitable rooks and jackdaws, to the farm buildings behind Chessels.

Then came a large range of old flint farm barns and hovels, bullock yards and threshing barns of old. Already becoming redundant as machines superseded horses. Next came Hoe Cottage, which lay between the Farmhouse and Lynton Cottage (later to become Flansham Cottage when Mary and I moved back) and then came more enormous elms and our sunken silage pits close to the frontage of the home meadow, before a large white house, a little like the superstructure of an ocean liner, stood high on the south bank.

High Standing, built in the early fifties, was the last house on this side before a pair of farm cottages ended the southern development and the lane again split. Now Hoe Lane continues west and another little track, Stanover Lane, slips below maple and hazel lined banks down to the Rife; the area in which, as Gerry Young surmised in his books, "provided a safe route for smugglers landing French brandy from the nearby coast".

Immediately beside these cottages, Stanover Villas, lay the remains of Flansham's old brickyard. This had been a thriving little family concern between the two wars but competition and lack of brick making earth caused it to cease production just before the second war. All that by then (early1950s) remained was the rusting remnants of a small bit of the tiny hamlet's history.

As kids we spent days playing there, despite parents warnings of wells, and cooling pits and later, as I grew up a little, I spent many hours with George Stoner and Jinny Budd ferreting the old earthenwork banks. They were full of rabbits and, being built above ground level, were always dry even in a wet winter.

Running south from the west side of the brickyard for almost a clear half mile was farmland, both ours and Langmeads, all fenced, since both farms still had cattle. Hoe Lane, as it now was, ran on westwards until it reached the isolated Hoe Farm House. Old and flint faced, with its range of hovels and another old timber barn, about the 1650s vintage, moulded from the redundant timbers of 1588 Armada. The village and its environs contained five such barns, all built to the identical design.

Then beyond Hoe Farm, and the flood plain of the Ryebank Rife, farmland stretched northwards, flat and fertile, until it runs up into the lower wooded levels of the South Downs to the villages of Halnaker and Eartham. Flansham however stopped where the Rife itself forms the natural and almost impenetrable boundary to man and beast. That some further half a mile from the Hoe buildings.

Back then down the north side of the lane, close to the Stanover Lane turn off, stood another pair of slate roofed Victorian villas, Langmeads farm cottages again, and then next, Gerry Young's Meadow Cottage, hidden on a high bank behind a row of maple trees on the ditch side. A long gap then to the (then) recently restored Retreat, owned by Mr Archie Harding, who imitated an early version of 'The Good Life' and was always asking father for use of machinery for his vegetable patch. A nice, friendly but lonely old man, who always had time to stop and chat with us children.

Our old milking barn, where, when milking ceased in the early fifties a number of big parties were held, towered over the two oldest cottages in the Village (part 12th Century), George Stoner's Yew Tree Cottage adjoining our Oak Bay Cottage. Then it was Walt Greens house, and even later to be where Johnny Field was to live. Then came Horns Cottage, sitting by the little village 'triangle', a grass island in the lane, which led the way to Langmeads' farmyards.

The rustic, but (quietly) a little pseudo, Flansham Manor, and its resident but friendly ghost Cuthbert, laid close along the left side of the lane here; then two burnt out shells where the half thatched Chapel Cottage and its adjoining property had burnt down before my eyes one evening at the end of the war. It had been the home of the Skeites family, who moved away from the place after the fire.

James Guthrie's old Georgian house, the White House, with his famous 'Pear Tree Press' in the back garden, stood cosily amongst a group of Langmeads flint and slated barns, with beside them an old granary on high stone steddles.

To the left of these ran the quiet lane towards the brooks and Bilsham while on the other side of these buildings was another deep short lane which slipped quickly into Langmeads fields behind the cottages. Again, rooks ruled here, and walking below these trees in summer was a considerable hazard.

Pat Morris's 'Pinks Cottage' came next, then 'Rookery Cottage', occupied by his father old Jim Morris, both stockmen for the Langmeads. All around now were clusters of stables, milking sheds, granaries and workshops, This was Flansham Farm and Langmeads farmyard. Behind them, on a high spot amongst huge chestnut and elms, stood Flansham House, Jack and Margaret

Langmeads' family home. A large three storey property, built up piecemeal over hundreds of years, with its big walled garden in the west.

On down the lane another two hundred yards, past a bend in the lane where we children spent hours each autumn knocking 'conkers' off the huge chestnut trees, and we are back again at Flansham Corner, today at the start of the big busy world.

As the rest of the Century passed on by, this and similar close little communities, became the focus of attention from the demands of an increasingly wealthy and mobile population. Incomers, and indeed longer standing residents wanting, not unreasonably, room for their tennis courts, swimming pools, double garages and horses.

From a look at the change of recent ownership, use, and often unsympathetic development, the negative result is obvious. While it is worthless to seek to apportion responsibility, it is perhaps a valid point to say that, in the days prior to planning controls, these and thousands more small settlements, evolved as places of taste, quality and great charm. Indeed why else would people find them so attractive in the late 20th Century? All that charm was created by responsible local landowners who contributed their efforts over generations. Without any help from planning officers.

Since the heavy hand of these town and country 'planners' has taken over, it is hard to find one new erection, in these two settlements (or indeed barely any that I know) that has actually enhanced the area. Indeed it perhaps would not be unfair to say that these planning officers total lack of understanding, either of the area, or their understanding of the word quality, has destroyed many good buildings in many communities. And truly reflected their ignorance of the countryside within which they sadly hold, these days, such sway.

The only thing I would offer in mitigation for the carnage within our villages is that as the Century passed, and mechanisation rendered farm labourers themselves redundant, the balance was likely to change. The pity only being that it was not managed by more enlightened officials.

However, I have seen other places, where in similar situations more forward thinking by the planners has allowed for the continued occupation by country families in the communities of their birth. Helping just a very few villages retain their mix of rural workers, whilst most have, sadly, succumbed to short term gain by others, and been forced from the communities.

Nick & Mike Reilly silage harvesting at Flansham in the 1960s.

Harvest at Madehurst in the 1940s.

Perhaps my family's closeness to the area fashions the way I think of my home. There must be many others who feel like me in other small settlements, yet there are a surprisingly large number of landowners who, despite these ties, are prepared to either sell off every plot or barn, sacrificing both their own privacy and the charm of the old villages. And in the bargain destroying the whole balance of the villages that have, actually been instrumental in giving their families what they themselves had in the first place.

To visit these two villages today is to see the result. Bilsham's farm cottages are sold and prettified, the Chapel and Granary developed, and old Walter Loveys' stables and buildings converted into dwellings. Not one active farmer is resident in the place. Every house and building has been sold off to leave Bilsham Farm as bare land. And barely a soul has any involvement or interest in the surrounding farmland on their doorsteps. There is farmland, yes. But no farm, nor longer any real heart to the little place.

Flansham of today now contains 26 new dwellings, all except two built for incomers. Of the remainder, only five are occupied by farm personnel. A place that in 1960 lived and died for farming is now a shadow of itself. A very different place.

RESPONSIBILITIES OF CAPTAINCY

The administrative side of the Golf Club was, through the seventies, taking an increasing amount of my time. I had already been on the Committee since the mid-sixties, with one short break when I resigned over some pretty trivial matter (though probably not at the time) but then came back and spent the best part of 14 years on the Green Committee, which means little more than that you get all the complaints for the state of the course from every Member who misses a short putt!

In the winter of 1973, Robert Linton, then Vice Captain and the next year's Captain elect, cornered me one evening and with a couple of his customary nervous blinks and "ah-has" asked if I would undertake to be his Vice Captain. I was flattered but since all Captains except one (Chris Martin) had been over sixty, I doubted the wisdom of his choice.

Consulting various confidential sources, I then decided it might be better done now, whilst I was a reasonable and keen golfer, than waiting for my dotage, therefore I accepted. The year in question was to be March 1975 to

March 1976 and I had a year to brush up my management of a Committee! The next year flew. Work, skiing, golf and more work and suddenly we were at March and Bob was introducing me as "Captain for next year..." The welcome was, to my surprise, very warm.

I 'drove in' next morning nervously, in front of a good crowd of members, and then had the traditional pleasure of playing my first official match with the pro, Harry Riseborough, against Bob, ex-captain and my own choice as vice captain, Geoff Renwick.

Harry had been pro at Bognor some 28 years. His father Herbert, before him, had been pro at nearby Littlehampton for even longer. The Riseborough name was revered in Sussex golf and Harry was a true gentleman in every meaning of the word. He had also had the honour that year of being elected to be captain of the Professional Golfers Association of Great Britain (PGA) and that entailed a lot of socialising and travelling.

Harry had not been too well for some years but never made a fuss, and was always the same cheerful soul, standing at the door of his shop offering a joke or a quip to everyone or offering to play them for a few shillings. He treated all the members as real friends and was in return revered and respected by us all.

Yet we within the club were worried about the new workload and so indeed was his wife, Yvonne, but such was the honour, both to Harry and, as a spin off, to Bognor Regis Golf Club, that he took it on whole-heartedly.

He was now away a lot and the customary Captain/Pro challenge matches were put off that summer to give him time to rest at weekends. When I saw him in June he was looking pale and drawn, but still, he assured me, he was 'fine and would be on top form for our later challenges'.

The British Open was at Carnoustie again that year and we went up and shared a house, again near Dundee with George, and Pat Heneghan. Harry too was up in Scotland representing the PGA and had a gruelling schedule: dinners, presentations, meetings, etc.

Mary and I ran into him on a stand behind a green one afternoon, watching the golf. We hardly recognised poor Harry. He was alone, hunched up in a big coat and looked awfully grey. When he saw us he immediately cheered up and became again almost the old Harry and we chatted quietly for half an hour before he had to depart for yet another meeting. We spoke about his condition as he left and then carried on with our viewing and socialising.

When we returned to Sussex, I had a message to ring the Secretary, Ken Thrift. Ken gave me the news that Harry had returned that weekend and had been rushed to hospital in Chichester. Perhaps I would like to visit him, but, he warned, "Don't stay long..."

Next day I walked into the ward, my eyes searching for Harry. Wrong ward perhaps? Then I heard a voice on my left.

"Nice to see you, Sir." It was Harry, attached to many 'drips' and looking terribly pale. Trying not to show my concern, I sat on a chair by his bed and we spoke quietly, discussed the Open and our challenge matches, which he promised he would be ready for in the Autumn. His smile, as always, lit his face, but his eyes didn't shine as before. Soon, following Ken's orders, I made my excuses and we shook hands.

"See you soon Harry."

"Goodbye Sir." And we parted. Harry Riseborough died a couple of days later and the following week, in a bursting Church at Yapton, a very emotional Herbert Hamnett spoke from the heart for everyone: for Yvonne, their children Yvette, Stanley, John, Richard and Mandy, for Bognor members, Sussex golfers and the PGA who he had represented briefly in the last days of his life. As Captain of his Club I read a lesson. Then we were in the Churchyard as Harry was laid to rest. It was a very sad day.

There was concern as to how we could do something to make a useful presentation to the Riseborough family. Harry had been a wonderful club pro, but he was not a businessman, and we knew things could be hard for Yvonne and a young family. Speaking to George Hammond after the funeral we tossed ideas about. We quickly came to a plan. Both of us were well-known enough, although he more than I, in golfing circles to organise a day to remember; a day Harry would have enjoyed.

We set to work. I rang Ken Scofield of the PGA. George rang friends in the trade. Within a few days Ken had the agreement of all the top players, members of the British PGA, to come to Bognor and play for a day in honour of Harry, their late Captain. George meanwhile had rounded up a large number of national, and even international sponsors, for a Pro-Am to be held at Bognor that Autumn. So it was that on Sunday 26th October 1975, twenty top players, including Max Faulkner, 1951 Open Champion and other rising stars, joined with sponsors and Club members for 'The Harry Riseborough Memorial Pro-Am'. We organised raffles and auctions, collected generous amounts from members unable to play, any way of making the proceeds up. As the dark grey Autumn evening closed around the last golfers coming off the course, we knew it had been a success. It mattered not who had won; we knew that Harry's memory had won. A week or so later, his family was presented with a substantial cheque.

We all missed Harry and we still talk about his ways on the course. Until he died we didn't realise that he had been having treatment for cancer for almost 20 years. Despite this, he was always there and always remained polite and cheerful.

We then had to set about appointing a new professional. Eventually we selected one of Harry's old assistants, Reg Moore but by the time he took up his post my year of Captaincy was over. Harry would have appreciated the fact of a whole year of had passed with the 'Captain and Pro' undefeated. But he, and all of us, would have far rather he had still been there with us.

On the subject of records it is possible that within two years a couple of trivial but rather unique records may have been set at Bognor. After my year of captaincy ended Geoff Renwick soon asked my Father to be his Vice Captain, and the following March, 1997, the name of O.D. Adames went on the 'Captains Board'. It would be interesting to know when, if and where, a father has been captain of the same club *after* his son?

The second involved a round of golf in the annual Gilligan open mixed stableford foursomes, where I played with a distant cousin, Mary Steel, married to another old golfing friend, Mike Steel, from Worthing. We had not been playing well after a good score in the morning and a good lunch. Mary my wife was playing with Peter Royle, the recent county champion from Ashdown Forest, and they were, so they said afterwards, beginning to feel sorry for us! When we came to the short par three fifth. Mary's tee shot was close and I holed for a two. Three points.

On the sixth, a 274 yard par four, I put the tee shot to twenty feet and Mary holed that for a two with a shot on handicap; five points more. Then on the 475 yd par five seventh, after a good drive by Mary, and my long wood second shot, my partner again holed out from some twenty feet. Another stroke on handicap and another five points. So we had scored thirteen points in the space of three holes. I have never witnessed a score close to that and wonder if that too may be a record. Perhaps some golfing reader could answer both these questions.

~ Chapter Five ~

IF YOU DON'T ASK...

In 1973 we were yet again back in Murren. By this time the parties were smaller but always a group of 'Murrenites' like ourselves made contact around mid-January each year, checked on travel plans and often met at airports before travelling on together. Two regulars were Tony Miskin and "Punch" Davis. I had actually holidayed in Punch's company since the first ski party in Kitzbuhel back in '59.

By this time we had moved from staying at the Palace Hotel, and had found more congenial and homely surroundings with the Von Allmen family in the Hotel Eiger. Mimi, and daughter Annelis, had cared for our party's needs for several years, while Annelis worked hard to fight off some of our late night advances with deft skill. A skill born of experience! She was a beautiful girl, fluent in almost every significant European language, and between them the family had built up a loyal following of guests from all the continents. Each year they invested heavily in the Hotel and each year we came back.

By this time Annelis had married Walter Stahli, and between them they made the hotel a welcome home from home for many of us who were, by now, personal friends.

That year I had had a particularly bad back the whole autumn and winter, brought on by the routine drag of bale handling the previous summer. Still the right machinery wasn't available and my backache increased. So in Murren the steep powder banks which we constantly explored, and regularly exploded into, made my back very tired and I soon decided that despite the constant need for a back corset, I needed a rest from skiing.

Mary had already decided that skiing was much too much like hard work. My efforts to persuade her that it was really much easier at faster speeds were ignored, and although she skied with a few like minded folk this was, after all, a holiday and supposed to be fun. The village had always had a thriving Curling

Club, the Tachi, and the curlers themselves were an outgoing, extrovert crowd. Very many in those days were Scots, Robbie and Doreen Easdale and Archie Holmes whom we had known since the early sixties, were always welcoming and hospitable when we visited them in Scotland.

Mary had begun playing the game on our earlier visit way back in '65 and being pretty and young was an immediate hit. On her return to the rink some seven years later she was treated like a long lost daughter, old faces almost forgotten surged around to kiss her, hug her and shake her hand. Before the day was out, she was in various 'international' teams for the duration of our stay. She soon became quite good despite the size of the heavy stones.

Meeting her one evening after a particularly hard day above the village, I kicked my ski boots off and joined her team in their regular post-match ritual, drinks. Her opponents were introduced and, among them were two Scots, Tom and Sheena Hay who, it soon transpired, were large 'tattie' farmers from Carnoustie, above Dundee, an area we by now knew quite well from golf. We four quickly set up an easy rapport and agreed to meet later that evening for a nightcap after dinner.

Evening meals were then an occasion to smarten up, and jackets and tie were in order; getting skiers out of their sweaty clothes, it served its purpose. During the first few years of our holidays in the Palace Hotel we always travelled complete with dinner jackets, and the girls with evening dresses, so to us the switch to jackets and tie was a welcome relaxation of the code. By now standards had changed.

We met Tom and Sheena in the little bar of the Hotel Alpina, which hung right over the edge of the cliff wall, a spectacular view but one that Mary couldn't face in daylight. At night she could pretend it wasn't there.

Predictably, for an hour, farming, as always amongst farmers, even when on holiday, filled our conversation and after a few beers, and being quite keen to learn to curl, I plucked up the courage to suggest perhaps we could make a team for the following event, the 'Jungfrau Cup'. This embarrassed Mary since she knew Tom and Sheena were excellent curlers and represented Scotland internationally.

Tom nevertheless accepted the suggestion without hesitation. And so the problem now was whether we would just be an embarrassment to them on the ice! The long and the short of this story being that, some two days later, with one match to go, the 'Farmers team' of the Hays and Adames were undefeated in three games. The last match that afternoon was the decider and we would win 'The Cup' if we halved or won that round.

As we sat in hot sunshine with our recent opponents, celebrating our morning win, and with the long lunch break in the offing, I decided that, rather than waste two hours of a beautiful day, I would grab my boots and skis and go up the mountains. Forgetting totally about my back. No need, I considered, to dress warmly because the day was so hot. Five minutes later I was on the next cable car and headed skywards. Soon the final lift to the top station, 'Piz Gloria', (of James Bond *On Her Majesty's Secret Service* fame) had been completed. I had judged that I could go to the top and still get back before curling began at 2 pm.

In those packed cabins you don't notice the fall in temperature, as you rise up through the high mountain air, but that day, on exiting from the station, the icy air hit me. I wore only a pair of summer golf trousers and an open neck shirt – summer kit that was adequate at Village level, but not up on the top of the Alps in February. It was a silly mistake. I had been up there many times before, but because I was pushed for time I didn't really think. My only answer was to get down some 2,000-3,000 feet to warmer air – and quickly.

The first snowface from the Schilthorn is, at the best of times, a quite evil 'black' run. Steep, windy and deeply moguled, but by keeping just below the piste, where I had long ago learnt there was almost invariably good soft snow, I hurried on down. At the end of that top face, a lady in some difficulty (out of control actually) came straight across the slope just as I was also turning above her. In an instant I too was also out of control. In avoiding her, my ski tips had crossed and sent me tumbling a good 100 feet down, one ski by now off the boot. A considerable prang.

The lady eventually stopped herself, and presumably wondered what I was doing, cursing at her from many feet below. As I straightened up my back went into a sharp spasm. The cold at work on loose muscles! Now I was in a quandary.

Putting my kit back on I considered the options. Soon I concluded that with extreme difficulty I may be able to walk back up and go down on the next car; but that walk, and the one through the village, would probably be more of an ordeal than to continue back carefully on my skis. So, the decision made I cautiously set off, with my target to reach the ice rink in the 12 minutes I had left.

The sun and warmer air, as I lost altitude, eased my back considerably and the rock gully and steep snow face, known as Kanonenrohr, through which the run went, although never easy, was navigated safely. The whole run is some five miles and I covered the last two in rapid time to finally appear above the ice rink, just in time to see my team taking the ice without me.

I called to them and shed my skis at the same time as I reached the side of the rink. Again my back twitched. Yet not so badly as to deter my participation, and we proceeded to play the last game relying on Mary, Sheena and Tom. I could barely put the stones down, let alone 'sweep' them, and felt hugely guilty at letting these new companions down. The only good thing being that such was the skill with which the Scots played their stones, we won the game. With it the Jungfrau Cup, and the elation made me totally forget my backache.

That night, after a long soak in a hot bath, we four were presented with the cup at the Jungfrau Hotel by the manager Rudi Meyer, and with it we each received an engraved pewter memento to keep for posterity. The only thing wrong was that, while the cup is still there in Murren, our name misses its 'e' and so appears Adams N and Adams M

In spite of this, that day cemented a long-standing friendship, and we have enjoyed many times together since, both in Carnoustie and Flansham. And we still, both families, display our prizes engraved with the words 'JUNGFRAU CUP 1973 WINNER'.

BUSINESS MATTERS

All these changes in the community took some time and during the intervening years life went on. Farming can wait for no man. It was, and remains, totally dependent on the seasons and the weather.

The Seventies now saw major moves in the farm business. Both herdsmen continued to improve the performance of the animals and the returns from the milk, at last, after perhaps 50 years, meant the family was again financially secure. Although we had always possessed land, seen by banks by now as an increasingly valuable asset, the value of it through those earlier years meant little. Until the early seventies land had crept from perhaps £60 an acre to £300, its value was still not really appreciated. It was only after Britain entered the Common Market that values increased at a more rapid rate, very largely as a reflection of the new ties with Europe's farmers who still exercised huge clout with politicians.

Even in 1968, when we had our showdown with Barclays Bank over a £15,000 overdraft, our assets were relatively small. The total land value, without any hint of development, was perhaps £35,000; increased by another £20,000 for houses. Live and dead stock added around another £15,000. So whilst the bank had cover adequate for their protection, neither the residual value of the holding nor its earning capacity was really enough to support two families since, for the effort put in by family and staff, the income the business generated was a pittance.

It was only the family tradition and our love of the job, the land and our animals, which ensured the business survived until the upturn in values and fortunes of the new decade. It was the same story across every farming community in the land.

Slowly the hardships, the low salaries, the foregoing of luxuries and holidays, and sheer hard work, began to show dividends. Buying new machines was no longer so difficult, HP and leasing were becoming more acceptable and the terms competitive. The National Westminster bank was a great improvement on Barclays, and despite the fact my overdraft continued to creep upwards, it almost always had the support of the managers. Always it was backed by the now more familiar and more easily completed cash flow budgets, increasing stock valuations and income.

Cattle sales improved as calf values went in a few years from £1.50 a head to £40 and cows from £60 to nearer £300. By the mid-70s milk sales were nearing £70,000 a year and rising steadily.

The real brake on income was grain production, which still occupied some 100 acres at Madehurst, rotated with the cows grazing land. Although grain, as mentioned earlier, had tripled in value in the eight years since the mid-60s, my general lack of interest in it, brought on mainly by my cynicism at the treatment farmers were receiving from grain merchants, meant that I didn't grow it enthusiastically.

Whatever deal was struck with merchants, it was only a starting point/price. Even though I largely trusted the people I dealt with, particularly my old friend Peter Pratt, now with a merchant in Lewes, he was however but a small cog in the big machine.

Once a load of grain was on a lorry, everything depended on the various samples that were taken from a succession of tests, either at its destination, a store or the docks. Almost without fail, despite the fact it had left the farm as a dry, clean and tested sample (Peter would have tested it and bid me on his results), the next link, miller or shipper, would always find reasons to dock the price: moisture, weight, admixture (rubbish), etc.

Once a load has been tipped there is no comeback, since it is mixed in a huge pile or dumped straight into a boat. If one received warning of a problem before it was tipped they would usually say, "You can have it back, but the transport charge will be 'x' (always exorbitant)." So what option but to take the price on offer? I kicked regularly; to pretty well no avail, and longed to be able to retire the combine, grass the whole farm down and be free of sharp grain traders for good.

Despite this 'running sore' at least things were improving, and my own confidence in the farm and how to handle bank managers grew too. Learning early that so long as you play a 'straight bat', and keep managers fully in the picture of all significant developments, good and adverse, and that they can also see you are not spending farm funds on exotic holidays, big cars or race horses, they too are pretty manageable!

I played to these rules and we got on OK. Tom Chadbon had gone by now, and Hugh Pressdee took his post. A really charming man, Hugh. Early on I invited him to visit the farms and Mary cooked a lovely roast pheasant lunch. After that he was an annual visitor! One day, walking the farm, when I was after yet another overdraft extension for barn building, he looked at the farm and suggested I could solve all my financial needs by doing a 'Sale and Leaseback'.

Effectively giving up the freehold in exchange for its then capital worth, or most of it. When I had recovered my cool, I asked him if he had noticed the proximity we were to the nearby housing estates, pushing out from the coast? And what value the land might have in 10 or 20 years time? As a case of short term thinking that suggestion will take some beating, and registered with me as a pretty short-sighted idea from a professional man. It was also an idea which I rejected outright.

Whilst Hugh and I got on really well for the years of his tenure, I never forgot that day and it made me aware that the quality of advice from professionals should never be taken for granted. When, within two years land values had almost doubled again, I reminded Hugh of his suggestion, rather cruelly I suppose, and he looked a little sheepish.

All our business financing since I could remember, had been done via the banks, and all on current overdrafts. Father never understood interest rates, mortgages or HP and initially, in the late 60s, I had relied on the same method. The problem was, as many found to their cost, that in bad times an overdraft could be recalled almost instantly.

After Hugh's sale and leaseback suggestion, I began to consider the alternatives and explore other forms of finance since I envisaged the need to expand significantly before long and needed a secure source of long term funds. Looking to finding more land, I had in '76 tendered for a farm at Sidlesham near Chichester, via the Church Commissioners, and was short-listed. My plan had been to run 200 cows in two herds, and the rather novel system I devised interested the letting agents headed by Nigel (later Sir Nigel) Clutton. Probably the scheme would have worked; on the other hand, perhaps it wouldn't. Fortunately, as it was to turn out soon afterwards, another farmer was granted the tenancy. He too kept cows, grew open ground roses, and was very successful.

In the winter of 1977/78 our landlord at Madehurst, Captain J.B. Kitson, died after a short illness at a very great age. He had been the original owner when Grandfather Owen rented the hill grazing farm in 1926/27 and had been a real gentleman to deal with and a wonderful landlord to boot.

Apart from the late 40s, when Alan struggled with a wife, a racehorse and little enthusiasm, Captain Kitson was always cooperative. He kept the rent to little more than 'peppercorn' stuff and paid for all fencing materials and building work needed every winter. He built two lovely cottages in 1947 for our staff, without putting the rent up. Father appreciated this and when the Captains wife died in the 50s the two men became quite close. Father would regularly drop in to Lower Farm and after being met by John Harding, the valet, would be shown into the old man's study.

The house was huge, with some 17 bedrooms, a snooker room and numerous large reception rooms, looking down across a hidden 'ha ha' wall over a wooded hilly field, the Down Field. The property, truly that befitting a gentleman, also contained a block of four flats, a stable block complete with cottage, another bungalow, a squash court and an acre walled garden. The two men would talk for an hour or so and as he left Father would be accompanied to his car by the old Captain who always enquired of "Betty and the family".

As I began working more and more around his farm, I often saw the Captain out walking or just standing watching us. Always I would wave to him and receive a raised hand back. When he was close I would stop the tractor and go across to speak to him. Always interested and very knowledgeable, he would ask me quite searching questions.

He had large land interests in Scotland and South Africa, and each year until age stopped him, the Captain would go to both. He took the Union Castle boat to the Cape, spent the winter there and turned up, like the swallows each spring, to summer at his beloved Madehurst. As age slowed him I saw him less and less.

Often I called in to see Harding and his wife in the back kitchen and enquire of the Master and one day they saddened me by saying, "The Captain's lost interest. He's really almost ready to go..." A week later Harding phoned me to say the old gentleman had died quietly at home. An era had ended and I wondered with great concern what was to come of the farm.

Father and I attended the funeral at Madehurst Church. Many people were there from all over the country including many grandchildren and great-grandchildren. We went back to the lounge at Lower Farm to pay our respects to the old man's family and were introduced to the Scottish lawyer who was the Captain's executor. When we were introduced he said, "Ah, Nicholas, the Captain spoke of you. He wants us to offer you the property, if you would like it? Give me a call back in my office next week and we will discuss it..."

I could hardly believe it. Father, who had always wanted to secure the farm for our future, was of course overjoyed. But what was it worth? We were sitting tenants but we could have been squeezed out if one of the Captain's family had wished to take up residence.

The following week I heard from Scotland. "The Family would like you to offer for the farm. If you like you can offer us for the houses and another block of arable land next door. Think about it and come back in the next month."

He gave the impression he would like to sell everything as one lot, so I spoke to an agent and also to Gay's husband, Antony, since I thought they may be interested in the house, or part of it. Antony was rather nervous about making an offer, but finally we agreed what, I felt, was rather a low price and we put in a package offer to include the lot. If I remember it was about

£175,000 – for 200 acres of farmland, the main house and all 6 cottages! Then we waited.

That summer we were again in Scotland for the Open and George, Pat Heneghan, Mary and I rented a doctor's house for the week.

Tom and Sheena Hay met us most days for the golf. We played golf on the links at nearby Barry, and met on several evenings for meals. One evening I sat with Tom discussing things and he told me he was about to buy another farm at Arbroath on the proceeds of another excellent tatty crop. "I've got four sons", he said, "this one will be for Charlie". I hadn't mentioned Madehurst to Tom, we were on holiday after all, but now I mentioned the offer.

"No doubt, Nick", says Tom, "You can't afford not to buy it. Land prices are going to go through the roof in a few years with the CAP." Then he added, "If you don't buy it, I will..." That made my mind up.

After another good Open, Mary and I drove straight home. Still there was no news from Scotland on the executor's decision. I dictated a letter to Mrs Kirby in which I reiterated my desire to buy the farm, even if the price for the lot was inadequate. Perhaps they could say what they wanted for it?

A week later, one evening, Captain Kitson's nephew, Alexander 'Dandy' Howard, rang. I knew him because he had been acting for the old man as 'agent' at Madehurst for the past year or two and we got on well.

"We've got your letter" said 'Dandy'. "The price you offered is not quite enough." My heart dropped. "However, if you will pay us £82,000 the farm's yours. We know uncle wanted you to have it... Let me know as soon as possible."

So there it was. All I had to do was find £82,000. Having no free funds I decided to contact the AMC with whom I had already briefly discussed the idea earlier that summer. Within a week they had sent their local agent round to see me and the farm to assess the potential and the risk. A week later AMC gave me their approval for the loan and I rang Dandy to tell him 'Yes, Thank You, I will meet the offer'.

It was actually all so easy. It didn't really feel I had spent anything! No emptying of pockets or piggy banks, nothing really changed. The farm and herd was already up and running, all that had changed was that instead of paying a very small rent I was now committed to monthly repayments to the AMC for the next 20 years at 11.5% fixed interest. The main thing was that, at a stroke, I had almost trebled our acreage of owned land and secured our future, free of worries of landlords and rent increases. The relief was wonderful. Security.

As a rather trivial postscript to this chapter, a couple of years earlier George Hammond had remarried after a messy, unhappy divorce. His lifestyle had led to travel and a routine that Ginny couldn't handle and he now lived in South London with his new wife, a South African girl, Lindsay. We continued to play a lot of golf together around the Country and Mary, as she did with everyone, got on easily with Lindsay. When they came down one weekend to stay they left a bottle of Dom Perignon champagne as a token. Such a good bottle was it, that we resolved to put it away for a special event, whatever. There's usually an excuse!

When the transaction at Madehurst was complete and Black Barn Farm belonged finally to my/our company, Mary and I decided that this was the occasion we had been saving the Dom Perignon for. We decided to invite Mother and Father over to the cottage one lunchtime to share it with us. He was still 'over the moon', as they say, very buoyant, and even Mother showed more than a little interest.

I unwrapped the cork and twisted off the wire, held the cork firmly and, with difficulty, it came out. Not with a 'pop', not even a fizz. It came out without a murmur. The whole bottle was flat ... what an anti-climax. Was this an omen, asked Father, ever the pessimist! Luckily we had another rather inferior bottle handy and, with the required 'fizz' we poured it round and drank to Black Barn Farm.

NO LITTLE PROBLEMS

About this time, whispers, imaginary ones perhaps, were going round about the 'sound of tiny feet'. Mary and I both rather felt it would happen in good time but, as time went on, it didn't. Mary's Father knew a top gynaecologist in London and after several visits it transpired that there was a problem. The prognosis was not very good, possibly due to a rather untidy appendix operation Mary had had a few years earlier. The two of us began to realise that the only way we were likely to have a family was by adoption. It was not a very happy period for obvious reasons and we didn't wish to do anything too conclusive too soon.

Not much was said, but over the next months it was clear we were both coming to the same conclusion. As a woman Mary was naturally desperate to have her own children. As a husband, but perhaps more as a farmer as well, with a long family tradition stretching back at least 350 years, a son, or sons, would be rather special. But already in our circle of friends we had seen the result of unsuitable adoptions. Unavoidable, but genes have a lot to do with personalities. However well a couple rear a child, its inherited genes don't change. We had seen one or two very sad cases of adopted children running off the rails and both of us felt that it was bad enough for the parents if the children were their own flesh and blood, to have it happen with adopted children would be too awful.

But we did consider it. Perhaps we could be lucky? Or perhaps not. Gradually, but without too much discussion or trauma, both of us sensed it might be best to be thankful for what the Lord had given us, to get on with our own lives and make the most of what we had. This was already a lot and we were very fortunate.

That decision could well have deprived a couple or three children of a very happy and comfortable existence, yet alternatively it could have saved us two a lifetime of frustration, disappointment and sadness.

We ultimately felt it was too big a risk to take, and although now in the coming months and years we are naturally sad not to have youngsters coming along to 'pick up the reins', we are also quite relieved that the biggest problem we have in the house is the spaniel. You will probably consider us selfish.

Both our sets of parents would have felt this disappointment equally as keenly as we ourselves. Mary was the eldest Darrington daughter and, as the one who worked in the shops, was very close to her Mother and Father. Grandchildren they were later to have, but, in this life, one has to be thankful for other things too. My Father probably felt the situation more than my Mother. However one would never know because she was always reserved and very matter-of-fact. Dad thought of the family succession, beyond me, more keenly possibly, at that time than I did. Being some 33 years younger, I had plenty of other things 'on the go'.

As time went on Mary and I found a tacit acceptance of this situation and whilst not often discussing it, we were naturally aware of our loss. Yet I suppose, through it we have had advantages that have passed our friends, since we have not had the worry of such as growing tantrums, bad exam results, broken teenage hearts or drugs... We think about it and then get on with life.

From my point of view as a farmer, looking at the way the industry is heading at the end of the millennium, I think that, had there been one or two sons, I could well have been guiding them in other directions away from farming. I am terribly afraid that the family farm has had its day. The old ways don't fit into modern thinking. As a return on investment, owning a farm is a pitifully poor return unless you are prepared to treat your work as a hobby and forget the rewards of City jobs. It does still remain a wonderful way of life. However at the stage we were then, back in the seventies, there was much else to fill one's thoughts.

For the next few years we worked very hard, only seeing each other from late evening till about 8.30 in the morning – and sometimes between golf at weekends. Mary was usually playing on her Tuesday 'day off' and when work allowed, in the light evenings. I played every evening as my work programme allowed, and sometimes had commitments for 36 holes both days in the weekend. Golf is a game that can take over your life, but I knew the farm was the clear priority, with golf somewhere further down the line, although it may not have appeared so to outsiders or to readers.

Mother and Father were now playing a lot at Littlehampton golf club and, for the first time since my childhood, they were actually getting along quite well. The only thorn they had to bear was Father's cousin, Nancy, who had been virtually adopted by his parents when her own died in her infancy. Nancy had lived with the family ever since, working all her life at the telephone exchange, rising to be Supervisor, which appeared enough to satisfy her horizons and on her retirement her long service was recognized in the Queens Honours list. She never married.

She moved to the old Lynton Cottage with my Grandmother in 1947 and then, after Gran died in 1957 my parents, unfortunately under pressure from Gay and myself, mistakenly offered her continuing 'house room' in the farmhouse. It was a mistake that lived on whilst she did. When Gay and I lived at home, Nancy was just 'there' but never really a problem. When we later both moved out, her presence became something of a 'demon', at least in the eyes of our parents, as she, often quite innocently, intruded on their privacy 24 hours a day.

With no outside interests, she really had no original conversation. Soon after she retired she unfortunately found that a certain clear spirit made things seem better and before long could be found semi-conscious at any time of the day. This was very, very sad and was not handled too well by Father or Mother, perhaps. Yet Nancy was, after all, his cousin. Amongst the strong feelings he had, I am certain he also considered she was still partly his responsibility.

The friction in the house was becoming almost intolerable as Nancy followed Mother round and repeated almost everything she said straight back to her. Father cut it from his mind, swore he would do this, that, or the other, promised he would talk to her, find a home elsewhere for her, but actually did nothing. This sore festered on and we seriously feared there would be a murder in the house! Sadly, this situation still had some years to run, although in time I would take a hand.

THE FAMILY GROWS

What probably retained their sanity more than anything else through this period was the fact that sister Gay had finally settled down and married in July 1972. Very soon the sound of the tiny feet Mary and I missed were to be heard running through the farmhouse. Gay had been working in Chichester as a private secretary and surprised us all by becoming engaged to, and marrying her boss, a solicitor, at quite short notice.

Gay and Antony moved into their new home at Halnaker, a small downland village east of Chichester, that Autumn and in 1973 they had a son, Robert Owen. Gay's life had suddenly changed totally and our parents were only too pleased to offer her relief from the stress by having Bob down to stay at the farm at every opportunity. This filled their time and gave them huge pleasure.

Then, in February 1977, Gay had a little daughter, Elisabeth, the arrival of whom decided Gay that two was quite enough, although I think our parents rather hoped she would produce more, such was the delight they gained from having them in the house, diverting their thoughts from the ever-present Nancy.

To Mary and I these were peripheral matters since business for us both was hectic. Her father George, having spent his life building up a large heavy engineering business in the north, manufacturing, amongst other things, road tankers, had now retired and set about diverting his energies into building up the dress shops, called after Mary's mother 'Kay Darrington', into a significant chain along the South Coast.

All this meant more and more work and responsibility for Mary and although she enjoyed the challenge, it meant a huge workload in both effort and time. She never resented it, but seldom was really free of it, and her days were not long enough.

Had we had a family of our own, doubtless things would have been different, but without children and with Mrs Kirby still doing all the farm office work, my wife channelled all her energy into Kay Darrington.

We had a largish garden at the cottage but at that time it held little attraction for either Mary or myself who, like most farmers felt gardening was something of a busman's holiday. Consequently, I cut the lawns and Mary bought our vegetables in the shops.

Any spare time we had was spent on the golf course, shooting (in my case) in the winter, or just trying to recharge our batteries. We were young, fit, had lots of friends but were both, although it may not always sound like it, workaholics. Only when the job was done did we pursue these other interests.

THE CATTLE DEALERS

As work and responsibilities grew, I was finding it more difficult to get to market so often and on recommendation began using a well known local cattle dealer, George Hoare, to take some of our week-old calves and occasionally some beef steers and cull-cows.

By the late sixties George had become a part of my life and he would regularly phone to ask what I had to offer. Always when he came round to see, and usually buy, an old cow, he would say, "And what else have you got to sell today young man?" Just on the off chance!

George was a tremendous chatterer and I knew that if he was expected it was advisable to keep a couple of hours free for our 'negotiations'.

He would arrive at the farm in his Land Rover and talk about everything and anything apart from what he had come to discuss or buy. We would eventually see some animals and he would quickly assess them but, apart from a cursory look, George would ignore them.

"Went to Guildford yesterday," he would, perhaps, say. "Lovely lot of cattle there but a difficult trade ... wrong time of year ... shortage of grass .. lack of space." Always a reason.

Or it might be "Old Bill is selling up next week. Wrong time of year really ... Too many cattle about at the moment."

Everything a reason for offering me poor prices!

Of course, if I was buying it would be: "Not many good cows about at the moment," or perhaps, "I sold some grand cows to so-and-so last week. Pity I didn't know you were interested."

And so it went on. Then, just before he walked to his car, he would say, "Take £45 a head?"

"I think they are worth a bit more than that, Mr Hoare."

Silence. Another topic. Then, after ten minutes more chat.

"Pity about that small steer, he lets them down a bit. How about £48?"

"No sorry, I will send them to market, I must have £55..."

"But then you will have to pay the transport and commission," he would say. That I knew; but I also knew that he didn't reach his final offer till he reached his car and changed his boots for clean shoes. And it was also where he kept his cheque book. Even then he wouldn't hurry.

George was in his late 70s then. He bought and sold a huge number of cattle every week, seven days a week at that, and he knew what every farmer in the area had or needed. His turnover was huge and he was very respected for his honesty and the quality of stock he offered.

As he went to turn on the engine of his car he would say something like, "You're a hard man. Take £52 10 shillings?"

"You have a deal, Mr Hoare." And we would shake hands.

It was a little battle we fought on each of his visits that could not be rushed. When George retired, well into his eighties, I missed his visits, his chat and his stories.

When I next needed to trade cattle, I returned to Chichester and the change stunned me. The cattle lines were three quarters empty; the pigs had gone. So too had the gatherings of farmers. A few dealers appeared to be sharing out the business amongst themselves and it was clear something had gone seriously wrong. The last bunch of calves I sent there was sold outside the ring, after the sale when most buyers had left, by one particular auctioneer to a small group of his dealer friends, for a pittance. Someone was clearly more interested in seeing the dealers 'right' rather than the farmers and it was clear that the old market's days were fast ending.

From then on I sent every animal to Guildford and received much more reliable returns and never again worried about dealers 'rings'.

Between 1966 and 1986 I never visited a market – I seldom had the time – yet I was never dissatisfied with the prices my animals fetched.

I missed George Hoare and was sorry when Chichester market closed and became a car park. However the writing had been on the wall for some time; farmers felt, and indeed could see, that some dealers were being favoured at their expense. After that, it was a lost cause.

Ten years or so after George ceased trading I looked around for another outlet for our old cull cows, since I was becoming progressively concerned for their welfare after they left the farm for the last time. After a life's service to us, I was very unhappy that they were regularly being sold at market, then hawked round from buyer to buyer, often despite their advancing years and sometimes frail conditions, rather than going, as I wanted them to, straight to the abattoir. I wanted them killed as soon and as humanely as possible after leaving the farm and that was not always happening.

Making enquiries of neighbours, several of them said:

"Try Arthur Harriott," or "Arthur has all mine and there's never a problem ... and he pays promptly."

That was good enough for me, so I rang Arthur Harriott at Arundel. This was in the early eighties, and to this day I have never had reason to complain. My old cows go straight to the abattoir with minimal distress and delay. As a farmer and a dealer Arthur's reputation is countrywide.

Despite selling to Arthur I still use the auction market system and will continue to do so as long as it exists. All our store cattle go now to Hailsham and have done for some years, again with no complaints. I totally support the need for and principle of the auction system and grow increasingly concerned at the inroads the supermarkets are making into its viability.

If the market is not there as a free-trading 'yardstick', I fear before long all farmers will be at the mercy of a few major buyers. That would be a disaster for stockmen, and one, if it were allowed to occur, that would be irreversible, due to the unhealthy influence of so-called 'animal welfare groups' and their wholly unhealthy and disproportionate power and influence over Government nowadays.

In the seventies, the development of really labour-saving bale equipment began to appear. This was something I had waited 20 years for, my back having suffered increasingly as years passed during the annual 'bale-cart'. Within two years I had identified and purchased attachments that took out every element of the hard work apart from the final stacking in the barn. Suddenly, harvest time, and indeed the whole of summer and autumn, was improved out of all recognition.

The 'flat-eight' bale system, with sledge, grabs, and a self-loading transporter capable of carrying 56 bales from field to stack, without the need to leave the tractor seat, was indeed a luxury. Soon after came a front-mounted 'squeezer', which picked up the whole 56 pack in one lift and placed them in the barn.

Suddenly we could complete the whole operation mechanically. The only time a bale had to be handled was as it was stacked in the barn, and if we were prepared to leave them outside in the rain, they need not be handled at all. However, wet straw means wet beds, a considerable health risk to milking cattle, so we still stacked them inside.

Naturally, with the introduction of these machines our requirement for labour began to drop. The labour force on the two farms, 330 acres now, since more off-lying land had come available, was down to two herdsmen, one tractor driver, one student and myself.

My herdsmen, from the early 70s, were Peter Simmons, who came to Black Barn Farm from a dairy in Berkshire in 1971 and Geoff Highnam a tenant farmer's son who had found himself out of a farm when his Father died and joined us in 1973 to run the herd at Flansham.

They were both very reliable, honest men, who came with their wives, and/or small families, settled in quickly and subsequently made the dairy herds their lives. This soon took away a lot of worry and gave me more time for other things.

The 'tractor driver situation', meanwhile, underwent a succession of changes. None stayed more than about three years, some much less. The problem really was that in those days a tractor driver was also usually expected to double as relief milker and the two jobs didn't actually go together. As soon as a relief milker became useful, he immediately thought he should be earning what the herdsman earned and always there were problems. A solution was near though.

Students had been a regular feature on the farm since 1966. The first one or two were so good and since there were so many youngsters seeking work at that time, it seemed to be a good way of training the next generation. I decided that they were worth the odd problem.

We had these lads, usually fresh from school, over a period of some 15 years. In the early days we found lodgings locally and they usually did one year with us before moving on to agricultural college.

Some were so good and bright that I really hated it when the time came for them to leave at the end of their year. As time went on, however, too many proved completely useless and the standard became worse until eventually we gave it up and let someone else break them in.

After one of them got his landlady's daughter in the 'family way' I had to find alternative housing for him at a day's notice. Not easy, but since he was a good worker in other respects too, I persuaded an elderly couple renting a spare cottage at Madehurst to take him in as a lodger. This worked well and they did the same for the next year's boy, Robert Davies, who although initially a little bit 'full of himself' and quite fiery, was an excellent lad and became after a while a very conscientious stockman.

Robert was convinced, early on, that I had it in for him. Probably I was a bit severe on him but he was so good with animals that I was determined to make him into a good stockman. To do that I had to really keep him up to the job, consequently, with his fiery temper and my determination, sparks often flew.

Problems arose with Robert's lodging arrangements when, while only half way through his year's stay, the old gentleman he lodged with was taken ill and reluctantly had to move at short notice; fortunately I had an alternative on hand.

A local woman in her early thirties and with the experience of running her own small farm had, shortly before, begun relief milking for both our herds. Pam Evans was a gem; open, reliable, honest and very good at her job, a little excitable at times, but ideal.

Ideal too as a tenant and landlady for that same cottage at Madehurst, into which she very quickly moved. Pam relief milked the two herds, reared the calves and at home looked after a succession of young men as their resident landlady; also being a superb stockperson, through and through. She got the measure of young Robert in no time and stood no nonsense from him. After that he became better and better, bullied by me at work and Pam at home – an ideal recipe for success!

At the end of his year we parted very good friends and he went on to make a mark for himself in stock keeping circles in East Anglia.

Sometime earlier I had built a specialist calf-rearing unit at Madehurst, a good investment which is still there thirty years later. For the rest of the 70s, Pam Evans reared all our replacement heifers, relief milked and helped on the farm.

We now employed a workforce who all pulled together as a real team, Pam got on well with Peter, Geoff and myself, with various tractor drivers and the students. In fact, so well did she get on, that five years later she left us, to take things 'a little more easily' or so she said and married one of my ex-students. They settled in North Devon.

AN OLD FRIEND PASSES ON

In 1981 we had begun to notice that my dog Judy was slowing down. Since Mary was out most days, Judy spent her whole time on the farm with me; on tractors, beside the combine, at heel with a gun, she was always there. If I was ploughing, or combining, she would walk every turn of the field, whatever the ground or weather conditions, so keen was she to be where things were happening. Sometimes in hot weather she would slope off quietly to a distant water tank and many was the time she could be spotted jumping in and swimming round to cool off and quench her thirst before returning to her duties.

She was a very independent animal. She didn't seek company or crave constant affection. When we came back to the cottage she would be in her box. Always as we opened the door she would wake, stretch, allow us to pat her, and then return to her bed. She worked hard for a dozen years as a gun dog, working incessantly until the last bird was picked up.

When she returned home at the end of a day, she would be dried off and fed. Then for a good two hours she would grizzle and charge round the house. In the early days she drove Mary and I to distraction, but once we understood it was her reaction to tiredness, we ignored her until she collapsed in her bed and snored.

She began to show signs of real tiredness in the season of '81. Still very keen to come shooting but by midday she struggled. One day I saw a lady exercising two spaniels at Madehurst and I stopped the car. "Pretty dogs; got any puppies at home?" I asked.

Within a day I had a new pup, Peggy. She was the most lovely looking dog I had ever seen, six weeks old and, I thought, by the next season, with a bit of help from Judy, we would be able to work her and let the old dog rest.

Both dogs came to work with me and Judy usually hung around by my car at Madehurst whilst Peggy got in the practise at farming! We had noticed how hyperactive she was. When Mary opened the door Peg was gone round the farm twice before Mary had her boots on. She was going to take some training....

The following March I was chain harrowing a meadow at Black Barn Farm, down below the A.29 which ran along the south-eastern boundary of the farm below the Rewell Woods. Stopping during the morning for the call of nature, Peggy too jumped off, and in a second was in the small 'Bluebell Wood' close by. I called and called but she didn't come so, expecting to see her any moment, I continued harrowing.

An hour later I was getting worried. Perhaps she had gone back to Judy at the car? When I completed the field I made to go back with the tractor, only to meet my herdsman, Peter, coming towards me. "Will you phone Mary". She had phoned the dairy back at the buildings.

Mary picked up the phone. "I've got Peggy here", she said, adding "but I'm afraid she's dead"... I made my way home with Judy to learn the story. It seemed a man was driving his car down the A.29 when suddenly, out of the woods, came a deer. He braked hard and as he slowed another brown flash shot from the wood in pursuit. The dog never had a chance. It hit his off-side front light and smashed that, killing itself instantly. Kindly, noting our phone number on her collar, he phoned and told Mary the tale. "I've got your dog but I'm afraid she's dead", same as Mary told me. He then wrapped her in a sack and brought her home, much quieter now. He was very shocked and sad. He wouldn't consider making a claim against damage, blaming himself. I never met him but thanked him by phone

I buried the pup in the garden that evening, and Mary and I both came to the conclusion that, with her hyperactivity, what had happened could be for the best. She was such a lovely dog, but probably would never have been more than an excitable pet.

So now we were back to square one. I rang every breeder in the South of England, searching for another Peggy. In the end we located a commercial kennels in East Sussex. When we found them it was a mess, the dogs filled the house which itself was smelly; disgusting. When I saw the pups I felt so sorry for them. What sort of life would they have.

Perhaps foolishly, but at least to give one a good home, and probably thinking of Judy years back, I again chose the smallest bitch. £65 seemed £60 too much, but we had made our decision. On the way back the pup 'smelt' the car out. Her coat just reeked, it made us feel quite sick.

The first thing Mary did was to put this five week old in a warm basin of water and wash her thoroughly. That night she was put in a small box by the side of Judy's bed. We were awoken around midnight by her cries, which quickly became worse. In the end Mary went down and picked her up. So small and so young was she that she was losing body heat away from her litter mates. By morning she could have been dead.

Old Judy and the second pup, Peggy, at the cottage.

Mary gathered her up and held her all night under the blankets. She was silent. For the next week she slept by Mary's side of the bed for comfort and a week later we decided she had grown enough to stay in the kitchen. We heard no more cries but Mary had made a friend for life.

Peggy came shooting the following season along with Judy. The strange think was that Peg was completely useless and only ever retrieved one bird without shredding it. Judy on the other hand appeared to be 'challenged' by the pup and continued for another two seasons, almost back to her best. Something to prove perhaps.

It became clear she was suffering from a group of mammary tumours and the Vet thought she could survive an operation. We thought it was worth a try and went ahead. When we collected her she looked awful, shaved, stitched and comatose. She would neither eat nor drink and the vet, Ian Haggis, said it was imperative she did and soon.

Mary had the idea of hand feeding her with some beef we had in the fridge and within seconds this attention worked. By next day Judy was eating and back to almost normal. She did one more day's shooting, as a 15 year old and then I stopped her. "You're a house dog now, look after Mary and Peggy". She seemed to understand.

A year later whilst she was still able to eat and see, but not hear, we took the final decision. It was a kindness to put her down. The vet came to the house when Mary was out. I held Judy whilst he shaved her leg and injected her. Within a few seconds and with one look at me she was gone.

By the time Mary came home Judy was buried in the garden, by the well where, for years, she had chosen to lay and watch us. Shooting was never to be the same for me from that day on.

A STAB AT HORTICULTURE

For years, Mother's family had an interest in a large open-ground nursery company at Barnham that had been 'Grandfather Goodacres' business. After he died in 1961 a general manager was employed and the directors, of which I had become one, apart from fairly irregular meetings, took a back seat whilst the business 'drifted'. It was extremely labour-intensive, still employing some 20 men and women, many near to retirement, who had spent their lives working for Barnham Nurseries.

It was also hard, un-mechanised graft. Investment in equipment was minimal. Spades, forks and hooks were still the order of the day. As a director, seeing the way that farming was now mechanizing, I wanted to move things forward, but the cash flowing in barely covered the wages. Something had to be done and done fast.

One day it was discovered that the trusted manager had been using the company's facilities, phone, customer list and even vehicles, to do a bit of 'freelance' work on his own behalf, supplying company stock, in the company lorry, to our old customers, who, in turn seemed quite happy to pay him cash, or cheques made out in his name. So much for customer loyalty.

I was despatched one morning to confront him and he immediately admitted to the sorry tale and cleared his office. Stage two was to try and keep the business going but in all honesty, the time had, by then, passed when it was worth saving. The staff had become set in their outdated methods and bad working habits and were not used to being organised. Not so much lazy, rather they decided what they wanted to do and when and how to do it.

The propagating department, with no directives, grew what they enjoyed growing and what they knew grew well and easily. The fact that the beds contained thousands of these unsold plants mattered little to them. Fruit trees were planted, grafted, trained at huge cost and then left to gather weeds because the variety had lost popularity perhaps 25 years earlier.

The only department earning more than their wages was the small landscaping group, who still managed to obtain garden design jobs and County Council contracts on the strength of the reputation of the business some 20 years earlier.

Since no other director had the energy, time or inclination, I was now thrust into the job of 'fireman' to see if anything could be done. A wholesale garden centre, one of the very first in the UK, had been set up to sell container plants in the early 60s. It could have been the salvation of the business but it was in a mess. Customers needed but one look to decide to go elsewhere, and understandably they did.

The open land 'crops' still covered 35 acres of overgrown, dirty, tired and sick land. Crops were not being cleared after lifting but being left to grow large and harbour weeds. Some trees had grown to thirty feet tall, so long had they been left in the ground after becoming unsaleable. Ideally they should have been removed and burned, clearing the area for the next plantings.

My first decision was to put the staff to clearing the container beds of all old stock, weeding and smartening the place up. Then we began lifting the overgrown trees and ploughing land, some of which had not been touched since the War. Any spare land, most of it actually, was taken in hand for cropping for the farm. Clearing large areas, I bulldozed, ploughed and sowed wheat, anything to get it back into workable condition and free of weeds.

The staff were, I suppose, a bit miffed. Routines they had hoped would see them to their retirement and then ensure them the continued use of the firms many cottages, were changing. I felt sorry for most of them because, basically, they a were solid gang of good hard working people who had been allowed to become lax. They had needed motivation, which the manager couldn't provide and the directors, of which I had been one for a few years, had largely ignored. We were all to blame through inaction.

We now re-engaged a salesman and tried new lines. We advertised our change of direction and 'tarted up' the public image. Some staff left. Some worked their hearts out. Things flickered from time to time, particularly the landscape department, but I could see it was lost cause. It was also taking me away from the farms too much. Eventually, after three years, my uncle Ken Goodacre, now retired to nearby Middleton, offered to come in for one last

Father gives me a lunch break during the harvesting of the bumper crop grown on the reclaimed Barnham Nurseries land, 1984.

effort. At least by now some of the land looked respectable, a better advertisement for passengers on British Rail, as they rattled past the nursery.

Four years later we closed the business down. An auction cleared the garden centre, the greenhouses and the pathetic collection of equipment. The staff were all paid their redundancy money.

Mother, who had attended the sale, vowed never to visit the old site again. She had known it as part of a thriving 300-acre nursery, famous across Britain for its quality and service. Her Father had given his whole working life to Barnham Nurseries, which at one stage had employed over 140 staff, comfortably the biggest employer in the area. Now, almost 100 years after its inception, it was dead.

Now the only things we have to remember the old business by are many trees around the farms and, more easily identified, the original ornate finials from the roof of the main office that was a local landmark for years opposite Barnham railway station. They were removed when the building was demolished and mother had them positioned on the corners of the farmhouse here in Flansham.

Mother was very sad about its going and true to her word, never did return. We sold off the cottages, many to the old tenants and I set out to finish clearing the three main areas for arable cropping, not just as little bits but as whole fields. After that clearance, ditching and draining, which we did ourselves with our excavator and loading shovel, the land was into wheat that autumn.

The following season, 1984, our old 500 combine, now in its 20th year with me, harvested 4.2 tons of wheat to the acre, proving what that land could grow if nurtured. It was a shame for all parties that such a decision hadn't been taken when Grandfather died. Management without equity never has the same motivation as it does when its own fortunes ride on the overall success of the business.

STRUGGLING TO COOPERATE

During the late sixties three of us local dairy farmers, Don Langmead, John Forse from Barnham and I, had investigated a co-operative venture, the flavour of the era, and had spent much time and money on a feasibility study aimed at obtaining a set-up grant from Government coffers. There was quite a lot of such assistance available in those days.

We had four dairy herds between us, some four hundred cows, and the plan was for me to take responsibility for the milkers whilst Don and John concentrated on the arable and their other varied interests. After a long consultation period the plan, in retrospect, luckily, fell on its face and we each went our own ways. Well, almost.

I say 'almost' because there was an exception which survived the break up, this being silage making. We jointly purchased a forager and mower and made available, in season, enough tractors and trailers as the gang needed. One man stayed responsible for the forager, but otherwise drivers changed as required.

The results were lower labour requirements and (usually) more speedy clamping of our grass. The latter didn't always apply however because the three farms had very different management structures. I worked with my staff. Don directed his staff and John employed a farm manager. The differences were noticeable and led to some friction within a few years. Don decided, upon the retirement of his herdsman Pat Morris, to sell his herd and backed out, which helped reduce friction within the gang substantially.

Yet I was very aware that, whilst there were many aspects of this co-operation that worked well and suited my business, the work rate, in output per day, was frequently very low and uneconomical and for the usual reasons: slow morning starts, long lunch and tea breaks, particularly if one of the farmers themselves was not present, and a general lack of motivation.

It was frustrating in the extreme, because the proximity of the farms made it a natural precursor to further joint ventures, but the poor work rate soon put an end to thoughts of any further schemes, at least for me, since I was closely involved in the actual silaging operation, often sitting on a tractor mowing grass in the next meadow and could see this lack of 'performance' as it took place.

Yet despite these problems, we persevered. When Don dropped out his cousin Keith took his place and by then we had made some improvements and it usually worked better.

By the mid seventies I had purchased a large industrial excavator and a loading shovel or 'materials handler'. My main reason for buying this excavator was for ditching and emptying slurry lagoons, but the loader soon replaced the various tractors used on grass clamps and therefore I now provided a man to drive the loader around the four dairy farms during silage making.

This helped me financially, since it increased our input of machinery, and hence meant we were 'net earners' from the operation when accounts were settled at the end of the season. All costs were jointly shared and split out at annually agreed rates on a per tractor/trailer/man/hour basis, with the cost of the harvester split three ways and running costs split on an acreage basis, so we only paid for the hours the gang was with us.

The only time in my life I have felt stress was when that silage gang was on one or other of my farms. Seeing the slow work rate, I strained to control my frustration as breakdowns, often caused by sheer stupidity at times, shortened the day. There was never any sense of urgency and they would think nothing of stopping work at knocking off time, 8pm, leaving only two loads left in the field, with clouds gathering, meaning that instead of having the job completed by nightfall they would hope it was dry enough to finish next morning. I had always striven to get a job like that finished as soon as possible. Nothing is more frustrating than for the weather to break with some small area of cut crop waiting to be cleared. With it done then you can make a fresh start on another job next day.

Had the men been directly in my employ it would have been an easy matter to get the message across, but when they are on loan, employed by another farmer, one needs to tread like as if on hot coals. As an example, Don once

The silage gang clearing grass from the Down field at Black Barn Farm in 1980.

caused a man to refuse to work on his farm again simply because, and probably deservedly, he had spoken sharply to him one morning. The whole gang was on a knife-edge for days.

Over the years I almost accepted this frustration as the price for getting the work done, but when a natural break came some 24 years later, I took it and made other arrangements. However, I suppose those 24 years must say it was a success. It was an interesting interlude that opened my eyes and perhaps tempered my impatience. Perhaps.

'WE MUST KEEP THE OLD MAN ALIVE, BOYS'

One of the most serious concerns within farming families has always been that of continuity; finding ways to pass on a farm without the exchequer taking a debilitating share. For tenants, the problem has been complicated by the even greater worry of trying to secure the tenancy for the following generation.

There are almost as many methods and variations to solving these problems as there are farmers. Many schemes work but many don't and a lot more cause the beneficiaries so many problems that they often wish they hadn't been set up in the first place.

Many trust settlements of the fifties and sixties come under this latter heading and while the farms may have remained largely intact, the restrictions as to how the children could sell, split or again pass them on often became insurmountable.

In our family's case, the transfer of the farm from Grandfather to Father, via my Grandmother, since the value of the holding was then so small, virtually avoided tax liability. One benefit of farming at a loss!

When in the sixties Father looked, on Mothers prodding, to try and ensure that I was able to take the business on without too much liability, the best advice was to consider forming a limited company with Father and I, initially, as the major shareholders.

At that time Father was still convinced that the Doc's diagnosis of his bronchitis as lung cancer was correct and he truly expected to go at any time. Those were the days of Harold Wilson, socialist dogma and jealousy that was determined to claw back every penny that a man died with, after a lifetime of paying taxes.

We did form a company, which was pretty progressive and forward thinking in those times and quite brave of Father. With his state of mind, his biggest worry then was that he survived the seven years the law required to ensure that what he had made over into my name wasn't lost by his premature death. It gave him one more thing to worry about too.

There were always black jokes in farming circles about looking after 'Dad', how to cosset him until the law changed or help him survive until time annulled the liability. To that end a nice little plagiarised ditty I once saw in a farming magazine went like this:

> *We've got to keep father alive boys.*
> *So keep him away from the bull*
> *And don't let him walk by the river-*
> *Its flooded deep flowing and full.*
>
> *He mustn't climb up on that combine*
> *If it jerks he could easily fall down.*
> *And he better not go to the market,*
> *The traffic's so heavy in town.*
>
> *Stop him from climbing that ladder,*
> *He'll be dizzy if he goes any higher.*
> *And keep him away from the augers, I pray*
> *As the grain rattles into the drier.*
>
> *He'll be safe counting sheep in the meadow*
> *Or is it too far to walk?*
> *And take out the key from the old jalopy*
> *'Cos he cant go far wrong on a bike.*
>
> *We must keep the old boy alive boys*
> *And not let him come to much harm*
> *Till the Tenancy Act is really a fact*
> *He's the Tenant you see, OF OUR FARM.*

Only fun, unless ones family was unlucky enough to be caught out by such an untimely death. There were of course thousands, a handful of whom I knew, who, having grown up and farmed on a tenanted farm, had a 'Notice to Quit' through the letter box a few short weeks after the sudden death of their father. Many Landlords were, not surprisingly, often very keen to get a farm back in hand, perhaps to ease their own financial situation, or pass it on to their own son.

In my own case I had sat both sides of the fence, potentially affected by capital gains tax liability if Father died prematurely and at risk of losing Madehurst to the Landlord when the same event occurred. The eventual fact that I lost neither was down as much to timing as to any avoidance measures designed by advisers.

Even with another, less generous Landlord than we had, a cynic could well argue that selling a farm to a sitting tenant at that time could well have been more financially astute than holding on to it. The Labour Government had, shortly before, introduced the new tenancy act, securing a 'three generation tenancy' within the original tenant's family, if they were indeed continuing to farm the land. The effect of such a sitting tenant was seen to reduce the value of a property to about fifty percent of its vacant value and the executors would have known it could be many years before those three tenancies were worked through. Fifty per cent in the hand immediately might well have been a more attractive proposition.

Had Father died but three or four years before, the pressure on the executors not to accede to the old Captains wishes, however sincerely he wanted them to, would have been great. They would most probably, as honourable people, still have done as he wished, but it would still have posed a dilemma for them. The fact was that had I then bought the farm I would, within one day, have been able to again put it on the market at twice what we had paid for it, since it could then have been sold as vacant farmland. But that was never on the cards.

So we had indeed kept "Father alive" long enough for that change in the law to help and I was most relieved.

So now in 1978 we had a situation in which Father still retained a 51% controlling stake of a significantly larger company. The possible CGT on that would have wreaked havoc with my fragile but improving finances. What to do now?

The ideal situation would have been for a generous new chancellor to bring in changes aimed at helping small business, but there seemed small chance of that.

Then Mrs Thatcher stormed to power and managed to turn the Country blue for ten years under her leadership and hopes were raised. Yet nothing happened to help our vulnerable position and Father grew increasingly less mobile. Worse still, the Tories then dumped the Iron Lady and everything increasingly pointed to a Labour revival under Mr Kinnock. At that stage in the early nineties, with John Major struggling, I was resigning myself to living the rest of my life with a new mortgage, paying off the tax bill that was inevitably coming soon.

Then against all the odds the Tories scraped home in the Spring of 1992 and within a very short time, and quite unexpectedly, they belatedly passed long needed laws on inheritance tax, which at a stroke totally exclude us from liability.

The euphoria was not long lived. The Tories soon ran into all sorts of trouble, largely sadly through their own arrogance and seemed most unlikely to last more than the one term if they were lucky.

Father though was showing all my family's trait of longevity, he was by 1993 into his eighty seventh year but by his own oft-said admission, was not wanting to live much longer.

The rest of this story will follow later but he had lived long enough to allow us to benefit from the expected tax changes and left his family secure. His timing was, as always through his life, by accident or design, impeccable.

And so it was that whereas countless sons, in a similar situation, lost tenancies, or their own farms had to be sold to pay for swingeing tax liabilities, by the grace of God and a fair wind we missed these dangers. Our farms had come through to the end of the twentieth century untouched by two of the worst fates that can befall a farming family.

A LITTLE WRITING

Despite cutting back considerably on my own input, I was still, in the nineties, doing most of the routine grassland work on the two farms – all the Spring fertiliser applications and suchlike which, along with a thousand and one other little jobs, kept me fairly well occupied. To do these entailed a lot of road work on tractors, travelling between the two farms. Previously seven miles apart, they had recently become a mile further distant by the closing of one of the quiet back roads on the way. Not only did this add to the distance, it also involved driving on a fast section of dual carriageway, running a serious risk of being a road-rage victim into the bargain.

Over the years there had been a distinct increase in the level of aggression shown to drivers of farm machinery by certain elements among the motoring fraternity. At the end of a long day bouncing up and down on hard summer grassland the last thing I needed was a road journey home with a cumbersome implement on the back of the tractor that provoked some half crazed 'oik' to start behaving as if he were on some television chat show.

To avoid this I more and more relied on contractors and, so well did they perform, that in a few more years I became practically redundant as a tractor driver. This helped me but at the same time there was a certain drop in my personal job satisfaction. There are few things more rewarding than doing a job, like perhaps mowing a field for silage, and seeing row after row of straight lines of fresh cut grass lying ready for turning or harvesting. Nor perhaps looking at well trimmed hedges after having tidied and shaped all the old growth each 'February time'. Yet the contractors were doing an excellent job and there were now many other things taking my time.

Back in 1983 I had become involved in writing a fortnightly piece for a local paper, *The West Sussex Gazette* (WSG) and quite soon found it demanding. For years we had read the paper but as Sussex became increasingly less rural the WSG followed suit. They had a 'Farming Page' that barely ever by 1983 had anything of interest to farming readers of whom there were, to my certain knowledge, still a few.

Consequently, I wrote to the editor, John Kendall and suggested that if he was to continue calling it the 'Farming Page' it ought to actually have something agricultural on it. He called me back and said that if I could put 700 or so words together that made some sense, he would publish them. Having written and rewritten that first contribution some half dozen times I sent it off and to my surprise he printed it.

For the next twelve years it was to continue.

It was not too long, however, before I began to realise what a monster I had created for myself. Meeting an fortnightly deadline when summer work presses and you cannot think specifically what you want to say is quite a headache.

Many a times I sat in front of the typewriter for ages unable to get started, only to give up. Anyone who has faced the same situation will know the importance of getting that first sentence on paper. After that the rest is easy. On dozens of occasions, while in this dilemma, I would be sitting on a machine out on the land when suddenly an 'opening' would come to me. I would frantically search for a bit of paper to jot something on, lest I forgot. Sometimes a few words would be written in the dust on the tractor or even my car, in the hope that they would remain until I finished, to be enlarged upon later.

Despite these problems I never actually missed a deadline in all those years and to be honest I found the whole exercise very rewarding. It is an excellent way to get things off your chest, like writing a letter to the newspapers, only in this case I knew it would always get printed and even more rewardingly, I would be paid for my efforts.

I always wrote from the farmer's angle, trying to express what farmers, or many of them were thinking, and I believe many read it. Not that I am suggesting it changed the world, but during these years many points I made were, before long, acted on. This was, most likely, because they reflected something approaching common sense, rather than that anyone took any notice of an article in a provincial weekly newspaper!

To be honest, it was a lot of fun. To see the letters coming back either to me or via the editor's letters page from someone I had stirred up. Mixing mild controversy with the real countryside filled many columns. After the first one was published, a distant friend, on hearing I was to be a regular contributor, said that she had read the first and enjoyed it, but what else was there to say about farming? Oh that it were that simple!

That particular run came to a stuttering end after some thirteen years without a missed deadline in the mid 1990s when a new, keen, young editor decided that the things I had to say were rather too controversial for the sensitivities of his newly green readership. The paper was by now becoming little more than a medium for advertisers and he appeared not to want any views that could possibly upset potential customers.

His efforts began to show in some pretty petty editing out from the contributions. On the phone he said that what he really wanted from me were little bits about "the flowers in the meadows" or about "old Daisy and her new born calf, etc." Twee little 'green' bits. I replied that farming in the real world was not quite like that, so he would need to find someone else to satisfy his perceived needs. This stand off went on for a few weeks, with bits edited out etc, until one week he felt the whole article was just too strong for his poor readers sensitivities and omitted to print the column. I never sent him another; which probably worried him no more than it did me. The WSG has since become the poodle that the editor was seeking – very negative, mainly adverts and with all its teeth drawn.

It may well not have helped that some months earlier I had been contacted by a London journalist who wished to start publishing a magazine for the 'over fifty somethings' who wanted to get the flavour of the Sussex downlands scene. Colin Dunne wanted me to do a loosely similar contribution for his *Downs Country*, although there the similarity ended, since the deadline for the articles from me was to be some six weeks before publication.

I had, for years, been afforded the luxury of being topical, since the WSG was printed some three days after I submitted. It meant that matters fresh in the news, or sometimes those which were only just about to break, could be aired. With the *Downs Country* deadline there was no way to be topical without an exceedingly good crystal ball. Consequently it is only possible to write historically. To try and predict would certainly mean ending up with egg on ones face. Just as 'a week is a long time in politics' so it is in farming, such is the speed that situations can alter.

Young pigs feeding at Madehurst (above). Autumn grazing in the Valley, 1985 (below).

~ *Chapter Six* ~

THE VET'S AT WORK

As I have attempted to show, over the past forty years since leaving school, my work and sport have between them kept me fully occupied. The farm and in particular the cattle, have been my first love. Many times, to the obvious bemusement of friends, following a long and unsuccessful weekends golf, I have said words to the effect of 'At least tomorrow I can get back to doing something I am reasonably competent at, and enjoy'.

And I really mean enjoy. Working on ones own land; being able to mould it how you want, plant crops and trees, form ponds, provide havens and protection for the creatures that are unable to come to terms with modern sprays, methods, machines, and often uncaring humans.

The joy of cutting a good crop of May grass; and perhaps being able to spot and save the life of a hedgehog, young leveret or a hen pheasant sitting on her clutch of eggs, by being observant to everything going on around. Watching a Kestrel stoop, almost under the wheels of the tractor as it spots a mouse, or perhaps even a worm, exposed by the mower, whilst it hovers 150ft up in the sky.

Of ploughing on a winters day with nothing for company but gulls, peewits and the odd rook, all searching for worms in the newly turned moist earth.

Of the recurring thrill from helping with a difficult calving, day or night. To see, what one often thinks of as the impossibility of extracting a huge calf, through the tight 'calving channel' of a tired cow. The excitement, as the calf's tongue flicks signifying life, and then the added urgency to complete the job before it succumbs to shock and dies

The anxious wait as the creature lies still on the floor before gulping its first breath; or sometimes to feel the sadness as all the effort has been in vain. When it lays there limp and still despite all our efforts, and those of its mother who, continues her frantic licking of the sad little body long after we have given up.

And yet one needs these times, if only to help appreciate more the days when it all goes well. When within ten minutes from birth a healthy calf is tottering to its feet like a drunken man and begins searching with its nose for the source of life. Its mothers teats.

Other days one can lean on a gate and watch a herd of cows lying contentedly in a bedded yard or a meadow of an evening; or filing through the milking parlour, patiently awaiting their turn to be fed and eased of their milk before returning to rest or graze.

To watch prime beef cattle grazing, young sucked calves nuzzling their foster mothers to rise and allow them to take milk from their udders.

And then, to live with, and accept, the cycle of life. Reluctantly coming to terms with the fact that an old cow, reared on the farm perhaps some fourteen years earlier, and treated like family and friend through a dozen calvings, has almost reached the end of her life. And must, as a kindness, be 'sent down the road'.

All these things are part of the farm life, natural and quite normal. All true stockmen will have the same feelings, and often those same feelings affect the way we approach our own lives.

We can, I believe, accept death more naturally, dare one say more easily, by witnessing the ever moving cycle of our own animals or herds. A calf is born and then reared with the best attention to its total needs. As a female it will calve at about two years old and becomes part of the team. She never wants for anything that a dumb animal can need.

If she falls sick, at the back end of her life, a human would enjoy the attention she receives. And then, when it is clear that, on several grounds but primarily welfare, the time has come to end her suffering, or even to stop suffering occurring, we are able to make that decision.

Animals unknowingly rely on us to make these decisions for them. The alternative would be increasing pain and cruelty, which would be unacceptable to all parties. In this we are light years ahead of the way the Human race handles the same situation, when that most important matter, quality of life, has dropped below an acceptable level.

Living in this environment naturally fashions ones own thinking on life. And death. In my own families case, and I am sure I am not alone, acceptance that the death of a loved one, sooner rather than later, would be a kindness and a release, has eased both shock and a little pain when the event happened.

Life and death are indeed the same cycle. We must be thankful for life and then at the end, grateful if death ends the prospect of long pain and suffering. If this is hard and callous in the readers mind I plead guilty. Guilty, to if nothing else, humane and realistic standards. I am able to live comfortably with my code.

As an example of the efforts we make to help our animals I recall the times we have spent over these years with what we call 'Downer' cows. These are cows that go off their feet after calving. This is not caused through sickness but simply by, in most cases, muscle damage, bruising and shock brought on by a difficult calving. There are many reasons for a bad or delayed calving, and all good stockmen will do their best to minimise the risks. Yet they still happen.

These downers are a worry, in as much as the longer they stay down the less likely they are to rise on their own and survive. Consequently after two days of rest and with the help of anti inflammatory drugs we always attempt to raise them.

This has only been possible since the advent of hydraulic lifters since there has to be some sort of frame overhead to attach the cradle onto. The farm has had such equipment for some twenty five years now and in that time I estimate there have been at least two cows a year requiring a lift. The method is to use a harness, which has in the past consisted of anything from ropes, old half ton fertiliser bags, or more recently we have tried a properly designed cradle which accommodates the udder and allows us to lift without risking damage to that sensitive part of the animals anatomy.

The plan is to slip the strap under the side of the animal and then roll her carefully over on her side, until we are able to pull it through so she rests centrally. The four corners of the cradle are then attached to the lifter and slowly raised until the animal is suspended in a standing position above the ground.

This has to be done very gently to avoid frightening the animal; when she is then in a standing position we slowly lower the sling until her four feet are each resting evenly on the ground. We have recently decided the cradle is less effective than old fertiliser bags.

Having been off their feet for perhaps two days the legs are usually numb and with no circulation, presumably similar to how one feels when you wake at night with a 'dead' arm. To overcome this we allow the animal to stand lightly touching the ground, whilst we massage the legs to increase blood flow, and it is noticeable how within ten minutes the previously cold muscles begin to warm, and movement increases.

At that stage we lower the sling until the legs have a substantial amount of weight on them. Initially the legs usually collapse, and we have to reposition them numerous times; but the more we move them the stronger they become.

The stress on the animal is clearly often high and twenty minutes would be the maximum for the first lift, and by then clear signs should be showing that the animal is on the road to recovery. Sometimes one lift is enough and the animal will remain standing once the cradle is lowered and removed.

At other times we may need to repeat the treatment for three or more days, perhaps twice a day. It soon becomes clear if the response is positive. If within two days there is no co ordination and no attempt to balance, the likely hood is that we will not win the battle. In these cases it is kinder to have the animal put down, rather than subject it to more pointless stress.

On the other hand if we see a good response we persevere and it will almost always be effective. Over the years we have had a very good success rate and I can recall only three cows that have not survived. The task is difficult and requires at least two men but when it works it is very rewarding. Not unreasonably, perhaps, I have found Herdsmen reluctant to try, or suggest, this treatment. They have a full busy day, particularly at calving time, and time is precious.

However once they can see the animal up for the first time their enthusiasm increases significantly.

Of the cows that we never raised the story of one is perhaps worth retelling. It was however not a classic case of a 'downer', and indeed it was just as well we didn't try to lift her as the story tells.

She had calved out in Chessels Six to the south of the buildings close to a public footpath. When she was found she had managed to calve but was out flat with milk fever, a calcium deficiency for which Geoff gave her the required treatment. We watered and offered her hay and she seemed bright but despite that made no effort to move.

Being on the footpath complicated things because one is nervous about the reactions of the Public to what we needed to do, and I didn't want to leave her there and have every walker coming to the house to tell us we had a sick animal.

Ian, our Vet was on the farm and I asked him to have a quick look at the animal, so we walked up across the meadows to where she lay. Ian felt her all over, took her temperature and listened to her heart and lungs with his stethoscope. "Not much chance I'm sorry to say," says Ian. "She's slipped a disc in her back, and as she cannot lay down until she recovers, because she will get mastitis, she will need putting down today".

I thought this was amazing. "How can you possibly diagnose a slipped disc, so quickly, on a creature that can't tell you where the pain is?" It was also a diagnosis I had never heard of before; it was certainly not common.

Ian explained "Firstly her hind legs are stone cold, no circulation..." he went on "Her front ones are quite warm and she can move them easily. Then when I ran my fingers down her spine she twitched, as if in spasm when I touched her there" he said pointing at a spot along the spine.

He added " I assure you it is a 'slipped disc', as we would describe it in a human".

Nothing for it then but to phone the knackerman to put her down and remove her. The slaughterman arrived quickly, and despatched her before too many walkers came on the scene. Before he departed I asked if they could do a cursory post- mortem when they returned to the slaughterhouse.

He phoned next day. "I could not find anything at all, except there was sign of severe bruising close to her spine". That was enough proof for me, were proof still needed, of the excellence of our vets in general, and Ian's experience in particular.

For many years I had considered that the monthly vets bill represented the best value for money of all the inputs on the farm and I had, perhaps unwisely, told Ian this one night at a party. Not surprisingly before long the rates went up! Yet the cost is one that I seldom if ever have had cause to question, and the stockmen have always been told to call the vet if ever they are concerned for the well being of any animal.

I never wanted to hear the excuse 'I didn't think it was worth the call' as we looked at a dead or dying animal next morning. With healthy animals, cattle, sheep, pigs, chicken, whatever, there is the chance to run a successful livestock business. With sick or under performing stock a farmer who spurns good veterinary advice is letting himself, his staff and above all his stock down. Neglect of animals under ones charge is inexcusable.

All through the 70s we still visited Murren each winter. Although the parties were smaller now, marriages and a weakening pound to 'blame', there was a regular group. Punch, Tony Miskin and we two would meet old friends from all over Europe. Indeed the world.

I still skied a lot with 'the Baron' Goran Akerheilm who was becoming no less eccentric as he grew older. There was still the high noise level in the cable car as he tested his multi linguistic skills on his fellow travellers. But the skiing we shared was always excellent and invariably both fast and exciting.

Another great companion on the mountains at that period was Norman Fuente, another Sussex sportsman in the mould of Jack Langmead. Norman and his wife Edith were the catalyst that had formed the old Middleton ski trips and had visited Murren since 1926, missing the War years obviously, and then always went for three weeks each winter with their son, Peter, and daughter, Pat.

Norman was a great skier, tough and would go anywhere until he stopped just before his 70th birthday. Peter Fuente was even better and was fearless and although we didn't ski too many years together in those days, we had some exciting times.

In 1966 Peter, Norman and I took my first trip, with a guide, by aircraft onto the high Petersgrat Glacier, across the valley from Murren, It was an unbelievable experience, and the view was almost beyond description. Then we had soft deep snow all the way back down to the valley village of Steckleburg.

Fortunately there had been a spare seat in the plane and, since it was my sister Gay's birthday, I treated her to the return flight. She too was mightily impressed. Gay was up in the village as nanny to Peter and Sarah Fuente's two little boys, Charles and David but didn't ski herself.

Another regular who I skied with for 25 years was a tiny Swiss lady, Rosalie Streiff. She skied like a feather over the powder snow, chatting and laughing incessantly, seemingly cherishing every second she was on the mountains with her English companions. She and Norman had known each other since the 30s.

She was a real 'live' celebrity all over Switzerland; and had been since winning the first Ladies World Championship in the nearby resort of Wengen in 1928. We were to continue to meet Rosalie in the village until 1994 when bad knees and general frailty confined her to a walking aid and finally kept her away from her beloved mountains.

Yet even at that time, well into her 90s, she was the regular target of European TV and radio crews keen to seek her advice on the latest ski sensation. She was a lovely bubbly personality and a really great friend of us English visitors.

Between this group, and there were many others too, we had pleasures beyond description high up on that sunny snow-clad wilderness. Alpine air is pure adrenaline, and once taken, is an addiction hard to give up. Coupled with deep powder snow and good companions, it is something to die for. Many sadly do, but there are worse ways to go.

We introduced many first time visitors to Murren, and its secret charms. To places the normal visitor never finds because of ropes or warning signs. To see their faces on reaching the bottom of some glorious private slope was worth the effort. We never took anyone down these runs unless we had ensured they were of the required standard, and whilst some had their own personal doubts, on the way down the rather 'special' tricky bits, we never had a casualty.

Peter Fuente still skies with me today, and his own children are superb strong, brave skiers, but the old faces are no longer there and even Hans Feuz is slowing down. Fortunately, for everyone who knows him, the same thing applies to his 'pit stops' and whilst we exchange greetings on the slopes as he teaches yet another group of youngsters, we have learned not to suggest a drink.

GREAT LOSSES IN THE FAMILY

So now we move on into the early eighties. For me they were generally quite a peaceful period. The family are all still around. Gay, Antony and their children, Robert and Elisabeth, live at Halnaker, a village east of Chichester, where Antony continues to work as a solicitor in the city.

There had been a few changes in the hamlet over the past few years and a few sad losses. Probably the most significant was the loss of Jack Langmead. Jack had known Father all the years since the twenties, and with his death father lost his oldest and greatest friend.

Since Fathers retirement in '66 they had spent so much time together, either fishing, golfing or just in each others company, and the Old Man was really lost. With golf Jack had introduced him to a whole new world. They

An Alpine morning in Murren

both had their own electric golf buggies which they would load up on to their respective car trailers and travel all over Sussex, Surrey and Hampshire together. The golf was seemingly unending and the companionship they gave each other was tremendous.

Whilst they had been friends all those years they were closer, over the past fifteen years than ever. The reason being that, since the earliest days, Jack having a larger farm was able to run it with the help of a foreman, and thus had always been able to find time to play his sports, Father had worked incessantly until his retirement and his only recreation was the winter shooting.

For some time Jack had worked hard on him to retire, and encouraged him to leave it to me, to get on and enjoy the years he had left to him. As he himself had earlier left the running of his land to his younger son Donald; and so, suddenly they were now both free, to live their lives and have pleasure. This they surely did.

Jack had lived life to the hilt. His body had survived considerable abuse, and in the last few years this high lifestyle, not unexpectedly, caught up with him. Sadly, encroaching and rather ignored diabetes, caused him towards the end to lose a leg, and his mobility was seriously affected. Father would see him most days and they spent hours chatting over the old days.

Then it became apparent that his other leg was also going to have to be removed and the poor old chap clearly felt that life was going to be pretty hollow. He went very quickly in the end and it left a huge gap around the district. He really had been a larger than life character; a dominant personality who made many friends and a few enemies but you could never ignore the man. He had certainly been a great friend to me and we all missed him enormously over the next few years.

By this time Mother too was playing a lot of golf, in the same way as she had always done every thing, by giving it 100%. Whether it was tennis, flower arranging, gardening or bridge it was always done enthusiastically. Tennis and flower arranging she had given up; gardening was her real love and now golf and bridge complemented it.

When she took to golf it was never quite as easy as she hoped but it gave her the opportunity to play with Father, since they were both members of Littlehampton, just along the road, and that period saw my parents closer than at any stage in my own life.

Her one enduring love was, as I mentioned earlier, her garden and over the years since we moved to the farmhouse she had turned the previously rather immature and formal garden into one which, to the visitor, was always full of new views and surprises. Not a straight line to be seen; it was to become a mecca for many serious gardeners who appreciated the wide variety of plant and foliage.

It was regularly opened to the Public during the summer's for various charity events and her enthusiasm never ebbed; there was always something new on her agenda.

It was about this time that we had finally managed to move cousin Nancy into her own quarters and the atmosphere in the farm house was improved out of all recognition. Friends could now call, without being constantly sidetracked by poor Nancy's heavy presence, and my parents were really happy with their newly regained privacy. They had not had such a luxury since the first days of their marriage some forty years before.

Early in '85 it became apparent that things were not too well with Mothers health. Some rather ominous tests, and her general demeanour, suggested that we may need, shortly, to steel ourselves for rough times. And so it turned out.

During the late summer she was operated on at King Edward VII hospital, at Midhurst and the family made daily trips to visit and encourage her in her recovery. The operation, we were predictably told, was 'successful, but...' And we waited for her to be fit enough to return south to her home.

She finally returned home some five weeks later and although she was still very weak she insisted, as we would have expected, on getting back into her routine at home, and looked forward to driving her car again. Being such an independent person we didn't like intruding too much and she would not have welcomed us if we had.

One day some two weeks later there was a knock at my front door. It was Colin, a regular golfing companion and our local Doctor. I invited him in, since he clearly wanted to talk. Colin found it quite difficult I think to say what he came for. Indeed, I think I had probably guessed it myself even before he told me the news. Mother had cancer that was not operable and at best she probably had six more months to live.

Even with the vibrations I had already, with my experience of life and death on the farm, I found it quite difficult to absorb. I was now faced with the dilemma of who to tell, and when, since I was the only one to know the worst.

That evening to spread the burden a little, I told Mary. We both agreed it would be better to say nothing to poor father since he was gloomy about health matters at the best of times and it was important he kept a bright-ish face in the house with Mum.

I was booked to go to Brancaster with Barry Targett and two other friends the following week and we decided it was far better that I go, than have questions asked as to why I had cancelled. After all there was not a lot I could do just then.

It was a nice break in good weather and after three days Mary and Peggy came up as we planned another two or three days in Norfolk before wandering our way homeward. However it was not easy to get this load off my mind for more than a few minutes, as I kept thinking of poor Mother back home at Flansham, and everyone so helpless.

I could not wait to get back to Sussex and the days, since it was a lovely Autumn, dragged as we made our way back south.

When we had returned we decided, on the pretext that Mother had to take things easily for the next few months, to try and find a help for her. Through necessity it would be better if this help lived in although, having not many

My parents, Jack and Betty Adames in 1985. One of the last photos of them together.

years earlier got Nancy out of her hair, I knew Mother, fit or otherwise, would rebel at this suggestion.

However I insisted, and shortly afterwards the daughter of a golfing friend, just split up from her husband with a babe in arms and needing a job, came in. It was not an easy situation but we managed to keep it on track despite regular protestations from Mother.

Christmas came, with no very obvious signs of her imminent deterioration and Father, Mother and Nancy came for a quiet lunch. It was a happy day but she was growing increasingly frustrated at her slow progress. She and I sat quietly alone on the couch in front of a lovely log fire and chatted for a while. It seemed to cheer her up, but not me.

After the Christmas holidays she began to weaken quite fast, and was mostly now in bed. The 'help' though, unbeknown to either parent was a trained nurse, and she now came into her own, and helped both of them immeasurably.

The cancer was now becoming debilitating, but Colin, when quizzed, felt that with her determination she could go on for many weeks yet. I visited her regularly in her bedroom and tried to cheer her, but she was very sad. "I wont see Bob and Lissy growing up" was her saddest comment. She now knew the situation, because a Macmillan nurse had come and told her the brutal truth. Rightly or no, I can't say, but they had told her the exact situation, leaving nothing in doubt, and she was naturally traumatised for some time afterwards.

The most poignant moment I endured with her was one afternoon when I went to see her after lunch. As I entered the room I found her scrambling back into bed with a wide smile on her face. Her face smiled but her eyes did not. I asked what had happened and she replied, "I had just dozed off and when I woke I looked at my watch and thought, Oh goodness, it's time I got up and went down and did the washing up." She continued, "So I got my legs over the side of the bed, went to stand up and they collapsed under me."

She had forgotten her dire circumstances during her nap, and thought all was well, only to again realise the awful truth. I too smiled with her but inside I felt terribly sad.

We had arranged to go to Murren at the end of January with six friends, and since this had been arranged for months Mother insisted, despite my protestations, that we should go.

"You both go, enjoy yourselves. You only have the one holiday and I will be OK for a while yet."

I asked Colin for his opinion and he, still feeling the end was probably some way off, suggested too that we should go; after all if things came to a head, we could soon be home again. So reluctantly we said our farewells and slipped away. Mum was well sedated, and didn't know too much what the day was by then, so eight days would soon pass.

Five days later we were having dinner with our German friends, Werner and Genia Mangelsen, in their lovely chalet, when the phone rang. Genia answered. She listened, went a little white and passed the phone to me. It was Annelise from the hotel.

"Nick," she said, "your sister has just phoned us. Your Mother has just passed away, please call your father."

Next morning we left the village early to try and get a flight back from Zurich. My concern now was for the living. Father would be distraught. He had guessed the situation over the past few weeks and had done a wonderful job comforting and supporting her. They had talked more than ever in their lives. Now he needed all the help we could give.

On our return we found him very subdued and naturally, even for him, such a hard man, a little tearful. Mother had gone very suddenly, even before the nurse could alert him; it was probably a blessing but I still rather wished, for his sake, that he had been there as she left us.

So now Gay and I had to motivate Father. He was 79 and we felt he could be pulled together but unless he was really 'kick started', given a reason to live, he could equally pass away within a few weeks.

The funeral was a private affair, at the crematorium in Chichester, with poor Herbert Hamnett almost overcome at the parting of yet another close friend. We kept it private for Father's sake and planned a memorial service later.

The next day Gay took the old chap over to Petworth where we had found someone advertising a litter of Springer puppies. When they came home there was a look of joy on his face. Under his feet in the well of the car seat was a little bitch pup, not six weeks old. He had a companion again, and against all tradition she was to be called Tara.

He had been staying for a few days with Gay and Antony, but really all he wanted to do was get in his car and drive home. Now he had his Tara there was no stopping him and next day the two of them settled back in the quiet old

Farmhouse. He was where he wanted to be, we were close by and could watch out for them, so we let him have his privacy.

Tara became his full time companion and they spent their whole life together. She was his eyes and his ears, and they were absolutely inseparable. She slept in his bedroom. They went visiting together, and she was the most gentle and tolerant companion.

For the next few years she gave him a reason to get up in the morning, something to care for, and something that needed him. And they were the greatest friends.

Yet our trials of that sad late winter and spring were not yet over. Only six weeks after Mothers death, Mary's own Mother, Kay, died suddenly at work in Worthing. She had been looking very frail, but had a great spirit and was not going to stop until she was forced to.

Mary and Kay had been very close friends, the more so since George Darrington had died a few years earlier, and they jointly ran their group of shops. The business was a great interest for Kay and she was, despite her increasing frailty, a very lively person.

This came as a terrible shock to everyone, particularly of course to Mary, who had been with her only minutes before she died. It also meant that in the one week not only did we have Kay's funeral, and all the family trauma that naturally entailed, but we also had the previously arranged memorial service for my dear mother at Yapton. It was a week neither of us will forget and by the end of it we were completely drained.

The latter did however give a chance for Mother's friends from far and wide, for representatives of the various organisations she had started, Flower clubs and 'The Sussex Kidney Trust', to attend. The old church was full and it was, by now, a little easier for Father to face people again.

Now Mary was faced with the prospects of running the business on her own and she was increasingly finding the whole thing a burden. There was nobody of a like mind to discuss things with and the question that kept reappearing was 'what was she doing it for'. Other, that is, than to keep the many staff in work.

She had barely had three consecutive days off work, apart from a very few holidays, in the past twenty five years and we began seriously to think that it may be time to find a buyer, and to finally give Mary a break. There was plenty to keep her busy at home now, with the farm office to run, the garden and her golf to play. Time soon goes by, and is not to be wasted.

INTO AFRICA

In the early days of '83, risking the wrath of a number of liberal friends, we had taken ourselves off on our first long trek out of Europe. We flew down to Cape Town, still then well under the control of the apartheid regime, to see for ourselves what we had been told was the most beautiful country on the Earth.

Apart from the usual inconvenience of long legs and short seats, the flight was rather a bore, apart from one aspect. As we settled in our seats Mary had said to me about what films there may be provided in the cabin to pass the time.

"What I would really like to see," she said, "would be *Chariots of Fire.*"

"You'll be lucky," I replied, "that film's only just come out." We settled down to our first meal and 12 hours of stiff-legged boredom.

Suddenly Mary nudged me.

"Look," she said "It's on!"

And sure enough, *Chariots of Fire* was to be on screen within the next few hours.

Despite all the wonderful sights we saw during the following weeks the one memory that comes back to me when we talk of Africa is associated with that film. As we flew in darkness, high above this great continent, away to our left there came the first red glow of the speed induced sunrise. Just as the film was ending, with its magnificently powerful 'signature tune' we were greeted by the most rapid vivid sunrise we had ever witnessed.

It was an unforgettable moment, with the increasing glow of the sun in the huge aircraft and this wonderful evocative music wafting through the earphones. Suddenly it was a dark continent no longer, and we looked forward to our first landing, to be able to stretch our legs in Nairobi shortly after.

From there we flew on to Johannesburg before again re-embarking for the two hour trip down to the Cape. This was a rough ride as the pilot constantly took evading actions to miss huge thunder clouds, and the plane, with only about four other passengers aboard, bounced like a cork in the ocean.

Shortly before this trip George and his second wife Lindsey, had divorced and she had returned home to Africa. Just before we left England we had phoned her for some information and she had insisted that we stay a few days with her, if we had the time. So our plan was that we would meet Lins at the airport, spend a couple of nights with her before then meeting up with two old Middleton friends, Don and June Hansford, who we were to meet us at the airport when they arrived, pick up our hire car and then spend the next night in a pre booked hotel before starting our trip eastwards to Durban.

We met up as arranged and spent two days being shown the area, had a couple of meals out and then a party, where we met a number of Lins's friends at her house. She lived only a few miles from the airport, at Newlands, under the shadow of Table Mountain, so it was very convenient.

The next morning, as arranged, Lins drove us to the airport where we met Don and June as they came off the plane. Then the wheels fell off. Neither our car, nor the hotel were booked; the travel agent had cocked up and we were momentarily flummoxed, eight thousand miles from home, at the start of a long trip and a little panic momentarily set in. However, almost at once, Lindsey came to the rescue.

Hearing our dilemma she immediately offered us her house.

"I am off to Hermanus tomorrow for the weekend, the house is empty, stay for a week if you like, and my maid will be in every day to tidy up."

What a wonderful offer!

We had, in the meantime, found two rooms in a Cape Town apartment block, and so decide to take them, then take up Lindsey's offer up the following day. Things were really looking up now; and with the newly hired car loaded we set off on the great adventure.

Next morning we found our way back to her house in Newlands. It was a lovely creeper-lined residence, set close to the famous cricket ground of the same name. It had a pretty garden full of fruit-laden trees, figs, apricots and vines and at the side a huge avocado, absolutely covered with the biggest specimens one could imagine. All for the picking.

In the back garden was a swimming pool where one could stand in the water and pick fruit off the overhanging trees at the same time. Lindsay showed us all around and insisted we used every facility. Needless to say the pool was the first and most regular one we took advantage of.

We all lunched together before Lins left on her own trip and then settled in to enjoy the Cape in some luxury. We had our 'card marked' before she left, and over the next few days we saw some of the very best eating places in the area.

There were several highlights but two stand out in the memory. One day we visited, and lunched, at Boschendal an old Winery which, in its early days, was Cecil Rhodes base in the Cape. Lunch was served at communal tables by pink turbaned, Asian waiters in flowing robes. Amidst stunning views of the surrounding mountains, endless vines and with excellent food, we spent a wonderful few hours.

Another day we drove round from Cape Town via Hout Bay, to Cape Point. An endless vista of wild, sweeping, sandy bays and rocky coastlines; hardly another person in sight. When we finally arrived at the point, and drove down the little winding road we were greeted by the sight of the most amazing azure blue water. It was, a colour which I had heard of but never seen in nature; except perhaps in the fleeting glimpse of a darting kingfisher, and it stays in my memory to this day.

On the beach to one side were a lone couple sunbathing and far away to our right on distant rocks were basking seals. All around was the cry and sight of huge sea birds coming in from forays from the distant southern ocean.

From there we returned via Simonstown, a quick look at Constantia and a paddle in ice cold Boulder Bay.

Another day we rode to the top of a baking hot table Mountain on the only cable car I was to see that year. Murren seemed an awful long way away.

A few days after this the four of us set out on our long drive along the famous Garden Route on our way to distant Durban. It was a very long trip on excellent, open, largely empty roads, and we made many stops. I well remember, after the cold Atlantic at Boulder Bay, dipping my toes in the water at Mossel Bay to be astounded at the temperature of the water. Now, of course, we were in the Indian Ocean.

After stops at Outshoorn, Plettenburg, Port Elizabeth and East London we were confronted with the dubious excitement of driving through the Transkei . A journey where, due to the very unstable political situation, we had been warned to take extreme care; not to stop unless we had no choice.

The 'black homeland' was bandit country in the eyes of local whites and most flew over it or went in groups. We did the trip alone and the only stop was for petrol in the little capital of Umtata . It was a tingling few minutes. Surrounded on all sides by the natives, many on horseback, many in traditional dress and none looking particularly welcoming.

It was a great relief to get moving again and within another hour or so with no mishaps we again entered safety, in Kokstad, Natal. People seemed surprised to see us in one piece. After lunch we made our way to Umhlanga, east of Durban, where we found a seaside hotel and settled in to unwind after a long tiring journey.

After another leisurely week bathing and sight seeing in the area, we said our farewells to Africa, and each other, and embarked on a plane bound, after a stop in Salisbury, for London Heathrow. Arriving there around breakfast time to be met by the ever reliable Ron Middleton in Mothers little car. Tired as I was I insisted on taking the wheel since I knew Rons' driving would shatter my nerves. It had been a great experience.

THE FINAL LOG-JAM RESOLVED

By the middle of the eighties, spare time was becoming easier to find, as gadgetry, almost always farmer-designed by practical men with an idea, took most of the remaining physical strain out of farming. In much the way that my Father had used wood, metal, screws and bolts all those years ago, now the main component was hydraulic power working within fabricated steel. At the time we were still annually struggling with the straw harvest, using machines that actually did the job well but the big setback was the sheer volume of bales we needed for the long winter months.

With the two dairy herds to provide for, I was baling for weeks around my neighbours stubbles, trying to gather together upwards of 25,000 bales. By the time these had been picked up and stacked in the fields, forming stacks of 56 bales, then lifted hydraulically onto the back of a transporter for removal to the farmstead to be manually handled into the barns or up onto the ricks, this all added up to three moves with machine and one move for every individual bale – a huge effort for such a low value product.

One day in 1985, whilst working at Chessels, I heard the sound of a powerful tractor working at great speed on neighbour Keith Hocking's stubbles, just south of our buildings and, always interested in something new, walked over to see what was going on.

There, towed behind a huge Fiat tractor was the largest machine, other than a combine, I had ever seen on a farm. Obviously a baler, it was rushing up and down the rows of straw at some 15 miles an hour, whilst from the rear end were coming the largest square bales I could imagine.

Walking out to the nearest bale I could appreciate the sheer bulk of it – four feet square, eight feet long and held together by six thick strings – and I knew at once that this was the future. With me was Kevin Scott who had been working on the farm for several years and who relished the annual bale cart about as much as I did – only I had been doing it for some thirty more years than him!

"That's for us!" I said with enthusiasm.

"Won't be much for me to do then," said Kevin. Which, of course, was what I was aiming for. More time for other things.

This was the revolution in straw handling that I had been waiting for all my working life and I resolved there and then that this would be the way for us from now on. I quickly worked out that with some 28 conventional bales to each of these new giants we would need to handle, at most, only a thousand each season. More to the point, it was a thousand bales that were too large to be handled by hand. A dream had come true. Now we could equip to do the job mechanically.

That evening I phoned the operator, Alan Barratt, a local farmer's son who was branching out into farm contracting, and was looking for business. He quickly offered to come in and bale a hundred of these bales for me to see how we managed with them.

Next day he was as good as his word. That evening I went out to inspect the results: one hundred massive half-ton bales.

Problem one. We were without any specialist machinery to handle them but we did still have the old industrial loader used for silage work. Although it was really too cumbersome for confined work, Kevin managed with it for those first few bales and the advantages were quickly obvious. The chance was not going to be missed and by the following season we had overcome our handling problems with the purchase of our first Kramer loader/shovel complete with attachments for every conceivable job on the farms.

So well did the machine handle the duties we put on it, that within another two seasons I had purchased another similar loader. Now, with one on each farm, the two herdsmen were able to do every task that confronted them. There was seldom need for any other help, or any other tractor power, and I often thought about what Kevin had said to me the day we first saw that huge Hesston baler. Indeed, there was not much for him to do now, and the following year, just before harvest, he gave in his notice. This would have given me a major headache in previous years, but in the end it caused me little inconvenience, such was the revolution brought about by these monster bales.

Summers would never again pose the strain they had done in the past and we didn't miss Kevin any more than we missed the drudge of handling all those damned little bales. Times had changed and now machinery really was taking the strain.

Such was the effect of this improvement that I quickly began asking myself why we needed anything more than the very basic machines on the farm. The trend towards using farm contractors was taking off very fast at the time, although contractors had been around for years, but due to the inadequacies of their equipment they had not gained a very good reputation.

Farmers generally were reluctant to get into the position of being let down and for a long time almost every farm continued to own and maintain their own machines for every single task. The cost of this had been high, but now the equipment was becoming bigger and more sophisticated by the month, and purchase prices correspondingly enormous. Here now was the excuse to 'bite the bullet' and trust the contractors.

Labour was leaving the land faster and faster and there was less need to consider their positions, as we did with our 'old retainers' who had been on the farms all their lives. Everything came together quite nicely in that respect. As staff left the farms in search of better and more rewarding work, we farmers came to rely more on the contractors. And as the contractors won more work they could afford bigger and better machinery, more regular, usually ex-farm, staff and consequently did a more reliable job.

These changes made it clear that I could now run the farms without any labour other than the two herdsmen and handle all the seasonal work peaks with contractors. I did occasionally worry that I was taking too much on again, but the thought of being able to run the farms exactly how I wanted really appealed to me.

Using what modern machinery we still owned I was able to do all the springtime grassland work, fertilising and mowing during the summer, hedge trimming during the winter and the thousands of maintenance jobs that always crop up without warning.

Another obvious attraction was that there were fewer wages to pay. In particular it was a relief not to have to pay a tractor driver through the winter months, when for much of the time there is little useful work for him to do, and often one is forced to give him unproductive jobs at a full pay rate. It also meant that, if I wanted to take a day or two off for whatever reason, it was much easier without also needing to make arrangements to keep a man occupied in my absence.

Contract rearer John Tangye up at Worplesdon was now caring for the young heifers, Geoff and Peter the cows and the silage arrangement with John Forse at Barnham worked well enough, so the system was pretty simple. It only needed phone calls to line up big balers, muck spreaders or fencing contractors and the specialist jobs would be done in a fraction of the time we were able to do them in the past. And usually better. More importantly there would be no more machinery breakdowns and repairs to concern me, since this was now the responsibility of the contractors.

Yet in spite of all these improvements I did manage to have some disasters and none was more spectacular than one caused by some big bales in 1989. The accident occurred in August, but the fuse, literally, was lit some weeks earlier when Alan Barratt baled some hay into those big Hesstons bales one late evening down in Marlhole.

The hay was very green although dry enough at five o'clock but had begun to pick up dew under overcast conditions when he finished baling at about eight. Ideally, it should have been left to cool outside but I was unsure how these huge lumps would react to being left out, particularly if it rained, so next morning I put them into the Dutch barn adjoining the silage clamp by the dairy.

Keeping my eye on them for a week or so, I saw no sign that they were warming up, as moist hay can sometimes do, and whilst checking every few days I thought no more about it as a problem.

We move on now to August when I was combining wheat at Black Barn Farm, working happily away in a fair crop in the distant Valley Field. As I was making my way back up the slope, I saw Father's car pull into the gateway at the top of the field, where he stopped and began waving quite excitedly at me. It was not in his nature to panic but just in case it was important I pulled the combine out of work and ran her up to where he was by now standing with Tara running excitedly around his legs.

"There are sparks coming out of those big hay bales" he puffed out, "You'd better come back and move them before they catch alight." "Sounds a bit late for moving them," I said. "Have you called the fire brigade?" Deadly silence. It appeared Geoff came up to report the situation and the Old Man decided the only thing to do was find me.

"Jump in, I will drive," I said, "But it sounds as if it will be well alight by the time we get back…" And without too many more words I sped homewards.

As we left Yapton, I cast a glance across the farmland towards Flansham, a couple of miles away. With no great surprise I saw a huge cloud of smoke billowing over the trees around the hamlet.

"Too late now, I'm afraid," I muttered.

As I pulled into the farm we were greeted by the sight of thick hose pipes snaking their way up the drive. All around were the many 'idle hands' who always seem to gather on such occasions and who like nothing better than good disaster to gossip about.

As we walked down the drive, Father was clearly becoming stressed and I told him to slow down, since there was nothing more he could do. He slowed a little and I walked on. As I arrived at the yard the whole thing was well ablaze. The roof sheets were popping like November the fifth and hot lumps of cement fibre were flying through the air.

Father was there by now and becoming more overwrought by the minute, so I again urged him not to worry.

"It's well insured," I said, secretly hoping that this was indeed so…

With that I got on the Kramer, cleared the people who were cluttering the place up and proceeded to dig a fire gap through the silage face which adjoined the blazing barn, in the hope of containing the spread. It would waste a lot of what was moved but I considered it the only logical step. Half an hour later, covered in soot and half choked with acrid smoke, it was done.

Then the firemen began pouring huge amounts of water on the silage walls and the adjoining barns to avoid them too igniting, whilst Father, by now a little calmer, was telling the local press all about my disaster. Yes it was mine! And I should have known that the period between two and three weeks after storing damp hay was the likely time for spontaneous combustion. I had not really taken the risk seriously.

Obviously the hay and some fifty bales of straw were, like the barn itself, a lost cause. What concerned me was the silage clamp and I knew that, were the fire to get into it, it could burn through slowly for weeks and we could loose all of it. The fire brigade were by now having a field day. Three crews had arrived, all from different areas, and each senior officer wanted to be in charge. Instead of letting it burn out, they insisted on damping it down for the next 24 hours and so kept the fire going a day longer than it needed to.

Having soaked it so that it would not burn they then spent almost another day shaking it out to dry it, so that it would burn. I was unimpressed and told them so and eventually they departed with 'the hump'. I was relieved to see them go.

When it was all over, the NFU again came up trumps. The local assessor, Hugh Brown from Donnington, came over a couple of days later and we quickly agreed on the losses. Within eight weeks a new barn was completed on the site – and I resolved never to make hay in big square bales again.

The most serious effect of the debacle was that Father, very upset and shocked, had a small stroke in his eye the following day. The doctor expected he would be OK in a few days but since he was 84, we feared for his ability to drive his car again.

In the event he did recover but had lost his confidence in driving, except to potter around the farm, so that emergency trip to Madehurst proved to be his last road journey as a driver after some sixty eight years of driving. That was to be a great loss to such an independent man and made him very, very, depressed.

So it was that he came to spend more and more time with Tara in the farmhouse. Although many friends would drive him around, it was not the same as driving himself, and he was really happier at home. His only independence now was in driving around the meadows and local houses in his electric golf buggy.

With Tara sitting alongside him he would creep silently around the place, often coming up behind me at odd times and places as he checked that I was still doing my job. I still got the old comments, like "You need to…" or "It would be better if you…"

Some things would never change, at least not while he had breath in his body!

Most Sundays he would drive the buggy, with Tara on the front seat, up to the cottage for lunch with Mary and I, but this was pretty well the limit of his ambitions and confidence. Life, apart from the odd hours with his grandchildren Bob and Lissie or a few very old friends, dragged. He would sparkle for a few minutes but then drift off into a silent world of his own thoughts, and seemingly could not wait to be alone again with Tara and his memories.

FURTHER DIVERSIONS

With the extra time, and with the business running quite smoothly there was also more time to concentrate on aspects of farming that, because of time pressures, had previously been impossible.

I had always been aware of the needs to keep improving the land and property under my charge, and of the old adage "Farm as if you are going to live forever, live as if you will die tomorrow"; and so now, with extra time, I resolved to do my best in maintaining the two farms as both attractive and functional stock units.

My two priorities were, then, and remain still today, to run profitable stock farms and retain the maximum environmental benefits for the creatures and plant life which share our land, depend on our farming methods for their own survival, and which give such pleasure to look at.

If in turn these things give pleasure to visitors that is an additional bonus and all I ask, and expect, is that they in turn respect what they see.

My lifelong passion has been for ornithology with particular emphasis on wildfowl. This interest began as a youngster when I first started carrying a gun. As of course it was vital to identify the species before it was shot, lest some rare specimen came over ones head.

This rapidly increased my awareness particularly of the native and winter visitors and in all the years of night flight the only accident was when I killed a Tufted drake, for which I felt very guilty.

In turn it was inevitable that all other varieties would feature in my interest and I have ever since gone out of my way to ensure these creatures are given space and conditions to thrive, in this hostile and increasingly alien and thoughtless world.

And some thirty years from when I shot my first duck, in November 1952, it was this awareness that persuaded me, indirectly, that shooting as practised in commercial shooting operations by the mid-eighties was no longer for me, and for a long time ended my involvement in the sport.

At that time we were using a large tracked excavator on the farm, which I used for ditching, drainage and reclamation work, emptying slurry pits and felling trees for both ourselves and many neighbours. Having some free time and the machine idle, I decided to embark on a scheme that I had dreamed of since childhood, to make a small lake, with safe islands, around an old pond in the meadow behind the Cottage, and to stock it with free winged wildfowl.

The old pond had lain overgrown and half forgotten for years. As children Gay and I had been frightened with stories from Mother of the 'Green Man' who lived there, and we thus treated it with the respect demanded of deep water.

When I was fifteen, about the time I was really getting into shooting in the first place, I began breeding Mallard. Then I set about clearing it by hand. However the task was far too large and within a couple of years other things interfered and the project was dropped.

In the intervening years willow trees took over, cattle trod the pond sides down, the old hole silted up, and we very nearly came to a decision to fill it up and enlarge the meadow.

However that did not happen because Mary and I decided to make a feature of it that, being close to the back of our garden, would almost be an extension of both our property and of the farmhouse next door.

So in the winter of 1979 I had set about clearing the whole site. The willows were felled and burned and with a clear picture in my mind's eye I set about digging a pond of just over an acre, which included two large islands where the birds could rest and breed undisturbed by intruders.

The spoils were piled up either on the islands, around the sides, or trailered away to fill in various holes around the farm. It was dug out to the same depth as the original pond with shallower areas to cater for species that dabbled rather than dived. The depth of the finished pond varied between a foot and some eight feet and was actually quite an impressive sight when the earthworks were finished some weeks later.

The following months saw fencing and wire netting erected round the perimeter, grass seeds sown, and reeds, shrubs and trees planted in strategic places.

The result was dramatic, in that almost before I had finished the digging, the evening sky would be full of wild duck coming in for the night's shelter. Within a couple of weeks, with some tail corn thrown in for bait, there were often up to two hundred birds in the sky for that magical twenty minutes of 'flight', just before darkness.

The noise of rapid wings, of circling birds calling across the meadows, and the electifying sight of ducks lining up and 'barrelling' into the pond from a great height had already made the project worthwhile.

In the February Mary and I drove down to the New Forest to visit Peter Mays, a wildfowl breeder we had heard of near Holmsley, where we hoped to collect a few pairs of suitable species to form the basis of our new collection.

The sight that greeted us was mouth watering, our imagination fired beyond our pockets, and after a long look round we departed with a few birds, but with a long list of specimens for the coming months and years. Our requirements were for birds that would suit the conditions, settle and breed easily but be attractive.

Amongst the first birds we brought home on that first visit were Pochard, Pintail, Tufted Duck, Wigeon and a pair of Barnacle Geese, and as we released them into the waters to settle into their new surroundings, the thrill was immense.

Later in the month we drove down again to Peter Mays and brought home four more varieties including the spectacular Mandarins and a pair of Hawaiian Geese (Ne Ne's). We decided to let all these settle in for the summer, before introducing any more.

By late April, I was incubating and later hand-rearing some 80 ducklings. Every species we had brought in, except the immature Ne Ne's, had laid eggs and for security from vermin I decided hand rearing was safer until we had sufficient breeding pairs.

Our garden was full of Father's hand built rearing pens as the ducklings grew enough feathers to withstand the night temperatures and the daylight hours were barely enough to cope with the extra duties, silage making golf and a little reluctant gardening.

In late July the first birds were released back onto the pond and as the numbers grew so the food requirements soared. Most of the ducklings settled well although the Wigeon were very nervous, however the pond was now alive with fowl and the project had really come alive.

That first season I decided to leave about half of the birds 'full winged', that is to say, not pinioned, so they would be able to fly free, and come and go as they pleased as they grew to maturity. The biggest problem here was in the 'role of Solomon', deciding which bird should have its wing joint removed confining it to a surface existence for life, and which should be free. I felt terribly guilty as I selected those for amputation and soon had to develop a compromise which involved cutting the end wing joint half way off, rather than to the actual joint. In this way I reasoned that it would unbalance the bird but allow them to at least fly short distances around the pond or even the meadow whilst restricting them from leaving the district. It also eased my guilt.

So for several seasons this operation was highly successful. The number of species increased until we had seventeen different varieties flitting in and out and around the district. Evening flight was spectacular and we would sit and watch the sky come alive at dusk as the tame birds and countless wild ones, flew home for supper.

Barnacle Geese, now breeding freely and nesting on one of the islands, had increased to some seventeen birds, and spent their days grazing grass in the adjoining meadow. They never ventured further afield because the old 'stock' gander, bought from Peter Mays, was pinioned and could not leave the confines of the pond. He acted as a magnet for his flock and would always stand close to the wire watching and honking at the birds across the meadow.

During this time the pond had been used by the River Board as an emergency home for a number of mirror carp caught from a drained lake elsewhere. Within two years the pond was alive with fish and the inevitable herons, who don't miss a trick when it comes to finding a free meal.

As one could imagine, the effect of this project on the local wildfowl population was quite spectacular. Neighbours fish ponds were soon acting as overflow nesting sites each Spring and the ponds and ditches on the golf course, just across the meadows, were full of breeding pairs.

Every duck in the district knew when feeding time was due; and without a dinner gong to rouse them, somehow managed to arrive home just as the daily bucketful of food was spread around the pond.

The reeds grew round the edges of the water, newly planted weeping willows began to feature, particularly in early Spring, and the whole scheme was turning out just as I had dreamed it would.

Unfortunately there were some clouds on the horizon...

To begin with the problems were caused by magpies, crows and the odd fox, but these were closely followed and then overshadowed by humans.

The corvids began the trouble by developing a taste for duck eggs and then ducklings, and despite all my efforts were impossible to deter. They knew where to look and as soon as a duck emerged from her nest they would drop down from the trees and fight over the spoils. Very few birds other than the geese, who stood guard all the time over their nests, were safe.

Magpies are particularly cunning, swanky, noisy, nervous thieves, and each morning I could hear them from the house as they went about their raids but could not deter them since they would spot me as soon as I approached. Over a two year period I shot 190 magpies from the windows of my bedroom but their numbers continued to increase apace, such was the growing problem.

The foxes were less of a problem since they could not get into the main area, which was protected by an electric fence for that sole purpose. The only birds they caught were those who found their way out through rabbit holes or gaps in the wire and then couldn't get home again.

If they had all just chosen to kill the common mallards it would not have done other than good, since they were becoming dominant. However the vermin seemed to have developed a taste for the most expensive and difficult to rear species, and it was depressing to find a headless bird when it was the only one of its breed and sex on the pond.

Despite all these annoyances the project continued – after all, these were natural pests doing what came naturally, and had to be considered part of the risk of everyday life for wild creatures.

Not so easy to control was the human element, and the final nail in the coffin came in 1989 when, despite my protestations, West Sussex County Council insisted on reopening a dormant footpath which ran some fifty yards west of the pond. When challenged by the NFU to justify the move one of the most memorable and galling reasons was that there was "a wildfowl pond close to the path..." and that it was "attractive for the public to see."

Such is the ignorance and naivety of our modern civil servant. Our argument – that the reserve was private and on private ground and that the shy birds would be endangered by walkers and their inevitably uncontrolled dogs, predictably lost the day.

The footpath signs went up and within two years the only birds left on the pond were the wild mallard. Our original Barnacle gander, the patriarch, who's

*A Barnacle goose (above) protecting its nest, and below,
a flypast of Barnacle geese shortly before they left us for the last time.*

presence kept the free winged birds there, was one day killed by a dog that jumped over the wire.

Within a week, with their main tie gone, the rest were beginning to fly further and further away from the pond. Within a month they had all gone. I just hoped they had flown north to join the rest of the wild population of Barnacle geese on the long journey to the Arctic Circle and that they would continue to breed and fly free. I half expected, or hoped to see them the following winter, but sadly they never returned.

So that was the end of the dream, a brief experiment. The pond is still there. Mallard and Moorhens live there all year and in winter for a year or two, the odd Pintail, Mandarin and Tufted Duck would look in – almost certainly my hand-reared birds, but each time they came they grew more nervous; natural instincts had taken hold.

They too have now given up, as have I. 'Given best' to the ignorance of the WSCC Footpaths Department. At least I gave it a try.

In most other respects, the home farm is much as it was in my childhood. The crops are better, the meadows cleaner, the hedges better trimmed, and many mature trees line the old hedgerows.

Proof of this hangs in our hall, where it has hung for over fifty years, in the form of a map drawn up by Gerry Young in 1945 (see frontispiece). It is of the hamlet and its pastures and fields as they were a hundred years earlier in 1845, which Gerry had carefully researched from the local archives.

It shows all the land holdings, the Tenants and Landowners of the day. It shows every hedge, every field name, and the acreage of each enclosure. Apart from a couple of minor changes, neither the field names, nor indeed the hedges on our holding have changed in the intervening 150 years.

The differences, compared with many surrounding farms, where stock farming has long since ceased and hedge removal has been carried out to accommodate large machinery, is startling. Unhappily, I must say that I don't think we can hold the line much longer. The writing is on the wall, writ large, for small family farms and for the wild creatures which share the land with us – for myriad reasons, which are discussed in later chapters. The sadness is that the general public won't notice the loss or see the changes until they have long become irreversible.

As the years pass it is inevitable that death will leave irreplaceable gaps in one's family and friends and through the mid eighties and early nineties we spent too long in sad graveyards and grey cemeteries.

One of the most distressing losses was that of George Hammond's third wife, Sally, who had come into our lives like a flash of light. Sally and George had known each other through promotional work and when, unsurprisingly, Lindsay and he parted in the early eighties, in a very civilised manner, it was not long before we met Sally, and realised an old friendship had fast become something more. George rented an empty cottage from us at Flansham after he split with Lindsay, and Sally began appearing at weekends with him.

Before we knew it, we were off to London in a private coach, Ron Middleton driving, to the wedding at St Columba's church, Pont Street, and then on to a spectacular celebration on a Thames Cruiser which, during a superb meal and reception, took us down the Thames and through the Thames Barrier.

It was a lovely day with many, old friends around and culminated in the happy couple being whisked away on honeymoon, James Bond style, from the boat on a high speed launch, which rapidly circled our boat and before making off at speed for the airport.

They settled into a lovely moated house in Edenbridge Kent and, two of a kind, lived life to the very hilt. In 1987 Sally bore a son, Christopher and George's life looked like settling down to a normal routine for the first time since I had known him.

When, only a year after the birth, we heard that Sally was having chemotherapy treatment we were shattered, but it was not until a couple of months later, when George revealed that his lovely wife was on borrowed time, that we really grasped that the situation was desperate.

When Christopher was a little over a year old, they all came over for a lunch party. We didn't know if Sally could come, but she did, and knowing what we had been told, we were amazed at her demeanour. She chatted, lunched and walked around the garden with Mary, before spending some time watching a game of bowls. She was clearly uncomfortable and seemed quite tired as they set off home.

Three weeks later Sally died; just 37 years old, with a lovely son, an ideal husband and everything to look forward to. We were all so sad.

A few months later we made the journey back to the church in which they had only too recently been married for a memorial service. As Sally would have expected, we were all commanded to a lavish celebration of her short life, before poor George had to face up to the reality of his new life, bringing up his baby son on his own. Times were going to be very hard, and our hearts all went out to them both.

The devotion with which they both came through that awful experience was an inspiration. Christopher, now almost a teenager, looks and behaves like a 16 year old. He is sports mad and George gives him total encouragement in every manner. Yet Sally's loss is still sadly felt and all the ladies go out of their way to spoil the lad; George too.

TIMES CHANGE

So much was happening that we began to think that our lives were edging again to more work, and that the sport of the sixties, seventies and eighties had gone out the window. Happily that was not the case, although both Mary and I had grown increasingly disinterested in the competitive side of golf. Some of the best days now were the trips we made to Scotland where Tom and Sheena Hay, and the two of us, would have our 'International' Challenge matches over some of the most beautiful links on the Angus coast. We would stay with them at their lovely farm house, Panlathy, nearby Carnoustie, and mix farm walks (with shopping for Sheena and Mary) golf at Carnoustie, Barry, Crail, Cruden Bay, and Tom's home course, Edzell.

Then sometimes they would come to stay with us at Flansham and we would be able to show them our local courses, the likes of the 'West Sussex' at Pulborough, Hayling Island, Bognor or Goodwood.

For several years around these times I had gone back to Hunstanton and Brancaster with three friends I had known and played with for years, Barry Targett amongst them. I had fallen in love with the old course, with its links which flooded at 'spring tide', forming huge inland 'seas', just leaving fingers of land to remind one it was still a golf course.

Redshank, Curlew, untold duck and the first geese skeins of autumn made it a magical place. Golf, always serious, nevertheless became secondary on this course where I had decided sometime earlier that, if I could only play on but one course for the rest of my days, Brancaster was the place it would have to be.

Every aspect of the place evoked the feeling of tradition, quality, class. At all times we found the members and the staff very welcoming and helpful. So different from many courses these days.

The Clubhouse too, over 100 years old, is really special. One day we arrived to see CLOSED on the lounge door. We knew the steward, John, was there, so we called out to him. "Sorry gentlemen, I'm relaying the carpets. The members have finally decided the smell from their dogs little 'accidents' are too bad and the carpet's being cleaned." He added, "Give me your order and I'll pass it out the window." Next day things were back to normal.

All round the main club room, with its large polished tables and chairs, stand the mens private lockers. Around the walls huge 'honours boards' containing the names of past Captains and Presidents. HRH Prince of Wales, HRH Duke of Kent, etc. Our minds boggled at the vision of an HRH changing his plus fours on the lounge carpet, as members concentrated on their drinks round the bar, and their dogs 'cocked-legs' on the chairs!

The latrines too were antique classics. Huge decorated porcelain jobs, large enough to bathe in, made by Shanks & Armitage to last for ever. One stood in front of them and thought "the old King stood here, with just the same thoughts in mind!" and "By Royal Appointment" took on a new meaning.

Brancaster is special. The Greens look as if they had been there since the beginning of time, and my we had some wonderful days on those windswept links.

Seriously competitive club golf had ended for me in 1987 when our scratch team lost in the County Team Competition for what was, then, "Whitbread Trophy". The fun of competitive golf to me was not just the game, in which we always competed hard, but in being able to meet in the bar with your opponent afterwards and, win or lose, have a couple of drinks. I had learnt the game in this manner, and made many good friends over the past thirty years.

I had been trained well in this by Jack Langmead, Tony Mote, Martin Christmas and as much as anyone, George Hammond. We had practised it hard in our circle, and were quite well-known for our socialising. Bognor Golf Club indeed had a country-wide reputation as one of the Clubs to visit, if not for the golf, certainly for the social aspects and particularly for the welcome visitors invariably received from everyone.

The trigger which caused me to call a halt, was during the afternoon singles. I played a quiet lad of no more than 16, and lost a close game when I carelessly failed to get down in two from just off the back of the 18th green. We shook hands, having barely exchanged a word for three hours on the course, as the boy seemed to find talking a problem, and went to off change. Going to the bar ten minutes later to buy him a drink, he was not to be seen.

I searched, and eventually found him on the putting green with a pint of orange juice. When he eventually came back inside he sat with his own team who never attempted to mix with us. I had changed my golf clothes(!) and we had no disagreements during our round so I decided that perhaps, the game was now being played by very different people with quite different outlooks and different standards, and that this was the time to bid it farewell.

We had played hard as serious amateurs but we always had fun. There didn't appear to be much fun in this new attitude and most of the young players seemed, incorrectly, to think they were all good enough to turn professional. Unfortunately, a number also behaved as though they were rather special. After that little episode I resolved, there and then, that I would give up competitive events and get back to playing with my old friends, enjoying the game as we had for some 30 years.

Instead of every spare evening through the summer being dedicated to practice and playing there would now be time for other things, like leaning on a gate and watching a smart bunch of yearling steers growing fat as the sun set across the meadows.

~ *Chapter Seven* ~

A BIT OF A BLOW

During the second week of October '87 four of us had again spent a few days at Brancaster, for our last few days of serious golf before the onset of winter rules and temporary greens.

The north Norfolk coast is exposed at the best of times but for those few days we were almost blown off the course into the North Sea, such was the ferocity of the wind. Each day we felt it must surely abate, but every day it became worse, and it was a relief to head homewards. Although it had by then begun to rain torrentially the wind eased slightly as we reached the south coast. The weather was indeed very disturbed but, at that time, we were perhaps luckily unaware of what was coming.

The conditions stayed this way for several more days and on the 15th of October Mary and I went to the funeral of Geoff Kirby, the husband of our old secretary, in the small, virtually disused, old church at Ford, between Climping and Arundel.

This is a tiny church we had never before been to. The solitary building stands out in the middle of the fields, way back from the road, surrounded by a low wall, and some large old trees in the little churchyard, which on that day, as we trudged across the sodden path, made a forlorn sight.

The rain, driven on a strengthening southerly gale soaked us well before we reached the church door, and the high trees bent alarmingly over the old roof. The building was warm, but very spartan, candles for lighting and in need of attention. Lacking more than a handful of parishioners this was understandable. It was however a haven from the weather and actually seemed almost the right setting for a funeral. Sad, old, and rather mournful.

After sheltering in the churchyard for the internment the small gathering were probably all as relieved as ourselves to bolt for the distant road, and the sanctuary of a dry warm car. By the time we had driven home, and changed into dry clothes, the heavy clouds had turned early evening into a dark forbidding night. And indeed what a night that turned into.

The hurricane of October 15/16 was the culmination of ten days of wet and very wild weather. When it came, with trees still in full leaf, and the ground softened by the rains, the effects were devastating. Changing the face of huge swathes of the South East for generations.

Mary and I had gone to bed around ten o'clock with the gale lashing our south facing window. Even so we left a small lattice window open on the east side of the room, since we always need to have fresh air, and went off to sleep with a steady but increasing Force 7 blowing.

About one o'clock we were awoken by what sounded like an off key piano tinkling on the roof, and we quickly realised that it was actually the sound of the clay tiles being raised up and then dropping down again as the by now ferocious gale roared across the Home Meadow in rapidly repeating blasts. It was as if a general was marshalling his troops beyond our garden and sending them, in great waves, to flatten the little settlement. And indeed he almost succeeded.

My inclination was to go out and see what was happening but the sound of considerable crashing and banging, and the regular tinkle of broken glass persuaded me otherwise. I suggested to Mary we had a cup of tea, from the faithful 'Teasmade' before the power went off. The timing was perfect because not ten minutes later, with a huge flash, all the lights in the district went out.

I remember saying to Mary 'We will know the damage soon enough when Geoff goes out to milk at 4.30'. Then we grabbed a short sleep, between the tinkling tiles, blasts on the window, and crashes in the lane. And all the while the wind was coming across the meadow in increasingly regular attacks.

I heard nothing from Geoff and by five thirty, with the gale slightly abated now, I pulled on some clothes and ventured out to see the damage. It was still dark as I walked down into the lane. Immediately I was confronted with an elm tree across my path. Climbing through that obstacle I pressed on, The lane was scattered with debris, sheets of tin, tiles and perspex roofing, which I quickly realised was from our nearby buildings. Approaching the dairy I saw Geoff.

"The power is still off but the animals are all OK although they seem in a bit of a daze," he said. "Mind you, the buildings too look a bit of a mess, and some are open to the sky."

That proved something of an understatement. The first thing I noticed was two large tin-roofed barns, including one that covered the drier shed, were no longer there. Flashing my torch across the scene I noticed the almost complete roof of the drier shed, upside down in the garden of the old empty cottage across the drive. It had lifted and flipped over in one piece, fortunately missing the house itself.

Half the slates were off the dairy, gutters lay everywhere, along with smashed roofs, sheets, branches and what seemed like a week's collection of plastic bags, blown across the meadows from nearby Bognor.

The cows now stood quietly in the collecting yard waiting for milking. They were, as Geoff said, in shock and just stood very still, with their heads down. Realising that the power was likely to be off for some time I told Geoff to let them back out in the meadow, and after checking the fences, wait for developments.

"Have you heard from Peter at Madehurst yet?" said Geoff. I replied to the effect that the phones would be down, and lets get some semblance of order here before worrying about that! However it had crossed my mind that there would certainly be chaos there too.

We had no generators on either farm, so as usual, we would wait for the power to come back "Should'nt be long" I said more in hope that expectation, and I sent him home for some breakfast while I set about clearing the drive and assessing the situation.

To be honest it was difficult to take on board what had happened, or the real extent of the damage, so at that stage, and still waiting for full daylight, Madehurst was something to sort out later.

Time passed, and suddenly at 8.30, Geoff called out, "The power is back," so I told him to get the milking done and get the cows back into their routine. That was a relief and now I could begin to think about Madehurst.

Going back to the cottage for a quick breakfast I was greeted by Mary. "The radio says the whole of the South East is at a standstill, roads rail and power lines, all blocked or down." I tried phoning Peter but although the thing rang there was no answer. The only solution was to get up there. But how?

Loading a chain saw and fuel and a long tow chain on the loading shovel, I resolved to get there one way or another, by road or if need be across country.

On the subsequent journey I cleared a dozen large trees, pulled several cars out of banks and ditches and found two main roads quite impassable. The chain saw and the chain proved invaluable and both then and over the next months, both would be in constant use.

Without the power of the loader, with its tremendous lifting capacity, the journey could well have taken two days, but I soon found it would lift and push a tree of perhaps three feet diameter, bodily across the road and by the time I had arrived at the next road junction, there would be a queue of grateful drivers behind me. It is seldom these days to find anyone grateful for a farm vehicle on the road, but that day was different.

It was like lifting a siege, and two and a half hours after leaving home I arrived at Madehurst via Arundel, approaching the farm from the only possible access, across the fields. By now I well realised that what I found was going to be bad, but the sight that greeted me almost made me weep.

All around the field boundaries, only yesterday surrounded by huge Beech trees, I was now greeted by the sight of white 'tombstones', Huge chalk-clad roots standing a dozen feet in the air, at the end of smashed and broken trunks. Every fence I saw had trees lying across it and my heart dropped further.

As I stopped the machine at the farm buildings Peter, looking anxious and haggard, appeared at the dairy door. The reason for his appearance was soon apparent. The buildings, which comprised four large barns, the dairy and a long-pole barn, were almost devoid of roofing. A huge tin barn still stood full of hay bales, while alongside it in the meadow lay the whole roof, like a huge upturned tin-lid. The pole barn, some seventy feet by fifty was simply gone, and on their way over the other buildings, the flying timbers had smashed over fifty percent of the asbestos sheets on the big cattle barns.

The biggest barn had some thirty heifers inside, but Peter assured me that miraculously every one of them seemed to be fine. He also told me the whole milking herd, some 90 cows were unscathed in the meadow opposite the dairy, but increasingly anxious to have their milk removed. It transpired that they were in the only meadow on the whole farm to be still stock proof at daylight that morning. A little luck, anyway.

The dairy building itself had suffered severely. The south facing gable wall had been moved bodily inwards, and was in danger of falling onto the bulk milk tanks and the small office beneath. The roof was almost gone, with the whole metal structure lifted. Of course there was no power, and to my certain knowledge, no chance of any for some considerable time.

So that now was the situation, and it was immediately clear that the first priority was to find a source of power, since past experience of storms on the hills told me it was never a quick job to get the lines reinstated. And this was clearly no normal storm.

By 1pm I had returned on the Kramer via Arundel and called in at Andrew Langmead's farm at Ford. Once before I had borrowed an old generator from him and I was anxious to see if anyone else had beaten me to it. My luck was now really in. The old machine was still there and all it needed was transporting to Madehurst and with some emergency wiring I could get Peter milking.

Finding a working phone I rang my cousin, David Sadler (son of Bogie) now boss at Goodrowes and asked him for an electrician, 'Urgently please', in the hope that before nightfall we could perhaps get the milk off the cows, before stress brought on a bout of mastitis in the herd. To his eternal credit, as I arrived back at the farm with the generator in tow, two of their electricians also arrived, on foot across the fields. "Can't get any closer," said Ian.

"Don't worry. I will come down with the tractor and tow your van in," I said. "Just get us up and running."

Peter went off home to get some food and the men started work. We set the generator up outside the dairy, running off a tractor, and miraculously, within an hour, the lights came on and the dairy sprang to life. Peter soon arrived back and went out to gather the cows and with their udders bursting with some twenty hours of milk, he began to get them through the parlour.

Thankfully the rain had by then stopped and, despite the lack of a roof, by 7pm they were all milked and back in the meadow. Meanwhile I had pulled Ian back out to the road, thanked him profusely and returned again to the farm since the day was far from done, either for him and his mate, nor for us.

The priority now was to get the back lane cleared and allow the local traffic to flow, particularly the milk tanker to empty the farm vats. The road was blocked by some twenty substantial trees between the farm and the main road so with the help of my neighbour Robert Green's foresters I now set about cutting a track wide enough to allow the traffic access.

The whole village came out to help, and everyone 'mucked in' and talked to each other (shades of the old wartime spirit) whilst working against the clock as the weather again began to deteriorate.

We finally opened the road around ten that evening and I got home and fell into bed around eleven. I was completely exhausted and had not eaten for over 24 hours but was content now, in the knowledge that we had power on each farm; and that all the cattle were milked and uninjured. It had been the most traumatic day of my life and I knew that the next weeks, and probably months, were going to be almost equally hectic as we struggled to get the buildings ready to house the herds before the worst weather came.

Already Peter had been forced to throw one days milk away, and I was keen that as little more as possible was lost. Each days produce was worth some £400 and there were going to be a lot of extra bills to pay. To make matters worse he also had a lame bull, being used on the herd, who had to be treated urgently. This was an added complication but one we were unable to delay. We managed to guide our vet down to the farm to sedate the old chap and roll him into a loosebox to enable Paul to treat and trim his feet – a job we could have done without at that particular time.

And it truly was a hard winter. Next day I recruited two extra hands, Phil Smith our relief herdsman and another local, Colin Sands. Both agreed to come in full time for a couple of weeks to make a start. We spent a day searching for, and salvaging materials from the buildings that had 'disappeared'. Much of the material had come to rest against a wood some six hundred yards to the north of the buildings and we brought it all back and prepared it for reuse.

We covered the hay with a large sheet and hoped it would keep dry, since I had already ascertained there was no hope of getting any new tin sheets for at least two weeks. Then we concentrated on the leaking roofs and particularly the dairy and the pole barn.

It really is amazing what one can do when motivated. The three of us got that whole area back together ('jury rigged' at least) and roofed by the following Friday, during which time Phil had given both Geoff and Peter a day off, and we had done a hundred other emergency jobs

The following weekend I took some time off from the farm. Instead I took the loader and chainsaw to the golf club and spent two days cutting, clearing and burning some two hundred trees that had been uprooted. By Sunday evening the course was again fit to play, although the appearance of many of the holes was considerably altered.

There was now time to think again, to fix the new priorities. The past ten days had been the first time in my life that I had seriously doubted whether I wished to continue farming. So much that I had worked for, built, and known, was destroyed and our lovely tree-clad downland farm had been changed almost beyond recognition.

As an example of the strain the community was under, a neighbour at Madehurst, who had been so distressed by the destruction, tragically took his own life a week or so later. I didn't feel quite like that but I was very depressed.

However looking back we were very fortunate. Many farms were unable to get power to their dairies and whole herds of cows were reported to have been lost to mastitis because there were no means available to get the milk out of their udders. Hand milking large herds with today's staff levels is impossible.

Fortunately our insurers had also come up trumps, and within a year we had replaced all the damaged cattle buildings with clear span structures, at their expense. And repaired those others which were repairable.

Over the next five months Colin and I cleared up, and burnt, some three hundred mature trees. We also reinstated over seven miles of barbed wire fences, so that by the Spring of 1988 the farm, whilst denuded of many of its huge trees, once again looked respectable and ready for the new season.

Peter suffered a stress-related relapse a month after the storm, doubtless brought on by those traumatic few days, but Phil Smith, as he had done for so many years, again filled the post by covering for Peter over many weeks until he was fit enough to return to work. Peter was sadly never quite so robust again but was able to continue steadily for another seven years.

And about the same time, some three weeks after that windy day when we attended Geoff Kirby's funeral at Ford, his widow, and our long serving and loyal farm secretary Dora (always Mrs) Kirby, also died, in Arundel Hospital. She had been ill a long time but concealed her problems from everyone. The good lady had given Father, and then me, some thirty years of wonderful dedicated work. We owed her a great debt and we all missed her a lot.

Much then had happened in those short weeks. It had been a memorable but sad time and not an experience I would ever wish to go through again. And most importantly the farm business had emerged from it changed visually but still operating.

It took the farms two years to recover fully from the devastation of the hurricane, the trees of course excepted, but in fact we found ourselves seeing new views and parts of the countryside we had not been able to see before, and so that was a small bonus.

Many of the trees we lost were long overdue for felling because our old landlord, Captain Kitson, would not allow us to cut any major trees down at Madehurst. He so loved the views from his house at Lower farm, with trees planted many years earlier by his late wife, that he had resolved to retain them during his lifetime, an understandable attitude.

As a result most of the trunks we had to remove after the storm were hollow and worthless, since there was now so much firewood lying around the countryside that nobody would give you so much as a 'thank you' for it.

In fact that the only solution was to burn the lot, apart from what we wanted for our own fires, and this made the job much easier to complete. It seemed a terrible waste but there was no sensible alternative and the bonfires burnt huge and lasted for weeks.

Clearing up some of the hundreds of fallen trees at Madehurst after the storm of '87.

Earlier that same year Alan, Father's brother, had died quite suddenly. Known far and wide since his youth as 'Buckle', he had lived alone in the farmhouse at Madehurst, since he and his wife Betty had split up some thirty five years before. He lived in conditions none of his friends could understand, and to which, despite occasional domestic help, he drifted back to within days.

He was the 'oldest hippie in town,' and had always been the same. Buckle lived for the day. He wanted nothing to do with, nor had any sense of, responsibility; had no ambitions that were obvious, and his only reason for getting up in the morning seemed to be to earn enough money to spend the evening drinking with his pals in one or more of his many haunts around the district.

Yet Alan was a rare man in as much as he was universally liked by everyone who ever met him, and he never had a bad word to say about anyone. His life centred around the old taverns within five miles of Madehurst and his regular friends as likely or not drove Rolls Royces and Jaguars. Many more rode bicycles.

Years before he had run the farm as casually as he ran his personal life yet, despite being such a frustration to the rest of the family, particularly to my father, one could not fail to like him. Alan was a gentle sort of rogue, and stories about him abound to this day.

One of my favourites concerned the supply of chicken food sold to a casual friend, shortly after the war, and is worth repeating.

Buckle had a 'nice little earner' going, by supplying sacks of wheat to a number of townie friends who would come down to Sussex at weekends. This was wheat that should have been sold off the farm, to the grain merchant, to keep the farms wheels turning but the temptation was too great, since it could better provide him with drinking money and a bit of fun.

His 'office' was usually the Spur at Slindon and all his regular customers would meet him there for a drink, before later tottering out into the car park to complete the deal, usually after dark.

On this famous occasion he and his customer went out into the Spur car park, where from his own car Alan lifted a full 250lb sack of wheat. Strong as an ox he transferred it into the open boot of his mate's car. It was one of those old boots that opened from the top and hinged backwards to form a level platform.

The sack was duly plonked on to the vehicle and "settled in", as he would have said, "to make it safe on the journey, no need to tie it, she wont budge from there me old cocker!" Then Alan pocketed his money, said farewell and stood aside as his pal, rather the worse for wear, drove off. As the car pulled away Alan, quick as a flash hoisted the sack off the boot and back into his own car. With, doubtless, a huge grin, he then drove himself back to the farm. The landlord, looking up through the window had seen all this happen and laughed to himself, as he again laughed quietly to me as he recounted this story some twenty years later.

The following weekend the two were back drinking at the pub. It seemed Alan had been summoned to supply another sack of feed wheat since, it appeared, his pal arrived home only to find the other one had "Bounced off the boot on the way home... You had better tie this one on Buckle!"

No doubt this had happened before and would happen again. The clients could afford the loss and Buckle's need was seen, by him at least, as the greater. Almost a modern day 'Robin Hood'. Except that he distributed the 'loot' to the local hostelries.

Alan lead a chequered life during which he worked both on the farm and at a factory in nearby Bognor until his 65th year. Then he took up charcoal making in an old wood at Black Barn Farm and for the next few years could be found, when the pubs were shut, chopping logs stacking his kiln, or bagging charcoal for his local contacts.

He was unfailingly cheerful, and always looked on the bright side, and I would stop over and chat to him several times a week. Although he was always easier to talk to before lunch, than after he arrived back from the pub in his little car.

He had acquired this tiny Honda, of which the description 'well used' would have been an understatement, and he didn't actually do a lot to maintain her. Several times the vehicle was parked in funny places, usually pulled in nose uphill on some steep slope. Nothing too unusual here, except that when he got in to move it he always freewheeled down the slope, before starting the engine.

When I asked him about it he smiled and said, "Ain't got no reverse gear, Cocker." Seemed reasonable to me. He then went on, " Funny thing is she don't need reverse to pass her MOT, they don't seem to bother about the gears, so I'm not going to bother about seeing to the old girl." He just had to be careful where he parked or he would have to get out and push.

In his seventy second year he suddenly began to look very slow and frail. The Doctors were quite unsympathetic since it seemed his reputation had travelled before him and his lifestyle was hardly likely to reward the doctors for their efforts. So they fobbed him off and did nothing.

A week later I saw him at the farm, walking up the drive with an old broom as a crutch. He looked quite awful and I immediately phoned Father. Within twenty minutes he had Alan in his car bound for home, and soon had the poor old fellow tucked in bed in the spare room. When Father went in later he was unable to rouse Alan who seemed almost comatose.

Calling our own doctor, a friend of the family, Alan was examined carefully, and with in half an hour was on his way to Chichester hospital with suspected meningitis. Ten days later, after drifting in and out of consciousness, Alan died. Sadly an unsympathetic doctor in the previous weeks, coupled with his somewhat relaxed lifestyle had finished the old boy off.

At his funeral service in the village church at Madehurst on the 12th of March 1987 the little place was packed. We sang his favourite hymn, "All things bright and beautiful' and then all trooped out to see him laid to rest in the cool chalk, in the next plot to his Parents in the quiet little churchyard just over the brow of the hill some four hundred yards from his home for the past forty odd years.

The end of an era, and a real character lost. He had led what to most might seen a totally unfulfilled life, but I have often pondered on it since, and I suppose one could argue that he got as much pleasure out of doing things his way, with no responsibilities beyond himself and the day, as even the most successful men in the World. Alan lived as he wanted to and had friends in every place he went. He was always happy and if he got in a tight spot something or someone always turned up to sort it out, although, unluckily for Father, that usually meant him!

For years after he had gone I would imagine I heard him, with his deep Sussex 'burr' saying, as I passed, 'Wotcha, me old cock sparra. Another lovely day,' or imagine him silently reversing his little car out of his garage in the cartshed by the farmhouse.

Later, outside the Spur, just down the road towards Slindon, Peter Smith then the Landlord, installed a lovely long hardwood seat, and engraved on the back it said: 'In Memory of Buckle Adames, who Fell off his Perch on March 4th 1987'. Old Buck would have liked that.

That was a sad period, as we lost several good friends around the late eighties. Peter Brazier, my old cricket, skiing and latterly golfing companion, died at the age of 51 after a long illness. Peter was a big friendly bear of a man, crazy about his sports and his cars. We had spent several ski trips together, and although he was always a little reluctant to adventure far 'off piste' we had a lot of pleasure in the mountains.

Peter, like Buckle, never had a bad word to say about anyone, and was the same to whomsoever he met. In fact he was too, in that respect so like 'old Buck', and his death left a hole.

Gus Payne also died quite suddenly, although he had not been too fit for a little time. He had called on Mary and I at the cottage and stayed for a night, not long before he died, and being so used to his cheerful, exuberant, outgoing personality we were rather shocked at how he had changed. Much of the spark was missing and we were therefore not over surprised when we heard about his death.

My, we had had some fun and games with Gus over those past 20 years, and his companionship had widened our horizons enormously. His parties were always full of celebrities, style and champagne, and his generosity towards us was unexpected, unwarranted but very welcome. As good friends of George Hammond we received the 'red carpet treatment' wherever and whenever we were in his company.

At the Golf Ball each winter at Grosvenor House Hotel, Gus, as a Sponsor, gave a great pre-dance party in his suite, and all golf's personalities would be invited. Players, past and present; Lords and Ladies; people from all spheres but all with one thing in common, we were all friends of Gus.

Golf events after Gus died were never again the same. Never had the same 'fizz', and within a year or two Mary and I decided that we had seen the best years of the explosion of golf, played our small part in it and would now leave it to the next generation.

Indeed there always seemed plenty of people practising hard in the 'Bollinger Tent' so the hard work we ourselves had put in there over the years would surely be built on and continued!

It is people who make these events what they are. Being with special friends make for special memories. As the saying goes 'When you have travelled first class you don't want to go steerage", which is probably now pretty outdated. Nevertheless, still true.

ITS AN ILL WIND...

Due to the extremely generous treatment we received from the NFU Insurance policies after the hurricane, treatment which we didn't really expect, we were, as I mentioned earlier, able to fund and erect a number of clear span barns where before there were only timber and tin buildings. This really revolutionised our operations, since we could use larger machines and handle our feeds fodder and purchased supplies in larger parcels, rather than the previous hand work with small bags and bales. Within a year we saw the end of all manual handling since everything could now be moved at will on pallets, or in half or one ton bags. Indeed we were one of the first farms in the area to insist on all fertiliser being delivered in these big bags and in the early days we often had great difficulty in finding suppliers able to comply.

One day I asked a fertiliser 'rep' why so few farms were still not taking advantage of the bulk system.

"Well" he said, "the difference is that on your farm it is you, the boss, who is doing the work, who has to move the bags. On many of the larger farms it is the staff's job, and the employers want some work for them to do". I remember doubting him but some time later a neighbour I quizzed had actually confirmed this to me, saying, "I've got the men and they need something to do." However that was a situation that changed quite rapidly as financial pressures grew.

And so for several seasons we had great difficulty finding suppliers of these big bags, but within about five years, as labour gave way, faster and faster to machines, or staff retired, old ex-industrial machines became more common on all farms, and the situation had changed.

No longer did a 22 ton load of feed appear in 880 small bags, each to be unloaded individually, sometimes taking three men two hours. Suddenly instead the lorry contained eighteen stacked pallets, which we could unload from the seat of a pallet handler in less than ten minutes. Then if we wanted them moved again it took but another ten minutes.

Similarly facilities appeared for bulk handling where the loads were tipped or blown and no labour was needed at all.

So our new buildings now allowed us to be at the forefront of this revolution rather than trailing along behind, as so often in the past. As a result Farming rapidly became a lonelier but much easier occupation. And it also made one realise the dedication and toil of the farm staff who had previously moved everything on the farm by hand.

It still amazes me, having done these same jobs by hand, how the sheer volume of work used to be completed. Every season in its turn had immense workloads, and almost always the work was completed on time, and always I remembered the good humour of the old men.

What they, and indeed later, I had too shared, was a level of comradeship and a feeling of a job well done, that would never again be the same for the coming generations on the land.

ITS ALL BOWLS

At the end of the 80s I had tired of the drag of playing competitive golf almost every weekend of the year. Not only did it tie up weekends, but to maintain a standard I needed to play as much as possible during the week and, to be honest, I needed a change. It had become increasingly hard to motivate myself or to concentrate; particularly as the game, influenced by television coverage, had begun to take nearer four hours for a round as opposed to the three hours we had always expected.

My handicap had been three for the past fourteen years and as I played less it began rising inexorably. Having been in single figures since 1960 this was frustrating; but so was playing badly as I frequently was by now, and it seemed sensible to accept that the days of serious golf were behind me. Now it would be with old friends and for pleasure.

There were other things demanding our time and the summers in particular were very busy. We were now spending a number of days flat racing at the southern tracks and were making a lot of new friends, losing a bit of money to the 'wicked bookies' perhaps but enjoying the experience!

For the first time in the twenty years since we married, Mary and I were able to find time, particularly on Saturdays, to do things like that together. I was free of the golf and Mary had finally sold off the dress shops and retired to be a farmer's wife and company secretary.

Selling the shops was a great relief since, after losing her Mother, there had been no real incentive, no shared interest, and as always once a business ceases to progress things don't continue on a level keel, they start to slip. It took some time to find a buyer, since she was very determined to try and ensure the staff all had secure jobs after she left.

In the end a family from Bournemouth purchased the whole concern and the day the contract was signed was one of huge jubilation.

That same year saw yet another innovation, the first season of bowls at Flansham and the first semi-organised sporting event here since the days of the inter-farm cricket matches or the gymkhanas of the fifties.

The idea had come to me a year earlier. Watching the game on television, I decided that it looked competitive enough to interest me and just as importantly, some of our friends. At the time I had never even held a bowl in my hand, let alone played the game.

The spot I had chosen for a green was the little paddock across the farm drive from the Farmhouse, where, at the time, Father was still living. It was under utilised because of its size, and I reasoned that if, or when, we moved to the big house, it would be a pleasant way to spend the odd summer evening.

After silage making was completed in the late May of 1888 and with the help of another resident, Richard Taft, I set about repeating the tennis court episode with Peter Pratt of some 33 years earlier.

All the elm trees that previously surrounded the small plot had died with the advent of Dutch Elm Disease and the sun now shone on the little paddock most of the day, helping the grass grow. The land was also very nearly level in the area I had chosen, and with the availability of a large excavator and the Kramer shovel, the work required was not going to be a fraction of that which Peter and I had expended on the court back in the fifties.

Because of the available size I decided to make a half green, enough for four rinks. The paddock was about twenty five yards wide at its narrowest and we needed twenty for the playing area so that was the governing factor.

We chose the central section and planned to leave the square nearest the Lane clear for a car park, whilst the farmyard end, to the south would still serve a use as a paddock for the occasional cow and calf.

Having sprayed the site with glysophate, to kill the meadow grasses, Richard and I set about cultivating the top three or four inches down to a fine tilth. As soon as that was done, and with the use of his 'laser' level, we drove wooden pegs in at regular interval to show us the finished surface we needed to work to.

The bulk of the soil was moved around the site with the bucket of the loading shovel, acting as a scraper, and within an evening we had the whole site down to within a fraction of level overall.

Here the harder work began. With the use of a 'straight edge' board and hand rakes we then had to work the loose soil across from the high spots to the low areas. Rake, rake, check levels, and then rake again. This led to about a week of evening toil, constant backache and once or twice to questioning my own sanity!

By this time the project was attracting some casual interest from among others, our immediate neighbour, Chris Maud, who spent many hours peering at these two grown men, apparently intent on making work for themselves. Word came back to us that he thought we were a 'couple of eccentrics'. Maybe he was right, but undeterred, we continued.

When we had made the playing area dead level, I brought in the excavator and dug drains along each side which we filled with gravel to act as soakaways. 'Experts', leaning over the old flint wall alongside the farm drive, questioned whether it needed drains underneath the playing area as well, but since I had never seen that area flooded, nor would we be playing in the Winter, their offerings were ignored.

Next we spread the expensively purchased 'Bowling Green Mix' with my standard grass sowing device, the farm fertiliser spreader, behind a tractor. Finally the seed was raked in to cover all signs of wheel marks, and the surface was rolled with the heavy farm roller.

And that, believe it or not, was that. During the Autumn I imported soil for the banks at each end, and formed the two end 'ditches' with sleepers; a panel fence was erected across the road end to hide us from the public gaze for when we eventually got to play.

So well did the grass take that the green was being mown by early September, and looked quite encouraging.

The next stages began to get expensive. Remembering the slog of hand mowing the old court, I resolved to find a mower that would be a pleasure rather than a drudge. Enquiring around, I soon found an ex-golf course machine, a triple unit, sit-on machine, with a five foot cut. Without hesitation I bought it, and it arrived, fully serviced, the following week.

Then we decided we should visit Worthing Bowls Shop and purchase some equipment. Bowls, mats, jacks and shoes. As well as that, the pro at Worthing, taken with the idea of a private green, offered to give us a few tips on holding the woods, and playing the game. Always a good idea to get the basics right.

We offered him the chance to come over the following season and see it for himself, in the hope that by then it might be looking reasonably good.

So now we were bowlers! The first thing we did on arriving home was to take the bowls and see what course they took when they were delivered. I cannot tell you the thrill it gave me when the first wood began to move with its 'bias', and even more when the next wood did the same. Mary and I played a couple of ends before discretion took over and we left the new green in peace.

That winter I had to rabbit fence the whole surrounds to foil the little perishers digging up a few chosen spots each evening. Eventually, those I couldn't shoot went elsewhere.

Many hours were spent on the green between October and the following May. Tons of top dressing was regularly raked in, low spots, as indicated by the arrival of a puddle after heavy rain, were marked and filled. Mowing began again in early March and the hand roller was dragged across in all directions on regular intervals.

Bowls at Flansham.

Towards the beginning of April the triple mower was set lower and the cutting was increased to a daily operation, now a pleasure that took but a few minutes.

By this stage the word had spread amongst many friends. A number of golfers had indicated they would like to try the game, so I suggested that Tuesday evenings would be a regular 'roll up' night and anyone was welcome.

That first season went well. We all learnt together. The pro at Worthing brought a team over and they were all polite enough to say nice things about the green. In the following seasons however I doubted their sincerity, because we never heard from them again!

That first year we had some thirty regular players, we played friendly competitions and soon the standard became, if not good, acceptable. Our biggest problem was our neighbour who became rather sensitive about people enjoying themselves, and regularly shouted to us to keep quiet. Once or twice with some justification! However over the following seasons he became more docile.

So that was how the Bowling Green arrived in Flansham. Over the past seasons the number of regular players has increased to around fifty. The standard has since become quite good and we play matches against a few local clubs who don't mind our eccentricities; like wearing what we want, drinking beer on the green and enjoying playing for fun.

Having said that, we do have annual competitions, fiercely fought but played in the old garden party atmosphere that Mother showed us back in the fifties. At five o'clock we break for tea, sandwiches and home made goodies, all produced by the efforts of the ladies. Then when that is over, its back to war. And I gave up golf because it was too competitive!

We have a small wooden garden shed for a clubhouse; with a large box for keeping the beer, a box incidentally marked 'Antarctic Expedition', from one of the great treks across that far off land in years past. Also in the shed is a diary where every player puts their name every time they play. At the end of the season I collect a game fee and we give the money to a local charity. That way some good comes from our pleasure.

A mixed-sex toilet completes the facilities of our little 'club', of which I am the general manager, greenkeeper, secretary, captain, president and general dogsbody. Mary is catering organiser.

Every year it grows as we find more players and the season ends with the players all contributing kindly to a dinner at the Sports Club where, as guests, Mary and I distribute the prizes.

People asked me what I intend doing with the green. I believe many neighbours thought that the place would be overrun with a busy public club but my intentions are to keep it private, as a place to enjoy spare hours with friends. It is a game to play in the evenings, to share competition, a drink and a laugh. If, too, it sees us into the evening of our own lives, it will have served its purpose well.

After ten years I have found it complements golf well. From May till October bowls takes precedence in the evenings after work. Through the autumn and into spring its golf at weekends. A nice balance.

OF SICK COWS AND MAD POLITICIANS

The nineties brought with it the culmination of the scare of BSE – a plague inflicted on farming by Government and the animal feed industry in equal measure and little did we know, as the first cows were starting to go down with their distressing and unusual symptoms, where and at what cost the problem was heading.

Let me say here and now, to be shot at, that I don't believe either that a single person who has died from nvCJD caught it from beef, or that it is unique to the UK. Nor even began here. BSE is a virulent disease of the media, shared to a large part by publicity, and fund-seeking professors; weak transient politicians and some animal rights groups who one day will have a lot to answer for.

As we see time and time again, hysteria guides the media, and they feed off each other. When Tory health minister Steven Dorrell made his ill-considered statement on 20 March 1996 his words were 'manna' to the media. Immediately, his words, which included "possibly" and "could" were changed to read BSE "does" cause new variant CJD and "does" pass between species. Wonderful stuff, but unproven.

Then over-exposed self-seeking 'experts' appeared on TV across Europe to scare the pants off, in particular, the Germans, who are pretty paranoid about their health at the best of times.

In quick turn these same European 'partners' sought, for totally nationalistic reasons, to destroy the UK beef industry and solve their own over-supply problems at a stroke.

These developments hit us on our two farms no more or less than any other cattle farmers. For days we were in a dazed state. We looked at our lovely healthy cattle and seriously wondered if there would be an animal left on the land in a month's time.

Visions of Foot and Mouth type pyres came to us in our dreams. The thought of that was bad enough, but we knew that there was nothing wrong with our stock. Any farmer in the country would have consumed meat from any properly killed beast, in total confidence. And fed it to their family.

Yet, day after day pundits, broadcasters and a relentless parade of 'experts' did their very best to frighten the world, and bury our traditional industry. Three days after the scare broke, the NFU rang me one morning.

"Could you find time to give an interview to a Swedish Channel 7 TV reporter today?" said James.

"Yes, of course." I replied.

The reason I was asked was because I had been writing my fortnightly farming column for the *West Sussex Gazette* and had a minor reputation for saying what I thought, popular or not. Within three hours, fresh off the Brussels morning flight to Gatwick, a girl's voice on the phone asked for directions to Flansham, saying she and her cameraman would be "there by lunch".

It was cold and spitting with sleet as I showed her around the stockyards. "Your animals look so clean and happy, I could almost sleep in the straw myself" she said. Tough people the Swedes.

Filming round the cattle, we then retreated to the warmth of the farmhouse. After a chat, she of course speaking perfect English, we did a 10 minute interview where I did my bit to convince Swedish viewers that BSE was a 'mad media' problem: and she was quite sympathetic.

As she waited for her taxi back to Gatwick to meet her 'deadline' for that evening's news slot, we chatted. Amazingly, by a strange route, we discovered that 'The Baron' with whom I spent so many winters on the Murren ski slopes, Goran Akerheilm, was an old friend of her family. A small world. I also found that this 'girl' was married with three teenage children. Well, she looked a girl to me! A month later through the post came the video copy of the broadcast, and I was delighted to see that my views had not been edited out – very non-BBC!

Now we were faced with months of rumour and uncertainty. My fax machine daily sped missives to the Minister, to MP's and Sir David Naish, then President of the NFU. I was initially impressed with the firm line with which he was guiding the NFU, in refusing to accept a selective cull of healthy cows just to placate politicians on both sides of the Channel. I was also impressed at the speed with which he would phone back, day and night, with his responses and support. He was under huge pressure from all sides and yet he could spare the time for individuals. Unlike the Ministers, whose defensive arrogance grew by the day.

As a consequence of my actions, or perhaps to shut me up, I was invited during the next week to attend a meeting Sir David was holding in London on 10th June. About 50 selected dairy farmers, representing all regions of the country were invited, and despite awful traffic I made it on the dot of 2.30.

Sir David was excellent at handling the somewhat heated and emotional speakers and summed up with skill. He stressed his total opposition to a cull of dairy cattle on the grounds that it was out of all proportion to the problem. There was unanimous support and after talking to a number of farmers, I came back in a better frame of mind.

It was very clear within the industry that BSE was, by 1996, affecting significantly less animals monthly. The probable source was likely identified as meat and bonemeal, inadequately sterilized because of relaxed rendering guidelines. However abattoir controls were being brought in line, rather belatedly by MAFF and the real situation was easing, But for the EU and the Press, who persisted in inflaming the issue outrageously, the situation could well soon be under control.

Farmers knew what to look for in their stock, and we believed that most of our cows, particularly the older ones, were totally safe. Those that were susceptible had already succumbed and the risk was probably now almost entirely with the younger cows, but diminishing rapidly due to the changes in feed ingredients introduced in 1990.

That spring and summer seemed eternal – every day brought further speculation. The various Ministers and Under Ministers attempted to soothe dairy and beef farmers at meetings around the land and only succeeded in making matters worse. The problem was that they were like parrots. They gave farmers the 'Party line' which, in the way they gave it, showed their complete ignorance of the industry. They could barely understand the difference between a milking cow and a suckler, let alone a steer from a heifer.

When it came to questions from the floor, all the answers we got were repeats, parrot fashion again, of their earlier blurb. We all left completely disheartened. If this was the way they were behaving in Brussels and Westminster, we had no chance. Within a month the Tories, through these Ministers' ignorance and arrogance, lost the countryside's confidence, and the following spring their vote.

The summer staggered on. Drought for the second year running destroyed thoughts of adequate silage stocks for yet another winter, and the Environment Agency announced the coming introduction of a South Downs Nitrate Vulnerable Zone, with very onerous controls on slurry, muck and dirty water spreading. Life seemed rather miserable.

My fax machine ran day and night. I wrote almost daily letters to the farming press, NFU and Ministers. I sought farmer support against what Sir David, denying to me on the phone but nevertheless still pushing for, what I now perceived as a 'U turn', on a selective cull. Quite vehemently he had said to me, "I am not wavering in my view".

Then two weeks later he announced his support of government plans for a cull and my fears were proved true. He had capitulated. My fax output increased further.

The Union were now behaving like the politicians, selecting the truth and the facts that suited their position, and in the process opening the door to the destruction of thousands of healthy herds that farmers had built up over generations.

I placed, so to speak, my own 'sword in the ground' and challenged anyone to kill my healthy cows. I suggested as an alternative that the suspect animals be put under surveillance in quarantine. Since, by that time, as all over 30 month (OTM) animals were being incinerated, there was no possible way that any of the old cows could enter the food chain. They were no risk, and what was more, by keeping them alive, the decline of the scourge could be monitored. If they were killed, it couldn't, and little could really be proved about the natural decline of this plague.

The problem was now that Prime Minister John Major had gone to Florence and offered 140,000 cows as 'sacrifices' – a figure out of the hat, no basis to it, and Brussels was going to screw the UK for all it was worth to get those 140,000 cows, and more.

Sadly, Sir David was in a hole, caused by his support for the EU/ UK agreement, and was finding it difficult to remember, or even admit, what he and the Union were saying so forcefully but weeks earlier.

That Autumn, Swedish TV rang me again; the same lady, asking to do a follow-up programme. When she arrived we did a similar format; and although I had to say we were little further forward she announced that she was! The next day she was going on extended leave to have her fourth child. Again within a few weeks she sent me her tape which was an equally accurate reflection of my remarks.

So the worst of 1996 was we hoped now behind us. In reality, the only animals we sold realised good prices, hardly down on 1995. These were beef steers, males, about 16 months old. The trade for females was however weak and so I resolved to put them all to the bull, keep them overwinter and hope for a better trade for in-calf suckler cows next spring.

The BSE crisis could fill another chapter but would achieve nothing of value so it will rest here. Except to say that the Ministry did not kill one of my cows as cohorts over the next three years, since they themselves found, or invented, an extraordinary loophole to cover my situation. It was a loophole I could not argue with, since it took the officials off my land and away from my healthy cows.

Needless to say it was as stupid and as crass as the whole inflated crisis, and astounds listeners when I tell them of it. My belief now is that by the time the same officials realise the sheer stupidity of their judgement all the cattle they wanted to kill will have left the farm in the normal culling process, having fulfilled their natural milking lives.

THE JOYS OF INFLATION

There is a lot to be said about being in the right place at the right time. Generally I have been. Some of this is down to luck, and I do admit to being lucky, for which I offer continued thanks. However just sometimes one can make your own luck by thinking about and identifying opportunities.

It is not accepted in the best circles but the best thing to happen to my business over the years has been inflation. It has its disadvantages but at crucial times it has helped me enormously.

When I purchased Black Barn Farm the price seemed quite daunting and I wondered for a few months how we could fund it. The cost was something over £1,000 a month, repayable over twenty years and at that time, the figure represented a big lump in our income.

For the first couple of years, things were indeed a struggle, but thankfully I had gone against my accountant's advice and opted for a fixed rather than variable rate of interest on the mortgage, fixing it at 11.5%. I quickly then saw interest rates rise to, at one short stage, over 20%. At that level, on variable terms, the repayments would have been debilitating.

However the effect of this meant that farm incomes inevitably rose in line with this inflationary pressure. Certainly expenses grew too, but with the mortgage pegged, it quickly became of almost minor significance. From being the biggest monthly outgoing at the start it was suddenly almost trivial and after five years, only a quarter of the way into the loan, it was of little concern. My only regret was that I had not had the opportunity to buy three or four times as much land, because along with all other prices, land too went through the roof as the eighties boom continued to grow.

Another significant and ongoing issue was to hit us at this time. This being the sudden and largely unexpected imposition of milk quotas. When they were announced, I was among the most vociferously opposed, to them, since due to our rapidly expanding output, we suffered a severe cutback in production.

Quotas were brought in by the EEC to stem the ever increasing production which was putting huge cost burdens on the European budget, the CAP. They took everyone by surprise and, most of all it seemed, the Ministry of Agriculture's advisory wing ADAS.

Suddenly, our freedom to produce was taken from us, most of us had too many cows for the quotas we were given and something close to panic set in. The aim was to control overall milk production by imposing individual national targets. Each country was to administer its own quotas and at the end of the year, each March 31st, the country had to be on or under quota to avoid a swingeing levy.

This levy in turn would be administered by the MMB and charged to every farmer who was individually over his own quota. The levy was set at something like one and a half times the value of the milk by which one was over quota.

Drastic steps were taken. Milk was fed to pigs and calves. Feed was cut to reduce cows' milk production. Cows were dried off early and many good animals were sold in their prime. Many ingenious ruses were considered, tried or discarded.

In the early days it appeared that these quotas were going to shackle us totally to our initial allocation and would not be transferable. This would obviously have made it impossible for any newcomers to enter the industry, if any foolishly even wanted to.

Due to the total unprepared state of the Ministry of Agriculture there were a good many farmers in a panic. ADAS, seemingly unaware of the noises coming from Brussels had, up to the day quotas were introduced, been encouraging farmers to enter dairy farming. It was still seen by them as the growth sector, and huge grants were available to newcomers, indeed anyone, to set up a unit.

The advisory wing of the Ministry, many of them failed at other jobs, were always a few years behind the times; so this attitude was unsurprising. However for those farmers who were now left holding the baby, having committed themselves to ADAS inspired expenditure (on the promise of farm grant aid) over a given period of years ahead, the prospects were dreadful. Quotas were being issued based on the figures of the previous years actual output. Clearly newcomers had no output, so received no quotas. There seemed no way out, and indeed for many there sadly was not. The uncertainty was worrying everyone and many legal brains were employed to find an answer.

The first person to find a formula was a farmer, soon to become an ex-farmer, living in Wales. Hedley Robinson was his name, and his initial efforts were to quickly create a huge 'industry within an industry' that, within a few years, was to become a monster, or a lifesaver, depending on where you stood.

Mr Robinson devised a way of transferring quota with a temporary transfer of land. When *Farmers Weekly* featured his scheme I immediately wrote to him at his home. A couple of days later he rang me back and we spoke at length. My main concerns were: firstly, was it legal, and secondly, would it work? If not how safe was our money?

He had some reservations because while he had taken top legal advice he felt the first transfers would immediately be challenged through the courts and this could be very expensive.

However I wanted to return my farms output to where it was being aimed before the picture had so suddenly changed, and therefore I showed interest in one of the first lots of quota he was offering.

I agreed to his client's asking price of 7.5 pence per litre (ppl) for some 200,000 litres, subject to the bank's agreement, which I felt I could now rely on. However, I had to confirm this, so agreed to phone him back within the hour.

Getting the OK from the bank I then rang back.

"Sorry Mr Adames, the man wants 8ppl now."

Damn! I reluctantly agreed, and with that sent a cheque for the required deposit first class to Wales.

Two days later Robinson phoned to thank me for the cheque but to say that his client now wanted 10ppl. This seemed a bit strong and not the way I liked doing business. Where would this stop?

To this day I curse the fact that I told Robinson to advise his client what he could do with his quota and to please send my deposit back to me. I think that was probably my most expensive mistake ever, since, with hindsight, it would have been the most tremendous deal.

I threw it away simply because I did not appreciate being 'gazumped' in that manner. So for the next year or two we struggled on within our existing quota. We cut inputs, matched output and paid no levy. Unsurprisingly, most others were doing the same. The UK output stayed below quota and no levy was due.

Gradually, I began to grow in confidence, increasing cow numbers and milk sales and only once over the following five years did we have any liability to levy, and then only tiny. However, suddenly the MMB figures began to show that many others had taken the same view and national output began rising alarmingly.

I again phoned Hedley Robinson and this time bit the bullet. The original 7.5 or 10ppl had by now become 26ppl but it had also become a fairly safe bet that the deal would go through, so in the short period following that I bought some 250,000 litres, the cost now almost as much as I had paid for the farm only some ten years before!

It seemed a huge price to be paying for something that nobody could see or touch. Just a right to produce. Yet it was being seen as an increasingly secure investment and with this purchase I could again encourage Peter and Geoff to increase their production, which was easily done with yet more cows and better feed.

That delay in buying, through my pique, cost me a huge sum of money, but in the overall picture of things we had not had to pay any significant levies. What was more, we now had what appeared a sound investment, in the way of increased quota, and during the following five years I again went out and increased our pool.

Through necessity, the stories so far have tended to overlap, since there would be little continuity were these threads to be put together in chronological order. However, as we move towards the last decade of the 20th Century, it is all coming together and we are really almost 'here and now'. Life should, now past my 50th year, be perhaps easing off a little, and indeed from the physical point of view it is.

Yet business pressures diminish less fast; or more to the point, as time and 'red tape' gathers, they increase.

Farmers are notoriously averse to authority and I have never veered from that aversion. Perhaps unfairly, I have over the years considered our industry as prime producers, creators of many of life's basic needs. As such, simplified, I see us as amongst the most important of the world's industries, but sadly one whose health is only appreciated when the country, or the world, is at war. Our traditions and our labour is valued almost as much, or as little, as our produce.

In turn, I see officialdom, clipboard holding inspectors, and most experts, as parasites who in reality contribute nothing, their only function being to create further pyramid-like levels of self-perpetuating wasters; wasters of the wealth created by the countrys' prime producers, their employment only helping to manipulate the national employment figures; though from most viewpoints their jobs are of zero value to the real working population of Britain. Thus the expansion of the, shall we call it, 'enforcement industry' fills me, and many like-minded middle aged citizens with trepidation, and not a little contempt.

When a specialist (I didn't say 'expert') for arguments sake in, say, farming has spent perhaps quarter of a century or more learning most aspects of their job, the appearance of a freshly qualified graduate, impressive as those qualifications may appear on paper, to then instruct the said specialist in his work, galls more than a little.

When one realizes, from experience, that the opinions they are seeking to impose on one's business are often just that – opinions – and likely to be just their own – and probably both unfair and outside their remit, it makes for anger. This is a situation farmers face every day from such bodies as the Health and Safety Executive, the Food Standards Agency or the Environment Agency, and after a while one becomes extremely dispirited.

Until the seventies, food from our island was needed, and we were encouraged – or at least treated as adults. Then, through the eighties, as food became available from many sources, often produced overseas by near slave labour under conditions that within our shores would be unacceptable, we became expendable, whipping boys for the enforcement industry's hangers - on.

These constant 'pin pricks' are responsible for the way, over the past ten years, my two farms have evolved, and still are too a large extent.

The reasons that primarily decided me to reduce my workforce and employ contractors were the overbearing requirements of the Health and Safety Executive (HSE). In many instances I found the law, if enforced, would make my business inoperable. Such things as training courses, herbicide application, general farm safety requirements, employment legislation, whilst possibly both justified and manageable on large units, were, to small operations like mine, the death knell.

The actual enforcement or supervision of many of these requirements would, if done to the letter, have required another member of staff to fulfil them. And what value, apart from making this small business legal, would that person have added to its financial success? We were not, and are not now, intentional law breakers. Our farms are probably above average in both efficiency and tidiness (tidiness itself relates quite directly to safety). We also know our land, our buildings and their dangers, and we also have as most other self-employed countrymen, COMMON SENSE, which has no letters after its name. But when one tries to debate a point with these Inspectors, who know many things but are invariably devoid of common sense, one can never win an argument.

Now with contractors doing all our work, we no longer require any but the basic minimal machinery. Where we farmers, previously, on every small farm, had equipment for every task, despite the fact it was seasonal and spent most months rusting, we now keep the minimum.

Contractors are in and out in a fraction of the time we used to take. They update machinery annually, paid for by full order books and working the tackle hard. Many of their staff are ex-farm staff, farmers sons, and increasingly college trained. Contracting is the growth industry in agriculture, of benefit unlike the enforcement industries, and competition for enough work to keep modern and efficient machines occupied ensures both reliability and keen pricing.

If safety inspectors call, they are now directed to the Contractor, who is bound to have things under control. And if he calls when the farm is quiet, nobody around except the 'boss', there are far less questions to ask and answer, and few worries over faulty equipment.

~ *Chapter Eight* ~

LOOSENING THE TIES

Taking the long view the eighties had, despite a few major hiccups, deaths within the family and storms, been a period of further consolidation for the family business. It was a period of stability in farm incomes, during which, with the two herds running profitably, we had been able to put the intermittent financial worries of the past eighty years to rights.

At the end of the decade the biggest threat on dairy farmers horizons was the major upheaval anticipated to follow the Governments dismantling of the Milk Marketing Board (MMB) in line with their policy on monopolistic powers.

As was well known, and accepted by the huge majority of dairy farmers, the old MMB had been the saviour of the dairy farmer when it came into being in the early 30s. The problem now was, by the end of the 80s that it had become as bureaucratic as the worst government department, and was spending huge amounts of dairymen's money on overstaffing and general extravagances.

My generation had been brought up with the stories our Fathers had told us. Of the days prior to the Board. Of milk thrown away some days just because it was not needed by the dairy, who would pick and choose what milk they bought, and from whom. Always for a pittance.

Of the only alternative to bankruptcy, which meant early morning milk rounds, selling a rapidly deteriorating product to local residents. And of the subsequent struggle to collect the money from many of those small customers in the depression years.

The Board had then, at its inception, welded the industry together; given us price stability and security for some sixty years. The trouble perhaps was that it had made things too easy for producers and had got many out of the habit of thinking, by taking all our decisions for us.

Every aspect of our job was catered for; cheques were paid 'on the dot' every month; management such as breeding policy, quality testing, and in recent years, quota transfers and leasing, were all taken care of.

In exchange we didn't ask too many questions, accepted its word and seemed unconcerned that the already low value of our product was reduced by another 1.5 pence a litre, about 9% of the total price, to fund its high spending, overstaffed lifestyle.

So it was that when it became certain the break from the MMB was coming, plans were soon being made by these same producers to improve their prospects. And for the freedom of choice for dairy farmers. Due however to political pressure and manoeuvring, both within the MMB and from a government who, having only recently lost Mrs Thatcher, were intent on navel gazing rather than pursuing policy, the reforms slowed.

This suited the MMB, who saw the whole thing as a threat to their own futures and careers, and for a year or two longer the plans went quiet. It was not until after the 1992 elections, when against all the odds the Tories were returned for their fourth term, that the move for change again came to the boil. The plan was to break up the monopoly by giving all producers the opportunity to contract and sell their milk to whomsoever they wished, as had been done successfully in Northern Ireland for some years.

The MMB was to be divested of its powers but, to us farmers, the management appeared likely to move most of its organisation, and personnel, into the guise of a new national 'middle man', to be called Milk Marque, buying milk from its old suppliers and selling it on to the manufacturing and distribution industry.

In the initial stages it seemed that a huge majority of the Country's 32000 milk producers would happily sign on, almost regardless of the terms, simply because they were suddenly beginning to feel vulnerable at the thought of having to make marketing decisions for themselves. Fearing the sudden loss of 'nanny MMB'.

Needless to say, the prospect of the bulk of producers simply switching from one monopoly to another and perhaps more aggressive one, started the warning lights flashing within the tight circle of the major national processing companies comprising the Dairy Trades Federation (DTF). Suddenly it seemed the pressure from the federation was going to make Mr Majors weak Government wobble.

Talk of monopoly power was anathema to Government at that time, and the view spread that the embryo MM was looking likely to be almost more of a monopoly that the old MMB. We farmers had waited long enough and now wanted the promised freedom. Consequently such rumour and delay concerned many of us.

As Summer of 92 wore on the whole process was in the balance. MM seemed to be taking a strong line, and in so doing attracted a huge majority of producers to their fold. This, a few of us felt, was bad news since it seemed certain (to us at least) that if the new MM gained the producers almost total support, which the pundits confidently predicted, the DTF faced with such monopoly, would force the Govt. to delay the change. And put the whole scheme back in the melting pot.

In the late Summer I went on a farm walk at Steyning. That was an unusual occurrence on its own but the real purpose of the outing was to sound out fellow Sussex producers on how they would view the formation of a Southern milk group, independent of the new organisation.

The two main points I made to farmers that day were, firstly, this certainty that if the MM received almost total support there was not a shadow of doubt the DTF would connive with Govt. to delay the process, perhaps indefinitely.

Secondly that here in Sussex, close to a huge population requiring our milk; and with a significant number of large dairy farmers in close proximity, thereby reducing haulage costs, it would not be unreasonable to expect our buyer, whoever it was, to pay something more to us for this convenience.

This proximity to the market was clearly an attraction to any buyer, and yet from reports coming out of MM it seemed that the old pooling system, whereby a producer in Wales, or the wilds of Northumbria, would all receive the same price as those in the populated South, would continue. Even if the lorry travelled fifty miles to collect 200 litres a day from one farm. Whereas here the lorry could often fill its full load within half that distance.

That may not sound neighbourly but being in the South we had to pay far higher land and fixed costs than, say in the Borders or West Wales, and times were changing.

Following that meeting at Steyning I had spoken to the then Chairman of the Southern NFU, himself a local producer who I knew well, and he readily agreed that we should set up a small meeting in a local Pub. This duly went ahead on Oct. 4th at the George at Eartham, up on the Downs.

From that meeting it was clear there were two very different schools of thought and we were astounded at the almost fanatical fervour with which the MM supporters defended their path. The room positively bristled with tension.

I felt some sympathy with them since I too had great respect for the way the old MMB had saved the industry so long past, but I found it hard to believe they were unable to even consider alternatives. Neither had we ourselves decided against the MM option. Indeed, at that stage, I thought it almost inevitable that we would ultimately finish up contracted to MM.

After that lively evening we two 'conspirators' picked ourselves up and took stock. While there was sound support for us the MM faction immediately began a campaign against the Chairman, accusing him, for some obscure reason of disloyalty to the NFU, and making his position very difficult. I had no position they could attack so missed the flak.

Deciding that we had to keep the ball rolling we then set up an open meeting of all the producers in West Sussex for November 8th, a meeting which was to be held here in Flansham, and on the big night some 40 farmers turned up to see what all the fuss was about. Some arrived rather sheepishly and others arrived bristling with MM inspired anger.

Again the meeting was fractious. Some saw us as traitors. 'Splitting the Industry'. 'Must support the old MMB's progeny.' That sort of thing.

After some two hours of noisy, largely destructive argument all we achieved was the setting up of a small working group of four, including the local NFU chairman and myself, to continue investigations of the options.

Twenty four hours later that group was down to three. The chairman himself, who had been under increasing pressure from some of the Unions traditionalists bombarding him with phone calls and letters, decided the pressure was too great and backed down from an active role, whilst still offering us some support in the background.

Over the following four months, into the Spring of 1993 we arranged meetings with all the main potential buyers; with the MM 'set up' and local and national processors, before reporting back to the farmers.

It was now very clear to us that there were some risks but never the less good opportunities in selling to other than MM. They, MM, were desperate to have our milk but we had found them both arrogant and quite immovable in their offers and we reluctantly veered further and further away from them as an option. More and more towards an independent buyer. But, the question remained, which one?

We were also realising more and more how complicated the formation and administration of an independent group was going to be. How hard it was going to be to pin all those farmers with a similar view down to agreeing to actually sign on the dotted line; to be counted.

Nobody seemed willing to commit themselves till the last possible moment, and the situation was becoming tricky. The main benefit to the group ultimately, was to get enough farmers signed up to ensure a good bulk bonus, on the milk price, from the chosen purchaser. If we lost too many 'waverers' to the persistent visits and phone calls we were all receiving daily from the office holders and local staff of MM, we would finish up with no bonus and no thanks.

By mid Summer a producer from East Sussex, who had become involved in forming a similar group, around a private processor/distributor near Lewes, phoned me. They had heard of our movement and thought it "may be worth talking?"

Three of us went over to a meeting in Lewes Farmers offices the following week, after which I had the feeling that we could finally 'see the light'. These East Sussex chaps were much better organised, in that they were all members of the well established Lewes Farmers buying group, and understood the disciplines required to work co-operatively. They already operated a well staffed office, fully computerised, and they would have no problem taking on the admin work for our group, whatever its eventual size.

Subject to the agreement of the board of Lewes Farmers, we agreed to run the two milk groups together, supplying two dairies, and calling ourselves Southern Milk Producers. All the admin work would be carried out at Lewes and we would, from November, be supplying our milk to Unigate Dairies. The Lewes farmers' supplying Woodgate Farm Dairy.

Further meetings were held in the interim to tie up the small print and Lewes Farmers Manager, Raymond Foster, with his quiet efficiency, persuaded some 20 West Sussex producers, large and not so large, to sign contracts with Unigate. So on the day the old MMB tanker collected our last days milk from my two dairies, on 31st Oct 1994, SMP members were contracted to supply some seventy million litres of milk annually to the two new buyers.

Unlike almost any other of the more diverse groups in the country, all our producers were clustered close round our buyers and we were one of the tightest knit groups in existence.

We also supplied, for our members, returns significantly higher than those available to many larger groups and in particular MM, who sadly and consistently, in the first few years since the breakaway trailed the field, so far as returns to producers were concerned

Possibly the most satisfying result of the whole operation was that our independence call struck a note around the whole Country and MM began on November 1st with only some 60% of all producers. Even then the DTF protested "Monopoly" but that call was quite rightly ignored by Government and the monopolies commission.

Clearly that would not have been the case had we all stayed faithful to MM, when with some 95% joining MM there would have been very reasonable grounds for an enquiry which could have set the whole industry back on its heels. Nevertheless, within another six years MM would be disbanded in a conspiracy between the DTF and the Government.

THE BSE CRISIS RUMBLES ON

Some two years after the fateful statements in the Commons by Minister Dorrell the saga still showed no signs of a sensible conclusion. What was really infuriating me was the continued insistence that all EU and Govt. decisions would be "Based on the best scientific advice" That was quite clearly and obviously a lie.

The Europeans, so keen to destroy our world markets were not interested in the facts although, in all honesty there were little enough to go on anyway. The nvCJD cases largely failed to materialise and a clear link between cattle and humans showed no sign of emerging.

In '96 Mr Major had dug a deep hole for the industry by his offer, plucked from the sky, of 142,000 cows as sacrifices, an offer based on speculation but one the EU grabbed at eagerly.

Slowly, we farmers began hearing the terms by which the Ministry would be assessing and then controversially valuing these 142,000 cows. They were to be known as 'cohorts' Reports soon rippled around the district that "so-and-so had been visited by the vets to select their cohorts" or "he's expecting the cows to be valued and killed this week."

From the mass of information flying around I had concluded that we would have in the region of 65 to 70 such cohorts, all cows reared in 1991/2 at Guildford by John Tangye and fed food that perhaps unbeknown to anyone, contained the agent that spread the affliction.

The thought of losing what represented over half our milking herd and all cows in their prime filled me with horror.

We had done our best to breed true to the old traditional British Friesian bloodlines and some of the families went back to my Father's youth. Buntys, Windys, Bettys, Olives, Midnights and many more represented a life's work and I was going to fight for them.

There were many others fighting too, but before long I realised that many farmers had quite different priorities. All that concerned them, mainly the younger farmers, seemed to be how much compensation they could claim, and clearly, if that figure was high enough, they would have ear-tagged the farm cat and their grandmother too, and sent the whole lot to the incinerator!

Frankly, I found this offensive. My priority was to resist the Ministry at every turn, actively delaying MAFF visits, non-aggressive obstruction or cancelling visits at the last moment, that sort of thing.

Let me be clear. Had I believed for one minute that there was any possibility that any of my cows was a health hazard I would have cooperated fully. Not happily, but fully. Yet since the issue was totally political and the last consideration was "best scientific advice", I was effectively at war with officialdom, not for the first time I must admit, but this time it was in earnest. Really a matter of life and death.

This went on for months and at the same time I had continued to be a small thorn in the side of both MAFF and the NFU headquarters, causing them, I hope and believe, some frustration.

As I write, this the matter is not completely dead, so I must be cautious, but, in short, by the time the Beef Ban began to be lifted, I had not given one of my animals up to the incinerator.

One phone call and one strange interpretation of the rules had exempted all my cattle and with huge relief I was able to concentrate on other more pressing things. We had suffered this death sentence hanging over the farms for over two years and finally it seemed I had got a result.

The whole thing has been a total disgrace and waste of public money What the politicians don't seem capable of recognising was that not a single one of these old cows had any chance of entering the food chain since every animal over thirty months was to be incinerated anyway.

Had they left the cohorts on the farms and quarantined them it would have been the best guide to the decline of BSE. If they were going to contract it, it would have been visible. Once the vulnerable cows were slaughtered there was never any way any data could be gathered.

As time goes by and the 'storm' of nvCJD cases predicted by yet more 'experts' declines to levels below those on mainland Europe, one can but wonder what all the fuss was about anyway ... and lament the cost and anguish suffered by so many cattle farmers across the country.

THE BUSINESS CENTRE IS DEVELOPED

Since the early seventies a number of empty farm cottages were regularly coming onto the market in Flansham, and numerous redundant buildings soon followed, as cattle and horses vacated the barns they had occupied for centuries. The next residents were not animals but town dwellers seeking a 'rustic pad', in some romantic farming village, and within a few years every disused roof housed outsiders, and had ceased to have any connection with the land.

The reasons for landowners proceeding in this way were probably all, at the time, valid and understandable. The problem is that the settlements suffer immediately the buildings change use, and the non farm based residents take over occupancy. Many have no interest in the farms that still operate and, indeed, often do their best to close down or restrict the farming operations by objecting to trivial problems, the ways of farm life that country people take in their stride.

In some respects I may, by some, be considered guilty of some of these errors myself, as I have thought long and hard about the best way to solve the problems presented by farming's changing needs, within our own farm situation.

Having seen the growing gulf between the two factions of the community, these thoughts featured large when, in the early nineties, the time came to consider what to do with a redundant group of buildings in the heart of the hamlet.

Consisting of a substantial Sussex barn built in 1656 and its adjoining low hovels, these buildings had long since ceased to contribute anything to the farm, and indeed were an eyesore. And I am sure, in most peoples mind would have made an ideal site for yet more converted dwellings.

The old buildings consisted of a rectangle on a plot of about half an acre, adjoining the lane, with good access for vehicles. In the distant past there had been a large Sussex barn at both east and west ends but, in living memory only the eastern barn survived. This being built of flint and timber.

The southern side was made up of low cattle hovels in which, for my lifetime, Father had used as workshops and general junk heaps; whilst in the north western corner stood a home made concrete and asbestos type barn, built by 'The Old Man' and myself back in the late fifties.

In my youth the buildings were all thatched; and indeed I myself helped strip the thatch in 1958 before we re roofed it, with asbestos on the main barn, and corrugated tin on the hovels.

After the hurricane of '87 the state of all the buildings was awful. They were by then so out of date that nothing but the smallest tractor could get inside and all in all were not worth spending money on.

However being at the entrance to the farm I had become increasingly aware that they gave the wrong impression for visitors, since the rest of the place was actually quite respectable; at least for a dairy farm, most of which are usually notoriously untidy, so something needed doing to improve things.

There was actually a lot of potential to the old sheds . The main barn was built, as were many more in the area, from the redundant remains of the old warships which survived the Armada of 1588. They had lain rotting along the south coast when someone had the idea of utilising the timbers, and then designed the first recorded prefabricated buildings, to the benefit of agriculture.

There were to my knowledge five such barns within two miles of Flansham in the sixties and all were built in identical method. Each support and beam, each brace, and each roof truss were of the same size and each was numbered by the old carpenters with roman numerals, to show the erectors where it fitted, and into which slot. Each morticed joint was held in place by two or three wooden dowels, pegs, which have remained there to this day.

All the timber is either elm or oak. It is as hard as iron and many still show their connection with the old galleons in the strange cuts and shapes that were modified by the skilled carpenters while they adapted it for its new life.

The hovels too contained some such timbers, but also showed signs of much modification over the years, nor were they built of the same quality as the barn. The whole complex is surrounded by neatly knapped flint walls, split by a central dividing wall, the flints for which, builders of today inform me, almost certainly came from the chalk Downs to the north since, so they say, it is very difficult to nap flint picked off the shore because exposure to the air quickly makes it even more brittle than it naturally is.

These walls then formed two substantial 'bullock yards,' and enclosed the buildings in a self contained unit which, through disuse had become overgrown with nettles, brambles and elder trees.

So that was the situation I faced, and something needed doing about it quickly before the whole lot collapsed. The problem was what?

With my increasing distaste of more residential units, particularly ones so close to the farmhouse where I would probably soon be living, the idea of houses was discarded before it was even considered. And so the options then became either a new farm building or office units, and I was aware that the latter were at that time not too popular with local planners.

The idea of a new clear span farm building, although useful to the farm, would not have gone down too well with the village, yet what does, and would have meant knocking down most of the old buildings, so this idea too was dropped. Now there was only one choice, and a battle began with the powers in the Town Hall to persuade them the scheme was worthy of their blessing.

To this end I engaged the services of an architect friend, Jim Bell, then resident in the lane, and whilst he drew the plans and engaged the planners I wrote a letter to all the other residents explaining the plans and asking for their support for the project. This approach would, I was told, help sway the planning office.

Very soon my fears were proved correct since the response to this letter produced a 50/50 split. The split too was interesting since, almost without exception, the old established residents supported me whilst the 'incomers', with one exception opposed. Even more surprising was that three of these people who, incidentally had their houses on the market, were the most vehemently against. That seemed particularly odd since they would presumably not be there long enough to see the development.

Even so the biggest hurdle was the planning officers who, despite new Government policy, guiding to them towards accepting 'change of use' of redundant farm buildings on a national scale, resisted my entreatments tenaciously.

One planning officer came out to a site meeting and said I should 'go for residential use on the barn' and 'knock the rest down.' An action which would have exposed the Farmhouse to the lane, radically altered the village scene, and destroyed some three hundred and fifty year old flint walling into the bargain. Even when I showed him two hundred year old maps, with the buildings as the main feature of the settlement, he was unmoved.

Then he said "If you had repaired them [after the hurricane of '87] and then applied for this permission, we could well have taken the view they were worth restoring. Then I could probably have supported the proposals."

By that stage I was well riled and, immediately, Jim and I decided on the course we would take. That day Jim withdrew the planning application, to avoid a refusal, and over the next six months I engaged bricklayers and carpenters to rebuild the hovels, which now became well maintained redundant farm buildings. Since no amount of restoration would have made them suitable for today's machinery

This saw the hovels re-tiled, with new flint and timber clad walls, which cost me some four thousand pounds. Again Jim Bell submitted the plans and within six months of that original planning visit the same officer came back to the site.

We said words to the effect that 'since the buildings were now so well maintained there seemed no reason for him to want them demolished and on that basis they should be suitable for conversion to offices'.

"Oh no, I cannot possibly agree to that... You have clearly only just restored them..."

"But," we said, "Six months ago you said if we had restored them before your visit you could have supported our application."

"Ah well, its different now," he retorted. "You are abusing the system."

The logic of a little Hitler; all power and no vision.

Clearly we were getting nowhere and we decided to pursue the application regardless.

By the autumn of that next year, 1991 we had, bit by bit, opened the door, and after an Inspector came down from the City and submitted a long and not totally unfavourable report, we persuaded the planners of Arun Council to grant permission for two offices.

The barn at the east, and Father's now disused workshop at the west end were to become offices/workshops, with a total of some two thousand five hundred square feet floor space. What we realised at once was that by granting permission at either end of the site it was going to be almost impossible to resist our next application to complete the infilling. However, that would wait until we had the first tenants.

Now I could see the light, and within three months had engaged two local builders, Ken Hames and Barry Buck, to make a start by the New Year of 1992.

Those were exciting days. And we set about making these old barns fit into the approaching twenty first century, to again earn some money for the farming business, and to ensure they stood firm for at least another three or four hundred years.

Before many days were gone the gang had removed the accumulation of ages from the main barn and a new hard base was laid, before the old sheeting was stripped from the roof and the frail rafters removed. All that then remained standing was the original structure of old ships timbers and fragile flint walls, and very soon the size of what we had undertaken hit me hard.

Walls were strengthened, drains were laid, new oak was lifted high into the roof to replace weathered old purlins. Toilets were built and a new fully insulated roof was put over the top of the oak frame. We found a supply of second-hand Welsh slates, at the behest of the planners, and Barry built huge wooden window frames where before there were large double barn doors.

He formed windows at each end below the gable ends and Ken plastered the huge area. Then painters, electricians and plumbers completed the job by the July. He then built some imposing brick steps down to the old cattle yards which in turn had been levelled, landscaped by Mary, and surfaced to highway standard by a local road contractor.

The effect was startling and reflected tremendously on the skills of Ken and Barry who, whatever the problem we came against had found a solution. I changed my mind on a daily basis at times as unforeseen problems emerged, action which would have been hugely expensive with a builder working to a contract, but the results were excellent.

Jim the architect had ceased to be involved once the consent was granted and we decided the progress 'on the hoof'; this was because I had decided that the building would be how I wanted it to be. Not as an architect wanted it. If mistakes were made it would be my fault and it would be me who paid the bills. To have paid an architect, to create something in his own image which subsequently I didn't like, would have seriously rankled.

The downturn in commercial lettings coincided with the completion and whereas rents in 1990 where predicted at some ten pounds a foot by the time the barn was ready this had dropped to between four and six pounds, if one was lucky.

Consequently another two years were to pass before the first serious tenant emerged and in the interim the barn was used for indoor bowls through the winter months and a couple of good parties. One was for our own twenty fifth wedding anniversary when some one hundred family and friends sat at large round tables to enjoy unlimited champagne and excellent food.

This was the last time Father, by now in his 87th year, sat with so many old friends and I found it satisfying that he was able to enjoy, even if he didn't really appreciate, the change that had come about the old building. A building in which he had spent so much of his working life. Had seen so much farming history rumble past.

Indeed, he often told of how, in his youth he had watched men flailing wheat with the medieval hinged flails, during the winter; beating the grain out onto the old oak boards on the floor. The same boards we had removed that year to make level the floors we now partied on.

Over the following four years, with the precedent set and the village undisturbed by the office staff we managed to persuade the planners to grant permission for the whole set of buildings. As I found tenants for one we would start the next and despite one or two hitches the whole lot was finally fully occupied and earning a steady rental income by the summer of 1998.

Thankfully most of those at the forefront of the anti campaign have moved away. All the comments we hear, seldom directly, are complimentary and since the tenants are happy to be working in such a pleasant environment, and pay their rent, I suppose it cannot be too bad.

Lest you think such a scheme defeats my objections to the development of another old farming settlement, my defence is this. At night and at weekends the hamlet returns largely to its original peaceful state. No noisy young children, more dogs or screaming traffic.

Flansham Business Centre.

(above) the old hovels and bullock yards before work began in 1991.

(below) a view from the top of the barn roof of the north side of the units.

It has created work again in the place and turned four old useless redundant buildings into the most valuable investment, earning far more on half an acre than traditional farming can earn on two hundred acres.

Father would have been pleasantly surprised at how much better the place looks without weeds and his hoards of old treasure lying around cluttering the site. And earning the farm more than he could ever have dreamed of.

TURNING THE CLOCK BACK

For a year or so back in the early '80s I had begun to have doubts about continuing to shoot. The sport was not giving me the pleasure it should and I began to question my motives.

Looking back it is difficult to pin this change of heart on any particular aspect but there were several events, over a couple of seasons, that finally decided me to break from the local group and put the gun away 'in the cupboard.

I had been brought up by Father and Jack Langmead to think of the sport differently from other ball games. It was done not for competition, neither for huge 'bags', and certainly not to satisfy a blood lust as the opponents of blood sports may believe.

Primarily it was done for companionship. To be able to spend time with others sharing similar interests on our own land. It was, indeed still is, a wonderful way to ensure, at the same time, that the countryside, and its flora and fauna are cared for and protected from outside intrusion.

The presence of a keen keeper, and a few locals who earn some cash for their winters beating duties, pigeon shooting or ferreting is a pretty good insurance against trespass, poaching, and hare coursing. If those rogues know the locals are interested in a particular patch they will usually look elsewhere for their 'sport'.

Good company, working a good young dog, being with kindred spirits and at the end of the day having enough birds in the bag to give each gun a couple of brace, and a few left for deserving causes, was all we expected or asked. We strove to encourage all the guns to only shoot high birds and frowned on low slow ones being blown to bits too close to the guns. It happened sometimes, but it was frowned upon.

As a small shoot, with no great financial involvement, there was no real pressure to kill big bags. Even when we were rearing 500 or so birds a year the cost was minimal. If we shot 60 good birds, the day was a success. If it rained and the birds didn't fly, it was no big issue, we just took an early lunch, or tea and sat round for an extra hour or two with a couple of bottles of scotch.

With Flansham being, by then, the only really worthwhile venue there was some feeling. Everyone expected to share the sport but didn't put in the effort to provide the cover. Too little thought was going into ensuring the best was made of the other farmland. Farms that a few years before used to provide excellent partridge drives, now yielded nothing more that one small covey and a hare on perhaps six hundred acres.

Beaters didn't enjoy tramping over endless heavy soil for nothing, any more than the guns enjoyed spending the whole day searching for a lonely pigeon to shoot at. Disenchantment began to set in.

There were other reasons too. I was sometimes invited to shoot away. Sometimes on days where the guns numbered other than farmers. The professional fraternity sometimes tended to look on a good days shooting, apart from a status symbol, as a chance to show their prowess and impress others.

One day I stood next to one such man in the 'line'.. Every time a bird he had shot at fell, regardless of whether it was he who killed it, he would shout, "That was mine!" Then at the end of each drive he would pick up everything he could find and tell every one else how many he had killed. It was a really obnoxious performance.

To my simple mind this was supposed to be a sport. Not a game where high scores won. I mean, if it is so important to score more than anyone else he should perhaps, rather than killing creatures, have instead been playing a ball game. In that way he could have been seen to have won. And not destroyed life into the bargain.

Another defining moment came when, after a frustrating days partridge shooting, during which the young reared birds insisted on walking past between the guns rather than flying, the total bag between ten guns came to less than a dozen head. Never mind that, I felt, we had had a pleasant day in warm autumn sunshine, a good lunch and good company.

But rather than accept the bag, enjoy the day and laugh at it, my host went into the rearing pens and killed another dozen half grown birds. Then, making them up into pairs, or brace, he handed them round to the guests. These birds were barely fully feathered, too small even to eat.

I thought if that's what a day's shooting has come to 'that's it'. I had seen the increasing effect of too much outside 'city money' changing the sport. Too many wealthy outsiders, often very poor shots, were involved with no feeling for the countryside or the game birds. They just did it, too often, because it was the place to be seen. And the thing to be seen doing. At that time the city was rolling in paper fortunes and money was no object.

The following week there was also a bad tempered incident on our own shoot, frustration probably, and my mind was made up. I stopped shooting that day.

So for the next year or two the old shoot struggled on since my farm was by then all grass, kale had ceased to be used as a winter feed, so there was no shooting value. I confined myself with a very few exceptions, to shooting magpies and crows from our bedroom window as they attacked garden song birds at nesting time.

Over a five year period I shot something over 400 magpies in this manner and the numbers hardly diminished. So much for local keepering standards.

The exceptions were that I went for a days shooting for a few years with John Gillingham who was now running a nice little shoot on his farm near Pulborough. Nice company, no pressure for big bags and always a good lunch.

It was there one day that a bitch I had, the second Peggy, who was totally useless but a good house dog, went off across the River Arun after a wounded, swimming, pheasant. The river was in full torrent and we watched from the banks in some trepidation.

Not only was Peggy useless but if she ever caught hold of a bird she would then tear it into little bits. This was rather embarrassing, to say the least, particularly if the bird had just been shot by the man standing on the next 'peg'.

However, she finally reached the cock bird some way down stream, on the far side of the river. Gathering it in her mouth, and presumably unable to chew it, since she would have swallowed water, she then struggled for a good five minutes back up stream with this bird, held in classic retriever style as high up out of the water as possible, until she approached where we stood.

Knowing what would happen as soon as she reached the bank I climbed down to meet her before she reached dry land. Not to pull her out, but simply to grab the bird before she made another exhibition of herself. It was a tremendous effort and those watching were quite impressed. More than they would have been had she had thirty seconds more to spoil the whole effort.

So for some eight years I shot very little and missed it not at all. Indeed the situation may have stayed that way but for the explosion we were seeing by the mid nineties in the rabbit population.

They became so bad that we were losing about twenty yards round the outside of each meadow, perhaps some 20% of the farms' grass going to feed the pests. Sometimes you could walk into a meadow and the whole field would 'get up and run for the hedgerow'.

After silage was cut in the May of '94 I had had enough. Cutting the grass myself I saw exactly what the problem was and decided to try to get it under control before they took over the farm. What decided my method was in seeing the way the pests sat there completely oblivious of the tractor as it passed them by. If they treat my Land Rover the same way, I reasoned, they will get a surprise.

That evening after tea I drove quietly round and round the cut headlands. Within two hours, shooting with the gun resting on the wing mirror I shot almost 150 rabbits. I did not enjoy the job and it was certainly not sport, however it had to be done.

So for the next few days, as time allowed, I had a purge. Sometimes the bag totalled over two hundred killed. What was more, since the animals were so unfazed they just sat still eating grass until their turn came. The shots never scared them. Since they sat still I was killing something over one per shot, sometimes two or three, such were their numbers.

Once I shot five with one shot and on another occasion stopped the car with seven rabbits busy grazing and, without moving, shot the whole lot singly. Bang, bang, reload; bang, bang, reload; bang bang, reload and bang. In those few days I shot over twelve hundred. All from the car, and all in daylight. I shot any size of rabbit that moved. No qualms, since I know a baby today will itself be breeding in a couple of months time.

The next season, after a mild winter I shot over fourteen hundred. Several mild winters in a row had encouraged them to breed through the whole year and numbers were out of control.

By 1997 I was shooting up to 3,000 a year, sometimes 300 in an evening, with the gun so hot I could barely hold it. My biggest bag was 315 plus or minus. When Ian Langmead once asked me how I knew the totals, doubting my counting ability, I told him 'I know how many boxes of cartridges I start with, then I just count the misses'. Sometimes in a whole evening I would miss only two or three, but then I would have killed several trebles hits.

Once I knew the pest was dead I left it for the crows, magpies and foxes. That way I kept out of sight and didn't disturb the waiting quarry, and the carcases provided enough food to keep the avian vermin off the fledgling birds each spring. Pretty ruthless I know but an extreme problem called for extreme solutions. At least now I had grass up to the hedgerows in most of the meadows again.

Word got round about this slaughter, for that was what it had to be. It took little skill and, as I said before, it was certainly not sport. However, amongst my by now regular bowling crowd there were several downland farmers who ran their own shoots. Hearing of the rabbit shooting one of them, Jack Kendall, asked me if I would care to join him for his own 'Guest day' that December.

Fearing that this would again be a repeat of what I had withdrawn from some years before I was in a quandary. I appreciated the gesture but nervous of what I would find. So I asked for a few days to mull it over.

When Jack rang me back for my answer, I explained my hesitation. "Bring your gun Nick," he said, "If you don't like it just come and enjoy the day, you don't have to shoot anything". That made it easier.

So some weeks later my first shoot for more than six years came round. I had really never thought I would enjoy the sport again yet so well did Jack organise it, and so well did the birds fly, I had to admit to myself that I really did. And so well did the other guests treat those birds; to respect even birds deserve, that by the days end I had really enjoyed the experience.

It was again shooting as I had known it as youngster. Done for the right reasons, in the company of real sportsmen. Never did I see a gun raised at a low bird, no shouts of 'That was mine'. This was a real pleasure.

Over the following years I received several such invitations. Every day was done in the same civilised and sporting manner. It was as though the clock had been turned back over forty years and I again began to get a real sense of anticipation.

My shooting was pretty rusty but it mattered not a jot. Nobody was counting, and the birds, so high they looked like the old Doc's starlings all those years before, were often too good for even the best shots amongst us.

This again was shooting as it should be. And I have to admit, I was enjoying every moment of it.

YOU CAN LEAD A HORSE TO WATER...

Barn Owls have not been seen in Flansham since the fifties, when the housing boom began in earnest, and old barns became the targets for developers. Since poorly researched rodenticides and pesticides filtered their poisons through the chain of life. Killing rats, mice, and then the owls themselves, without differentiating, These shy and beautiful birds have suffered cruelly at the hands of change. They have lost thousands of arguments with cars on the highways in their search for food, and have lost most of the natural rough pastureland from where mice, voles and small invertebrates previously supplied the bulk of their diets.

On balance it seems most likely that within a few more years they will be lost for good to all but the most rural areas of the country.

Yet despite my pessimism, in 1990 I persuaded myself that we could perhaps encourage them to live with us again in the hamlet; and I again tried to 'buck' a trend. There was an article in a magazine relating the story of a couple in East Sussex who were being so successful in rearing these birds in captivity that they were looking for farmers with empty buildings to adopt a pair in an effort to recolonise areas of the county.

Mary and I drove to Hastings one autumn day to be vetted by these people and, we hoped, deemed as suitable candidates for the experiment. Two hours later we were returning home with a pair of the birds in a box on the back seat of the car, and on the whole journey were alarmed at the anguished noises emanating from the rear.

In anticipation I had, before leaving home, prepared the loft over the top of our garage in the garden, sealed all exits with wire netting and laid in a solid floor. So when we drove into the drive the only thing needing to be done was to release the owls into the loft and ensure they didn't escape in the process.

Having done that and fed them with some dead day old chicken we had brought back with us from Hastings, the next task was to find my own source of chicks to feed them for the duration of their stay, which we were advised could be up to a year. A task which luckily proved quite easy, since I soon learnt that most poultry hatcheries sex and kill young male chicks at hatching and there was a good demand for them from bird rescue centres and the like.

They were deep frozen, but Mary was not too delighted when I slung the package into the domestic freezer. I stressed to her they were clean and healthy but dead, and I could not quite see the difference between them and frozen meat.

The two birds would, we were told, eat two chicks each a day and would need water, apart from which we should interfere with them as little as possible.

I had fixed an old tea chest up on the back wall as a nest site and strewn sawdust on the floor so they were quite comfortable in their own way. Daily I would climb up the garden step ladder and peer at the inmates before tossing the food inside. As I appeared they would sit still and silent with their huge eyes unblinkingly alert.

After a week or so they became a little more trusting and, as the food hit the ground, would be on it in a flash and, to my initial amazement, within a second or two would have swallowed the fluffy carcase whole in three or four gulps. Their mouths opened to a size I found it hard to believe.

As the winter came on, and then turned more quickly than usual into spring so the supply of dead chicks was maintained, whilst life on the farm passed as usual, taking most of my attention.

By the time spring had warmed the earth again and the songbirds were nesting around us I began wondering if anything was happening in the loft. At the end of April, with some trepidation, Mary suggested I climb in and see what was going on in the dark recess of the roof.

As I crawled in I could see the female was sitting tight in the box and as I drew closer she began to hiss a warning. That was enough for me and I concluded she had probably got some eggs but it would be better if I didn't disturb things at that stage.

The incubation period for Barn Owls is some 32 days; although this is somewhat complicated by the fact that the female starts incubation from the day the first egg is laid. This is unlike most birds, which wait for the clutch to be completed before they go broody, and then sit, therefore starting incubation simultaneously.

This in turn means the chicks hatch off over perhaps the period of a week and make it quite hard to spot when the first one is through the shell. With this knowledge I would go quietly into the garage beneath and listen for some telltale sign in the darkness above, signs which did not come.

After some four weeks I again climbed to the loft and this time, wearing sturdy gloves reached under the still tightly sitting bird; and found nothing but some broken shell and one clearly addled egg which despite her protestations I removed. The only lesson so far was that she could lay eggs. The question was if the male either knew his job or was fertile, or both. Time alone would tell.

A week or so later I noticed that the male took food to the hen in the box, since she was clearly not going to leave her nest. Encouraged I again left them well alone for another four weeks, and went through the same procedure as before, but again nothing was stirring.

This time, when I felt under the hen I found more eggshells, and also an egg with a dead chick inside. Whilst disappointing, this was a further step in the right direction and, although summer was by now well under way, I resolved to continue the wait and feed the birds better.

By July she was broody again and noting the date began counting the days off, the last few in some trepidation. Over those last days I began slipping quietly into the garage and listening for telltale sounds and then, on about the thirty fifth day, caught a sound that sent shivers down my back. Not of fright but of excitement. A sound Johnny Field and I had heard all those years ago in the loft of the old barn above the cowshed. Similar to a high pitched 'meeow' of a cat it came in short bursts and with a lot of scrabbling around overhead which convinced me that finally we had a family of barn owls in residence.

Immediately the supply of dead chicks was doubled, and every day they were removed within minutes of being put in. The male would be seen flying around the loft with food in his claws before presenting it to his mate who I supposed was then feeding it to whatever she had produced.

After ten days of this my curiosity overcame me and I decided to go up and investigate. Not knowing how the adults would react I put on gloves, a heavy overcoat and ski hat in case they decided to attack me.

In the event the male sat to one side with complete indifference and the female moved to the side of the box to reveal three of the ugliest creatures one could have ever imagined. I had never seen such young owls before, and I was quite shocked at them.

They were covered in light fluffy down, in parts bald. With huge hooked beaks and gangly legs I thought we had bred some flukes of nature. Some deformed beasts. After prodding them gently with a stick, and ascertaining their numbers I retreated down the ladder into the daylight.

Returning indoors I read up what I could and was reassured to find that the ugly creatures were in fact just what they should be; and so with relief broke the news to Mary of the new born.

For the next three weeks I continued feeding the owls what they would eat to ensure the young grew fast and strong.

The whole purpose of the experiment was, as I have said, to release Barn Owls back into the wild, in the hope they would recolonise the locality. I had no intention of keeping wild birds captive a day longer than need be and so, now, about five weeks after they were hatched I had a big decision to make.

Figuring that by now, some nine months after they were brought in, and with their own offspring to feed, it would be safe to open the trap door and let the parents begin learning their surroundings and how to hunt, the die was cast.

That evening at dusk I threw the food in and at the same time opened the door before slipping quietly back to my office which looked straight out at the loft. Mary joined me. We did not have long to wait.

Three Young Barn Owls await feeding over the garage in Flansham Cottage, 1992..

Within two minutes a bird appeared at the trap door. It looked around and without a moments hesitation flew straight up over the high trees alongside to the north, and away. Seconds later the second one did the same.

So, stage two was now completed. We sat and waited for the first one to return; either with some food, or even just return. We waited and waited. Nothing. Yet I imagined they would heed the call of their brood, or just instinct, and be home by morning.

Next morning the noise from the loft told me something was wrong and the young were hungry. Looking inside I saw the three chicks, by now bundles of down and feathers, sitting together on the floor of the loft in a screaming huddle.

It seemed pretty clear the adults had had quite enough of the place and the chicks and were not going to return. So much for the maternal instinct, and with no alternative, I decided that I would now have to foster the chicks myself.

Luckily they were growing well and appeared able to feed themselves if it was presented to them. Also the evenings were warm and they were able to maintain body temperature so all that should be needed was regular feeding.

Throwing three chicks in they immediately waddled over to them and the largest bird tossed the little body in the air and caught it in its huge jaws. It then began what appeared the impossible task of swallowing the carcase whole and I became convinced that it was impossible and the bird would choke.

Just as I was about to enter the loft I looked up to see the bird take one last huge gulp, and the meal disappeared down its throat. What a relief. And then the other two, having watched the proceedings began the same process. I decided I had seen enough and left them to it, retreated and shut the door.

This went on for another three or four weeks and by this time I had three stunningly beautiful, fully fledged young barn owls flying round the loft and sitting for hours at the exit watching life outside.

One evening I decided the time had come for the final act. Putting some chicks outside on the top of the step ladder I opened the trap door and again waited in the office.

Just after dusk a white shadow flopped to the ground outside. Another followed and landed on the roof of the land rover, slithering off its shiny surface and joined its mate on the ground.

The third, watching all the action, then flew straight to the food supply, grabbed a chick and returned to the loft. The others, without finding the food, followed and I was hugely encouraged.

That evening I saw them several times floating around the garden and by morning the chicks had all been removed and the three birds were sitting happily in the nest box.

Over the next two months the owls became a real part of our lives. Every evening they would swing silently out across the garden and away over the home meadow and from time to time could be seen hovering and quartering the rough ground where the old brickfield lay to the west.

So regular did they become that we could almost set our watches by them, and as this went on I reduced the food supply to encourage them to hunt. This was more likely to happen on an empty stomach than a full one.

By early December there were suddenly only two birds, one had either moved or been driven away and happily we found no dead body. In fact we expected that the dominant bird would probably drive his two mates away and we hoped perhaps set up home and even bring his own mate back in time.

A week later one bird only remained. It had become set in its routine and could be seen all round the farm and our old buildings. So we were most encouraged when, just before Christmas we left with the Mote family for Murren and ten days sunshine.

When we returned the bird was still there but very unsettled and nervous. The reason for this became obvious the moment it grew dark that evening. In our absence our immediate neighbour had cut down a tree adjoining our gardens, no problem there, but on his garage to the east he had installed a security light. When this was set off it shone straight into the trap door which lead to the loft, where the owl was in the habit of sitting for hours watching the nightlife.

Blinded by that light, within another day the loft was vacated. We watched and hoped but the bird never returned. The experiment was clearly over and we sadly decided that, at the end of the 20th century, man and his toys could no longer mix with these rare, shy and beautiful birds. Certainly not in over populated areas, such as this spot in Sussex.

Several people who knew of our quiet experiment suggested that I try again but my conclusion was that we had done our best and it had failed. The owls had voted with their wings and that was it.

We never found any dead owls, nor had any reports of them. Occasionally we heard of sightings in the direction of Yapton to the north of us, and I came across a pair living in a barn near Littlehampton a couple of years later. Could they be ours? Indeed who would ever know.

Then one December evening in 1995 I was on my evening rounds of the cattle last thing before bed. They were all inside the large bedded yards, lying quietly and I leant on the gate watching them. Suddenly I had the feeling that many will know, of being watched.

Moving my eyes round the dark shadowy buildings, lit only by a single 'night light' for the animals my eyes settled on a creamy object on a far roof beam. It could have passed as one of the many feral doves that had moved in over recent years but it was somehow different and next moment it took to the wing and silently swung round the barn and out into the night. It was indeed a barn owl

Next evening it was there again and this time I retreated so as to leave it undisturbed and it just watched me cautiously as I went.

Over recent years I have seen a bird there quite regularly, sitting in the barns and sometimes flitting quietly across the evening sky as I walk down the drive to the buildings. He has not settled in, or so far found a mate but I know a pair has bred within two miles quite recently, and so I keep hoping.

Perhaps our experiment was not the total failure that we first believed. Maybe one day they will return to the nest boxes, which we have had up ready for them in several barns since 1992.

'THE SUSSEX FARMERS'

We have passed some memorable times in the Alps with the many friends we have made and met out there. Not the least of them have been with the Mangelsens, Genia and Werner from the Island of Sylt at the northern tip of Germany.

Werner is an architect who built himself a beautiful chalet in Murren and the family use it as a bolt hole from the pressures back home. They slip quietly into the mountains and disappear from civilisation while the batteries recharge.

From their top balcony they are completely unseen, all that one can see are the tops of chalet roofs below, while away in the upper distance are the great mountains of the Bernese Oberland. Glaciers, vast rock walls, snowcapped peaks. The air is full all day with the busy lives of the alpine choughs or tachi's, and regular sightings of a pair of golden eagles who circle along the valley walls in the middle distance.

Through the ever handy telescope and with a steady aim it is possible to pick out chamois and mountain ibex scavenging for moss and sustenance under the deep winter snows, as they search just below the lower reaches of the ragged glacier and well above the tree line.

We have had the best and worst of times in that chalet. It was there in '86 that Genia passed me the phone to hear the news of my Mothers death. I can see to this day her face. She was as sad for us as if her own parent had died and tears welled in her dark Bavarian eyes.

On other happier days we have celebrated Werners birthdays through many seasons. The champagne flows, Swiss and German songs are sung, and laughter fills the chalet and the crisp village air.

Werner too is a hunting man although his game is larger than my own. Heads of moose and ibex adorn the walls, On the stair well hangs a stuffed great bustard, shot on the plains of Spain, which to be honest is not to my taste, yet the money that cost him may have gone to benefit the local Spanish economy and wildlife.

The Sussex Farmers in action. Mary Adames and Peter Mitchell on the Curling rink at Murren.

On the curling rink too we have shared much laughter. We have joined with these two at times as an 'International' team and had many good results against the best teams in the alps

One game in particular always comes to mind, although on that occasion we were not playing with the Mangelsens.

We had gone out there with Ian Langmead and a couple of other friends, Peter and Margaret Mitchell who had been several times before. Peter Mitchell had become quite a keen curler.

We agreed to make up our own team, Mary, Ian, Peter and myself as Skip, and called ourselves the 'Sussex Farmers'.

The tournament began and we played the first two games with variable success. We lost the first and won the next, so we were in the middle of the pack. Next morning as we arrived at the rink there was a largish crowd of both Swiss and Germans and it was clear they had come to watch us play.

They stood in two quite large groups one at either end as we began our third game and to be honest I was puzzled. 'Funny' I thought, 'There are much better teams than us to watch' As the game went on more gathered. A cheerful crowd who spent a lot of time giggling and laughing quietly as they walked by our scoreboard with the names of the teams highlighted. We just could not make it out.

After a bit more of this I could stand it no longer, walking up to a Swiss friend, an old Swissair pilot, I said, "Heiner, what is all the interest for? We're not doing that well."

"Its not your curling," said Heiner, "It's the name of your team!"

It transpired that not knowing of our old English county, they had the idea that the emphasis was on the second half of its name. Sus-'sex'. What on earth they were expecting to see I don't know; an orgy or a strip show perhaps? When the true explanation went around, the crowd looked rather deflated and within a few minutes had all but gone. But it certainly made our morning!

Two of the best things about our curling over recent years has been that being the only English still to be regularly attending we get exceptionally friendly treatment. The other is that since the prizes go down almost to last place we always have something to show for our time on the ice.

Almost all the events are sponsored by local hotels, businessmen, or Swiss companies and their generosity is overwhelming. The top prizes are regularly something like a weekend for two fully paid in the best hotels but right down to the lower prizes, are really worthwhile and valuable.

As you rise as a team to receive your award the room erupts with cheering and clapping. There is indeed always a warm friendly atmosphere and over many years we have renewed old friendships and made many more.

A GREAT DANE

Another dear friend we have known for many years but who now no longer comes, is Mogens Moller, known throughout the village as "The Great Dane". A huge amiable man, Mogens took his family, sometimes as many as 18 of them from their home in Denmark to Murren for many years. He and his charming wife Sally would stay in the top hotel and the remainder would live at the other end of the village for a bit of quiet in the evenings I think. Very often they would walk down to our hotel, the Eiger, just down the road for a drink, or a coffee and chat after dinner, and Mary and I became great friends with them.

Mogens was amongst other things both a landowner and a large ship owner, and his huge tanker and freighter fleet sailed the World under his own name. He was known also as 'Captain Moller' which, for some time, we took to pertain to the shipping side. However we found out that it was because he was, during the second war, a captain in the US Army and although he only ever told me bits of the story what he did relate was fascinating.

Desperate to enter the war against Hitler but unable to in Denmark, he crossed the Atlantic and applied to the US services. As a fluent German speaker he was accepted at once and used as an intelligence and liaison officer. As the war drew to its conclusion he was seconded to General Paton's drive for the Rhine and accompanied the big man most of the way from the Normandy beaches. As the German resistance was finally on the point of crumbling, after the battles to take and cross the remaining bridges over the great waterway, Mogens was suddenly withdrawn. He was whisked to London and then back by air to Denmark as the first Allied Officer back into Copenhagen. The first to show the Danish population that the bad days were almost over, and the first to greet the returning Royal Family back from exile.

He was a giant of a man. Humorous, kind with a mind like quicksilver, he loved England and spent many times here. He shot regularly on the best estates in the land and several times a year would travel to his local London hostelry, Claridges, where he and Sally were treated like royalty.

Sally tragically died there in the mid-eighties and after that Mogens was naturally very lost. Whilst he still brought his family to Murren and skied every day with his full-time guide, Hilti von Allmen, he was not again quite the same.

The last time Mary and I saw Mogens was on the day, against all the predictions, John Major won the '92 election. He had invited us to Claridges for lunch and the reception we received was astounding. Had we been royalty ourselves the treatment could not have been better.

He was as always the perfect host. He complained through lunch about the hard times Danish farming was suffering and about the exorbitant taxes they were charging him. However, I was sure it was to make me feel 'at home' since I don't really think it affected his way of life much. He was just making noises he thought I would like to hear.

He saw us off in our taxi and that was the last time we saw the Great Dane. When we returned to Murren he was missing and on enquiring, were told he could no longer face the trip. He was by then 86 but behaved like a fifty year old. Over the next few years we exchanged Christmas greetings but then they stopped and we presumed his time has come. But what a life that man had seen.

The Great Dane, Mogens Moller, on the mountains with his teacher, Hilti Von Allmen casts a shadow as large as his personality at the age of 83.

In '93 we spent Christmas and the New Year in Murren for the first time. We were in the company of Tony and Sue and their two children Tim and Emma. This was the first time they had been there, and the first time back for Tony and Sue since those early days.

We flew out just before the holiday and arrived against all predictions into brilliant sunshine. Deep snow and, to our surprise, the village appeared almost deserted.

That was the first Christmas we had been away from Flansham, and it was the best one of our adult lives. Tim and I skied all Christmas Day in crystal clear blue skies, on freshly fallen powder snow. All the lifts were running and if we saw twenty other people all day that would have been the limit.

Never before or since have I had such a day. Everywhere on the mountains was skiable. And Tim, who had arrived in Murren two days before as no more than a competent piste skier, developed in front of my eyes, to his surprise as much as mine, into a first class 'downhill go any where' performer.

By the time we were finally forced down to the village that evening, by the closing ski lifts and my aching legs, he was the new 'king of the mountains'. Never had I seen anyone develop at such a pace and he was clearly thrilled. The conditions were as good as I have ever skied in, Tim took full advantage, and learned more that day about the sport than he would have in a lifetime racing down the hard pistes.

And the weather continued; Emma and Tony, no mean performer on the pistes joined us frequently whilst Mary and Sue curled and walked and socialised.

We celebrated the New Year, which is the main day of their festivities, and stayed another few days beyond. Tim and I kept going hard, all and every day. I will never forget one afternoon after a good fast run down from the Schilthorn station, high in the cold clear sky, when, reaching a natural resting place I stopped for a moment, to rest my crying legs.

Tim pulled up alongside me. He too was feeling the pace. "How old did you say you were?" he gasped. "Fifty four " I answered. Then we were off again down to the village for a drink in the Eiger Stubli and a hot bath.

As I lay back in that bath I chuckled at his comment. I felt fifty four at that moment, yet it was a sort of compliment; and made the whole thing really worthwhile. To be able to pass experience and confidence on to a youngster, who responds, and then learns so fast is very rewarding; and it rounded off the holiday.

That was the 34th year since I had first risen in the clouds above Lauterbrunnen, that January day in 1960; to this day we get the same thrill every time we take the same journey, only nowadays we feel we are coming home.

I have had some wonderful days up on those snow-clad mountains. I have skied with some great companions of whom most are now no longer with us.

I think particularly of Rosli Streif who was the first Ladies World Champion, back in '28 and who skied with Norman Fuente and I for many years until well into her late seventies. She skied like a feather, shrieking with laughter as she hurtled down the deepest gully. I only ever recall seeing her fall once and even then before we reached her she was up and on her way again the air full of girlish giggles.

I think of Norman too. Such good company. So encouraging to me in the early days and such a good all round skier. He remembered Murren when he could only ski down from where he had previously walked up, since there were no lifts when he began in 1924.

He retired from the sport in the late seventies and each year after, when Christmas was on us, and he realised we would soon be off again, tears came to his eyes at the thought of those happy years in the high mountains with his skis and his close friends.

There were many others too. Being a member of the old Kandahar ski club, based around the old resort, made sure you got to know these super skiers and each year many came back. Goran Akerheilm 'The Baron' was a real one-off character. You need people like him to help you believe you are fairly normal! I can see and hear him to this day, with his booming voice and running nose, conversing across the crowded ski cabin in four different languages. With me pretending I didn't know him as he held court and dominated everyone until his was the only voice heard. A few days a year it was fun! As were the times we toured the mountains ignoring the 'run closed' signs and opening tracks for the unwary to follow.

It was a dangerous game and we were frequently warned, if we were caught, or by those few locals who knew full well who it was. Totally irresponsible of course, because it could have lead less experienced skiers into serious trouble. Well, I see that now!

Then there were other experiences. Those trips by light aircraft, and later helicopters, which took us across the deep valley alongside the village and high up onto the glaciers. We did this a number of times, depending on the snow conditions and the availability of guides.

My first trip, which I mentioned earlier, was with Peter Fuente in '66 when we flew in a fixed wing ski plane from a slope behind Murren. We flew to the top of the Petersgrat glacier and landed on a steep virgin snow field, then after disembarking watched the tiny plane slide off down the slope and over the edge into an abyss. They knew what they were doing but it looked terrifying.

From the top we could see seven countries. All clothed in an ultra violet light. Austria, France, Czechoslovakia, Italy, Hungary, Germany and of course Switzerland. Daunting. The trip down through powder snow and later steep rock and tree lined slopes was unbelievable.

We did it again by helicopter in the nineties, this time to the Ebnafleu across the valley, with Ian Langmead and Peter Mitchell, taking off from the nursery slopes above the village early before the classes gathered.

There was one memorable trip when Ian, who skied on then fashionable but ridiculous short 'Fat Boy' skis, despite warnings to use proper equipment, jumped out of the chopper on to the glacier at eleven thousand feet into deep snow and almost disappeared up to his waist. The guide looked on in amused apprehension, and without other than a warning to 'Keep close to my tracks' to avoid crevasses took off down the gentle glacial inclines.

Peter and I followed as instructed and we pushed on for about two or three miles before the guide stopped and we pulled alongside him. He was looking up the hill. "Good skis huh" he said. We too turned round. There in the far distance was Ian! Still two miles behind, a mere dot.

"I think I radio the pilot to pick him up," he says.

"Oh give him time, he's a good enough skier, he just needs some steeper slopes for the skis to run" says Peter.

When Ian finally arrives he is quite exhausted, pouring sweat. The skis were so short that, as we had warned him, they just sank, unable to bear his weight. It was not till he got lower that they came into their own and he was able to again travel over the surface.

We actually did that run and another trip by chopper to the Petersgrat that day and again Ian struggled but to his credit kept at it. By the end of the day we were all down safely, to the guides obvious relief, Peter and I happily tired. Ian though was almost finished. He had learned his lesson. He vowed that having done it, he had the best ski experience of his life, although he would never do such a thing again. It was a hard way to learn but he had.

Glacier skiing is now becoming increasingly popular across the world, as ski technology improves and specialist deep snow, and carving, or turning skis, make for much easier control in extreme conditions. At the time we were doing it we were pretty much on old multipurpose skis and it was more tiring. However this had the advantage of keeping the high snow fields almost clear; and it was most unlikely we would see another human being when we were up on the peaks.

It will not trouble me, but it will be a sad day when the helicopters are ferrying up hoards of youngsters on snow boards. I imagine it is a certainty but the damage these things can do to new snow fields is immense, and I think could well lead to some serious accidents.

The only certain thing is that they wont be able to travel any easier on the top fields but will have all their fun on the steeper lower slopes. Having destroyed the powder for all other skiers.

~ *Chapter Nine* ~

THE NONSENSE OF BRUSSELS

There were many other considerations to take into account in the mid nineties, particularly regarding my planned major restructuring of the farms for the start of the coming century. Some of the most important being the consequences emanating from the introduction of the major EC Farm Policy reforms which brought us "'Set Aside'.

From the start, the thought of growing weeds, as a subsidised crop, on land which my family had worked and tilled for so many years, repelled me. As did the thought of yet more paperwork involved in the new scheme. Known as The Integrated Administration and Control System (IACS), it was clear at an early stage this paperwork was going to be both onerous and time consuming.

IACs came into being in 1992, the season we ceased growing cereals, and by grassing everything down we had no need, or obligation, to enter the scheme, set land aside, or get involved in the latest paper chase.

However this attitude of spurning compliance, was going to cost us some considerable income, but I took the view that the loss was worth it and there were other ways to reap some of the money IACS generated, without actually taking it as a direct subsidy.

Much of this was a personal thing, since I had for years found myself disagreeing with subsidies; largely for the stigma they brought to agriculture. I had always countered accusations of 'feather bedding' by suggesting the main beneficiaries of subsidies were the housewife, who was able to buy her weekly food at a lower price because the subsidy we received was actually what, realistically, she should have been paying direct to the producer. They were clearly vote catching subsidies to help the public get cheap food, and then be able to turn the blame onto the farmer! That view provoked some discussion and dissent amongst fellow farmers, and even non farmers, from time to time.

Now I saw an opportunity to spurn these handouts, farm my farm how I wanted, utilizing every acre, and still make a fair living.

There was undeniably an element of support in the milk price, but again only because the price was too low. Not so many years before, in my youth, the price of a pint of milk almost matched that of a pint of beer. By the nineties we were receiving 6 pence a pint for our milk (beer was £1.20) and in the shops milk retailed for some 28 pence a pint. Perhaps even more pertinent was the fact that so called spring water (mineral water) was now selling for more per litre than milk. And people are silly enough to pay.

Then, from '92 I could, hand on heart, say that we were neither claiming nor getting any other state handouts, although the level of support under IACS for arable farmers was causing increasing embarrassment and concern at its generosity. Artificially enhanced in the first years because the grain prices, despite predictions continued to rise. Yet the subsidies were being paid on the assumption that prices would weaken by some £40 a ton. That this had not yet happened was immaterial since it was only a matter of time. This was clearly a deal that would eventually end in tears.

When, as described later, the herds were amalgamated, 'Cattle Identification Documents' (CIDs) and then later passports, were all we required to ensure our returns were gaining the maximum benefit from the paperwork of other farmers.

Simply, this new system which put two payments on a beef steer, subject only to age and the colour of its CID, meant we could sell an animal with its original green unclaimed CID, and the buyer could then claim one or perhaps two subsidies due on the animal, dependent on its age.

The payments would come to him in the April of the following year. However, the value of these 'unclaimed' steers in market reflected, within a few pounds (£s), the subsidy value and, what was more important, we received payment direct through the market, perhaps 6 or 8 months before the Ministry or Intervention Board paid the fattener.

So we benefited without more than the minimum of form filling; unlike the purchaser. As you may imagine, this was rewarding and gave, indeed still gives me quiet satisfaction.

Within a couple of years, the fact that we had not registered any of our land under the IACS scheme began to look a little risky. Although none of Flansham, and a lot of Madehurst did not qualify under the rules, being long established grassland, we did have some 120 acres at Madehurst that probably should have been registered: not for now, but for the future. As an insurance.

Were I struck down, and the land sold, farmland registered for IACS was worth far more. Even as letting land, the value was significantly higher and it seemed stupid to ignore this.

There was a fast approaching deadline to register under the 1992 IACS and just before it closed I asked our Land Agent to deal with the matter. The outcome was that in 1994, with no intention of making claims or using Set Aside, we registered these 120 acres.

Since the initial registration was all that is required, all further IACS forms, bar one a year, are 'binned'.

The significance of our steers travelling on green CID's was made very clear when during the BSE depression of 1996 these animals were realising the same values as the year before; and the beef unit, using Simmental bulls on our stocky traditional British Friesian cows, was making a healthy contribution to the Exchequer. Ours, not the Chancellor's.

Having seen the value of our beef cross calves for some 15 years, since we switched first to Limousins, and then to the docile Simmentals, I quickly realised that they were quite special.

Most dairymen have steadily moved their breeding programmes across to the modern 'hatrack' Holsteins, today's fashionable long-legged, bony, milking machines that produce perhaps 8500 litres in a lactation. Some up to 12,000 litres. Our sturdier little British Friesians will comfortably give around 7,000 litres. And last much longer.

Also the calves from the Holsteins, before the distortions of the BSE crisis, were worth around £75 at 14 days, whilst ours, from traditional dual purpose dairy Friesians, were at that time reaching up to £280 at the same age. The reason being that fatteners could not get any decent 'finish' on Holstein animals whereas, on ours, the job was easy and the cattle were in huge demand by butchers, who themselves had increasing difficulty finding quality stock that 'killed out' well leaving a high proportion of saleable meat.

So, progressively, this policy has improved our overall farm returns. 'The bottom line'. More Holsteins, less quality beef; and the greater the demand for our cross-breeds. With the reputation these animals have built us, and the Green or unclaimed CID, to further enhance their attraction, the farms run more easily. We look after them, and they return the compliment.

However a real difficulty has been in finding the quality we want through the AI Services as less and less British Friesians semen is available. And the choice of available blood lines becomes limited. Yet having said that, more recently there seems to have been a move towards the more traditional dual purpose animal. Signifying perhaps that even the more progressive younger farmers amongst us can begin to see the hidden benefits.

ALL CHANGE AGAIN

In mid October 1993 Father was visited by our old, now retired, vicar from Yapton, Herbert Hamnett, who had been christening, marrying and burying members of both Mary's and my family for many years and had become a real friend to all of us. He and his wife retired to Suffolk and once a year they drove back down to Sussex to visit old friends. This was one such reunion.

Earlier that afternoon he had called in for half an hour and a cup of tea with us and we had told him how hard Father was finding things since he was progressively immobilised by arthritic knees and general aches and pains.

As Herbert said his goodbyes to Father, the old chap hobbled out with him into the drive, using his by now obligatory walking frame. Although he sometimes managed on two sticks, the frame gave more security. He watched Herbert drive off and then, accompanied by his ever present spaniel Tara, made his way indoors.

We had, by this time, developed a system of phone calls. Every morning when we rose, which was always after him, even at 88 years old, we would give him 'two bells'. At this sound, Tara would know it was her signal to run around the meadow to our garden, where she would meet up with Mary and set off for their morning walk round the farm. At the end of the walk, she would then say her farewell and slope off back across the meadow to rejoin her master.

Again, every evening when he got upstairs to his bed he would give us two bells, so we knew he was safe for the night. Since he always retired early, we usually got this call around seven and if we did not I would just walk quietly round the farmhouse garden and look inside to make sure everything appeared normal.

When the phone rang on this particular evening at about six thirty, we assumed it was Father, but when it went on beyond the two rings Mary answered it to hear Nancy, father's cousin, on the line.

"I think something's happened to Jack," she said. "I can hear him tapping on the window with his stick but cannot see him".

Mary thanked her and we immediately went round and let ourselves into the kitchen. There we were met by the unhappy sight of father lying on the floor with an anxious Tara close by. He was clearly in great pain.

"I was making my supper and just twisted round to reach my plate when my right side collapsed," he explained. "I called and called to Nancy but she had the TV on in her sitting room across the garden and couldn't hear. Then I slowly dragged myself to the window and managed to just reach high enough to tap the glass with the stick."

He had been doing this for about an hour when, luckily, Nancy went outside to find her cat and heard the urgent tapping coming from the house. That was when she phoned us. Immediately we saw him Mary and I guessed he had broken his hip and decided to just give him some pillows to make him comfortable while we called the Doctor.

The doctor arrived within fifteen minutes, examined the old boy and confirmed our fears. He phoned for an ambulance and left around seven thirty. We then called my sister Gay, who came straight down, and together we tried to ease the old man's discomfort, but he was clearly in great pain. At nine there was still no ambulance, so I rang the doctor. He was amazed and apologetic and promised to chase them up. Shortly afterwards the hospital phoned to say that they were on their way. By this time we were all pretty mad and I told them I was on the point of lifting Father into our cattle trailer, calling the local press and bringing him in myself. The caller did not seem amused, but I think she got the point.

Eventually the ambulance did arrive, and the attendants carefully loaded the old fellow on a stretcher and up into the vehicle. Slowly it pulled out of the front driveway and I can see to this day Father raising his head, with obvious effort, to take a look at his old house and slowly waving at Tara, who sat attentively in the drive watching him go.

The two of them had a very close relationship, with her acting as his full time companion since we had bought her for him, shortly after Mother had died eight years earlier. We did not know it, but that was to be the last time he saw Tara and they both pined for each other.

We phoned the hospital later and made sure he was comfortable and next day went over to Chichester to hear the news. It seemed they would not operate for a few days, for reasons best known to themselves, and we could do little more.

The situation came as a great shock to him. He was completely disorientated from the first day and could not understand where he was, or why. A few days later he had a hip operation, which made him even more confused and then for the next four months, despite kind nursing, never got back on his feet for more than a few weak steps. All the while his body remained as strong as ever but his mental state declined rapidly. Our impression was that he realised his situation but had decided that he didn't really want to know about anything any longer.

We tried kidding him along, promising to get him home and convert our little cottage into a downstairs apartment for him, since it was clear the big house was far too large for him now. He cheered up a bit when we spoke of him having Tara back, but would soon slip back into his own little world.

In January we heard that Doc Ferris, his old friend, had died up in Scotland at the age of 100. It seemed he had decided that he had reached 'the end of the road' and had refused to take any more pills. This speeded his end and he died in a couple of days.

The old Doc and Father had been sending tapes to each other through all this time and one day Father asked about Doc, since he didn't think he had heard from him for a bit. We told him gently that his old friend had died, and about the pills.

Within another day Father too, having obviously taken the idea on board, began refusing to take any of his pills. Every one the nurses gave him the old man spat straight out again, defiant to the end.

Very soon he became almost totally comatose and when we last saw him, apart from a momentary grin as we woke him, he drifted off very quickly. On 20th February he suddenly and unexpectedly faded and died quietly in his sleep. I was involved in an annual golf match at Hayling Island and when Mary arrived for lunch she took me to one side and told me the news.

I was not shocked, but upset that we were not present, and keeping the news quiet from everyone, we finished lunch and sped home. The fact was he had had more than enough of hanging about. He had himself decided, months ago, he did not want any more and just wanted to go. This he made clear to me, and had he been a dog or an old bull, I would have known just what was needed.

A week later, we crowded into the little Madehurst Church to see him off. The place was packed and in the aisle by the front row, held firmly by his granddaughter Lissie, sat a shaking and very subdued Tara. We all swore she knew just what was happening and she behaved as always, impeccably. Very soon afterwards, as we lowered the old man's coffin gently into the chalk alongside those of his parents and his brother Alan, we all thought of happier times.

Later on we repaired to the farmhouse at Black Barn Farm, where Gay and Antony now lived and where many stories were retold. We also chuckled quietly as we reminded ourselves how he had always said he would die in February. We always laughed and told him not to be so silly, and every March we told him "You will have to wait another twelve months now!"

However, in the end he was right. He really hated February.

Life, though, went on. We had been forced to begin making arrangements for the unlikely possibility that Father may come home, and we had resolved, come what may, to move ourselves into the farmhouse in readiness. We had already called in Ken Hames and Barry Buck and began a major renovation. The house had gathered items of family history since 1926 and on top of that many of the chattels, brought from Chessels at that time, had been stuffed up in the huge loft and forgotten. To make room for the repairs we needed to empty the place from top to bottom and this was a monumental task. Fortunately, I had recently finished converting Dad's old workshop into a nice double office and this now became very useful to store the hoards of old items.

We must have made a thousand journeys down from the house, across the garden to the old building, carrying trays of glass, porcelain, silver cutlery and suchlike. We removed all the furniture and a million treasures gathered over the past 45 years from the old boy's pockets. Nuts, bolts, brackets, knives, watches, pipes, photos and a thousand other things, almost all worthless, but to him relics of his past. He was always able to put his hand on anything, even if it had not been used or seen for years. Now it all had to be sorted and removed; a very difficult task.

In the first three months of 1994 the men totally restored the old house. We re-roofed it, re-wired it, reorganised it internally, repainted it and did all the jobs that needed doing and which had not been done, mainly to avoid having to disturb Father's peace. He would not have wanted anything changed anyway.

By early March the kitchen and our main bedroom were almost ready and every time we went across the meadow we carried various items with us. "Never waste a trip, take something every time" I told Mary, and between us we moved about half our possessions before the final move took place. On Saturday 12th March 1994, I woke early. It was a lovely bright day and I was playing golf that morning at nine.

"This is it, up you get!" I said to Mary. "We are going to move now and have lunch in the new house."

Within ten minutes I had the Kramer at the front door, with two pallets on the front forks. The neighbours, had they been watching, would doubtless have rubbed their eyes in amazement. We loaded the bed, sofa, chairs and tables, the linen, crockery and kitchenware and a hundred things besides. By eight thirty I had moved some six or seven loads between the two houses and the majority of the move was complete. By nine I was at the golf club and by one thirty back to our new home where Mary, after struggling with the 'Aga' for the first time, had prepared a hot lunch. What service!

Over the following few days we moved the office, papers and files across, and all the while things went on as if nothing had happened. Tara was back in her own home, a little put out at all the changes but nevertheless making herself comfortable.

It had been a sad few months and nothing would ever be quite the same again, but there was a farm to run, and a living to make.

In 1995 we also lost my cousin Nancy. She had remained in her mobile home and ill-health crept up quite fast. The old lady was taken off to hospital and died soon afterwards. She had lived an uneventful life without much ambition or indeed much to show for some eighty years, which was really sad. Beginning work at the Post Office in Bognor in April 1925, she spent her whole life, except a short spell in Brighton, in the same employment. There were rumours of an unfulfilled romance, but she had no outside hobbies or interests and was always just a shadow in the background. The only harm she ever caused was in the way her presence almost destroyed my parents' married life; yet she realised none of it. Her going represented the end of a whole generation and one less person to carry on our old surname.

Now Mary and I were the only two left, although from time to time other distant relatives appeared from many corners of the globe; to see if the family roots were still hanging on, from where their own ancestors had emigrated during the past two hundred years.

My first recorded ancestor, the only other Nicholas in the whole family tree until I came along some three hundred and twenty years later, was by family 'tradition' washed up off Pagham Harbour, some time around 1620. The story told of him as a Scandinavian privateer, freebooter, whatever, the sole survivor from a gale in the Channel.

Certainly it made a good family story, as did more recent suggestions as to the derivation of the spelling of the name. Perhaps the idea of him being 'a Dane' – ADANE – had a bearing? It would not take too much time for the spoken word to have converted that by casual usage, to ADAME, or something belonging to him or his wife Sarah as ADAME'S. Fanciful you think? Well, the family from around the world seem not unaware of the theory, so perhaps there is a touch of the Nordic races in our blood. All seem to have been tall, in my memory over 6ft, and until me, tending to blondeness, so maybe it is not so fanciful.

TOUGH DECISIONS

The herd at Flansham was around this time causing both the vet and me increasing concern. For the past two years we had suffered persistent environmental mastitis in the cows and Geoff was finding it increasingly

Tara, waiting in vain for her master to return.

difficult to control, despite all too regular visits from the vet. We had also, due to the low level of the land and the proximity of the main waterways, been attracting the unwelcome attentions of the Environment Agency inspectors with regard to slurry from the milking unit finding its way into water courses. This was particularly bad news, since I knew that to try and overcome the problem, would be highly expensive and, more likely than not, unsuccessful.

I could see that in the longer term, whatever we did, the dairy was going to come under extreme pressure as legislation became more and more at odds with reality. As a consequence, alternatives were having to be considered but I knew some of the likely effects were not going to be to everyone's advantage.

The situation was not helped by the ever increasing intrusion from dog walkers and persistent local trespassers, or the silly vandalism creeping out from the encroaching coastal development. Wires cut and gates removed at night are not conducive to the smooth running of a herd.

Nor indeed were things ideal at Madehurst, where Peter was beginning to struggle with creaking knees and general aches and pains. So bad was he at times that the poor chap had to creep around the farm with a walking stick and was unable to milk without resting. He had always milked at twelve hour intervals, 7am and 7pm, but latterly I worried about him being alone on the farm late into the evenings.

Sometimes I would drive down the main road that runs through the woods south of the farm at perhaps eleven thirty in the evening and see the parlour lights still on. It was obvious this situation would need resolving before long and before Peter had a serious relapse.

These things weighed heavily on my mind for many months as I went through the available options. Geoff had been running the home herd for over 20 years, Peter had been at Black Barn even longer, 23 years. Both had given their best years and been very, very loyal. I dreaded making the decisions that I knew were needed.

Yet, by the summer of 1994 the die was cast. Peter had been waiting for a fairly major operation which would, at best, see him off work for some months. Our regular relief, Phil, was willing, but I knew he too was not really fit for such a long stint. Now was the time to move.

It was the most difficult task I have ever had to do, telling two loyal and honest men that their jobs were to end. I had many sleepless nights considering how to break the news gently, to Peter in particular. Geoff knew things were not going too well and I had signalled to him the likelihood of what was to happen, yet that made it little easier.

But the deed was done, and on the 28th January 1995 all the in-calf cows on both farms were dried off using long-acting antibiotics. They were all loaded on Jeff Standing's lorry and ferried to Chessels, whilst all the non-pregnant animals were moved to Black Barn for Peter to continue milking until the end of March.

Geoff became dry stockman and filled his days repairing fences, on full pay, until he too stopped work at the end of March.

On that day we again did a complete swap of all 180 cows. All the dry animals were taken back to Madehurst to be run outside until they calved in June and all the milkers came back to Chessels for one last burst of activity. They were now to be milked by Phil for ten weeks with the help of our second emergency relief, Avis.

In the meantime, a new modern parlour was to be installed at Madehurst in place of the old abreast units that Peter had used for milking for all those years. In my diary entry for that day I wrote:

'The end of an era, Peter Simmons and Geoff Highnam retired after twenty four and twenty two years respectively, not a bad recommendation.'

But it was also the end of the beginning of the new era, with a new Herdsman and a new parlour due to start work within weeks and the old dairy at Flansham closing down after being in existence for one hundred years. Time waits for no man.

On 24th May the milkers again mounted lorries. By now they were running up the tailboards like seasoned travellers and went to spend the rest of their milking lives at Black Barn. Phil milked his last cow and our new herdsman, Tony, took over responsibility. It had been a traumatic few months for everyone concerned but now an exciting new phase in the life of the farms had begun.

Meanwhile, Peter and Geoff and their families continue to have the use of their cottages as long as they require them and continue to play their parts in the communities they have been part of for so many years.

That seemed the least I could do to thank them.

I am often reminded of the old saying, 'Better be born lucky than rich'. How true. With luck one can become relatively wealthy, but with (or indeed without) wealth and no luck, things are always going to be difficult. With luck there is also an element of helping things along by taking the right decisions at crucial times. Sometimes the decisions are not easy and sometimes they are excruciatingly painful.

It appears to me, and I hope you don't consider this to be trite and pontificating, that a critical part of making key decisions is on how hard they actually are. Very often I have remembered what my mother taught me as a child; that the right choices are often those that are the most difficult and inconvenient, whereas the wrong ones, at the time, appear to be the easy route.

It is often only in retrospect that one is able to see clearly, and by then, if the decision was the wrong one, the damage will have been done. Think back yourself. How often can you remember such situations?

A good illustration of a small-scale decision on the farm might be working that extra hour in the evening when the golf course beckons, perhaps to clear a field of hay bales. The forecast says 'dry' but it seems right not to leave any exposed to the elements. Then with the job done, you wake in the night to hear a huge thunderstorm raging. The easy choice would have been to go and play golf, but then the hay would have been lost.

Much more serious choices have to be made sometimes, such as ending the services of two long-standing and totally loyal herdsmen when it would have been far easier to struggle on despite looming difficulties. The act of breaking the news to them gave me the most painful few weeks of my life. Their families would be affected for a while. Loss of confidence in their worth might trouble them and despite financial help and a guaranteed roof over their heads there were bound to be money worries for a time.

I felt such a heartless heel, yet many other considerations had to be taken into account. Other lives were affected by the alternatives. It was the right decision but I loathed taking it and how sorry I was for all those concerned.

Ultimately, such things convert into the wellbeing of a business and help ensure that it continues to prosper. A loss-making operation may well, in the short term be a more cosy place to work, but losses don't give long-term security, support jobs or settle debts. A profitable business is a secure one and ensures a future for all concerned.

That is a key strategy that has guided me for over forty years. Think long-term and think hard, don't be over concerned that on the way some feathers may be ruffled, be consistent and treat others with the fairness with which you would like to be treated.

With my father now gone and no other dependants, other than Mary to concern me, with the farm running as well as it could and my fifty fifth birthday past I was finding myself spending time thinking to the future. My ongoing irritation with the burgeoning enforcement agencies was coming to such a pitch in the middle of the nineties that I was moved to really consider which way the farms should go. Indeed if I wanted any further part of the industry.

The catalyst for this doubt was the twin attack of the EU in Brussels and the Environment Agency who between them were beginning a full blown assault on hill farmers in particular regarding what the politicians saw as the scourge of nitrate levels in water supplies. As always, the farming industry was being made the whipping horse for everything that was wrong in the whole country and here was another opportunity for them to throw their weight against small individual businessmen to show the public how determined they were to save the world.

The Ministry of Agriculture, or what was left of it after the BSE crisis, determined to implement the EU legislation on nitrates trying to reduce levels in natural water supplies to the arbitrary levels recently set in Brussels of 50 parts per million (50 ppm). To secure this target they were in the process of designating new Nitrate Vulnerable Zones (NVZs) across the country, particularly covering areas such as the South Downs.

The first I heard of this was a visit from an EA inspector who wanted to speak to me about our dirty water and slurry handling facilities at the dairy. His particular concern centred on the fact Southern Water had in recent years installed a large borehole in the bottom of the valley just beyond the churchyard at Madehurst, some four or five hundred yards from the dairy.

Despite the fact that we had been here first, and that they had no proof that our cattle were responsible for any perceived increase in nitrate levels in their water samples he implied that we would shortly be asked to either close down the dairy or else spend a large sum to seal all effluent from running into the soil. Needless to say they would not be helping with this financially, despite the fact that the only benefit to anyone would be to themselves, in the form of even cleaner water, since we would not get another penny for our milk.

This did not exactly fill me with joy. Even less so when the man then told me about the prospects of the NVZ designation which, he cheerfully told me would, more than likely, require us to meet even more onerous demands.

When I asked him what those may be he said he had no exact idea but never the less still outlined a few!

What was emerging was that the EA were going to require me to spend some £30,000 to £40,000 to 'line' our slurry and dirty water pits before the NVZ requirements were made known. I quickly saw that if the latter were more demanding than the EA requirements it could well be that we would need to break up all this initial work to increase or modify or accommodate the system to suit the NVZ demands. Clearly this was a ludicrous situation.

If one could have seen a return in the form of an increased milk price or some financial assistance it would have been less unreasonable, but to expect us to comply to the first set of demands, whilst not even knowing when or what the NVZs would entail was totally unreasonable.

For a few days I cogitated about this. I spoke to William White of the NFU at Liss in Hampshire and he took up the cudgels on my behalf. The more we had site meetings and correspondence the more unreasonable and badly thought out it all seemed.

That summer was again very dry in the hills, the second semi drought in two years, and we were struggling to find enough grass for the cows. I was growing maize by this time and that was looking well, but lack of summer grazing can become very wearing.

One day I was talking to Andrew White, the contracts manager for LKL, the firm who was providing our herdsman. Feeling frustrated by all these matters I tossed some ideas around with him, I suppose to pick his brains.

During the conversation he asked me if I had thought of contracting out the farm, or going into a share farming operation with someone else who would take over the responsibility for the day to day work. I said 'I was thinking of all sorts of things' but partnerships and the like were about trust. About having someone you could rely on. I would have to have a lot of confidence to put that much reliance on another man to make such a scheme work.

Quick as a flash Andrew said "I think I might know just the man.. Would you like to meet him?" This I agreed to do and within less than two months contracts were drawn and I was off on a new venture. A 'joint venture' actually in which the other farmer, a dairyman from Hampshire, was to take over the management of the farm whilst I retained full ownership of all the assets. For this we agreed that all profits should be split in a way as to reflect the risk and financial involvement.

It was not a complicated agreement and one from which we both agreed we could pull out if we became unhappy. Otherwise it was set to run for an initial five year period starting in the Spring of 1996.

This was at the time of the high milk prices following the break up of the MMB and before the escalating run of BSE scares began ravaging returns from cull cattle, calves and beef. There was a significant amount of money being made and prospects looked really great, for the first time in my farming life.

The herdsman went with the farm and, much to my surprise, got on really well with my new partner (actually to avoid the grasp of the taxman, my 'Joint Venturer'! We couldn't say the word partner.. for tax reasons...) who quickly appeared to be spending less and less time at the farm but relying increasingly on the herdsman to undertake the total management of the unit.

This concerned me a little but I was assured that it (modern farming) was 'all about delegation ... about giving responsibility etc.' So I let it run on and watched from a distance although never really taking my eyes off it for too long. Since we were still responsible for the calf rearing, either my stockman Wally Elvin or I were on the farm regularly, he rearing calves in the calf house or me collecting them for the trip to Flansham when they were weaned. Between us we didn't miss much, despite the fact the herdsman seemed to think he could hide almost anything from us!

This went on through the next two years during which again the weather turned in favour of grass growing and meadows and cows produced huge quantities of grass and milk respectively. We received our payments from the share of profits and I was able to put the obvious problems of management in the background.

A LITTLE SIGHTSEEING

My freedom increased to such an extent that in January of '99 Mary and I, in the company of Tony and Sue Mote, were able to embark on a monumental trip around the globe. The trip, as the saying goes, of a lifetime. Tony had recently retired, and with my new situation of 'semi retirement' we four concluded that the trip that had been mooted for some time should be put into being whilst we were still all fit and young enough to really enjoy it.

We had made up a list of the places we each thought would be nice to see, that we had hankered to visit through the years, and then sat down with a good map and worked out an itinerary. All our movements needed to suit the airlines schedules and to follow a westward or eastward only direction, so this immediately excluded a number of stopping points, but we eventually came up with a plan to which all four of us could agree. My only concern was the amount of flying we would be doing, which with my long legs I was a mite apprehensive about.

And so it came to pass that in early January 99 the four of us piled our cases into the Land Rover to be driven to Heathrow by Wally to board a jumbo for Los Angeles. Some ten and a half hours later, stiff and tired from inactivity, we landed, found luggage and a taxi and on to a hotel for a two night stopover.

Next morning, after a full Yankee breakfast, we had the idea to do a rapid sightseeing trip of LA, which already appeared to us to be a fairly uninspiring bit of freehold. Tony located a taxi driver who came with the reassuring recommendation from reception that... "You will have your own bodyguard!" We awaited his arrival with interest.

Within twenty minutes we watched with some amusement as an enormous stretch limo turned in the hotel forecourt.

"There's your man," said a girl in reception, and a burly fellow with designer stubble jumped out and opened the doors. We walked out to be greeted with, "Hi, I'm John," in broad Yorkshire tones with the edges rubbed off.

As we piled in, John proudly showed us the facilities he could offer and without further fuss we set out on our mystery tour. John was a fount of information. He spent his days and nights taxiing celebrities to and from studios and social functions, knew all the stars houses (as if that was important!) and all the places to go. During the trip he also explained how some years back he had gone out to LA for a short holiday from the UK and had never returned.

Over the following four hours he drove us seventy miles around the sprawling city, left us to have lunch on Rodeo Drive and then took us on to see the old *Queen Mary* anchored at Long Beach. By mid-afternoon he had returned us to the hotel with a promise that he would pick us up at 7.30 and show us 'an authentic little Italian Bistro'.

And so he did. His choice was excellent and what is more he came back later and for nothing more than a beer took us back to the hotel, our only disappointment being that he didn't have to act as bodyguard. I reckon he would have done a pretty good job.

The next afternoon, after a lazy day by the pool, we found our way to the airport and jumped on another New Zealand airliner bound for the Pacific Islands. Roratonga to be precise, where we again arrived, via a welcome stop in Tahiti some twelve hours later to be driven by an old bus to a seaside hotel and the sound of breaking waves.

Next morning the heat hit us as we opened the windows. We were some dozen yards from the beach where we looked through the palm trees, out across the flat waters to a white spray of waves hitting the distant reef. I half expected to see Bob Hope or Jane Russell walking up the beach!

For the next two days we saw what there was to see of the Cook Islands, of which this was the capital. We took the bus round one way and then the other, stopped at the main settlement and explored the supermarket, which as far as I was concerned was the best way to keep cool, such was the heat.

We also located what appeared to be the only place on the island where the locals understood what the word 'service' meant. All the other places thought it meant 'tomorrow'! The shanty in question went by the name of 'Trader Jacks' and was run by an Englishman, strangely also called Jack. The place looked like it might serve some pretty mean fish, so we booked for a meal there that evening.

They did indeed know how to both cook and serve and it was an excellent evening in cheery company. This was the island hot spot, the centre of Roratongan society and a great send off.

An early night saw us up at five fifteen and on the plane for the next little hop to Auckland, North Island, NZ where we landed some four hours later to find some of our luggage missing. A frustrating hour later we were away again in our hire car to find the Sheraton in the city for a one night pitch before starting our journey in earnest.

The hotel was memorable for its claustrophobic low ceilings and its excellent and generous food, but both we were pleased to leave early the following morning having seen no more of Auckland than the waterfront. It all appeared very derelict but we were assured that it would be 'all fitted up ready for the Americas Cup' that following winter. We took their word for it.

Then began the first of some sixteen days driving and resting all the way down to the bottom tip of South Island and back up to Christchurch. We hired a mobile phone, bought a book on bed-and-breakfast places ('home stays' they call them) and made our arrangements as we went. We stayed with some of the most charming and kind people imaginable and brought away a host of happy memories.

On the way we stopped to meet Ellie, an old friend of Mary's, who with her husband Ken ran a fruit farm at Havelock North near Hastings. Ken was having a desperate time with sun scorch on his apple crop and the waste looked like being soul-destroying. My heart bled for him. He did find time to show us around his local pride and joy, the Art Deco town of Napier with its strange assortment of buildings. An acquired taste!

We watched, saddened, where the severe drought had burned the vegetation down to the soil, as thousands of scraggy sheep, underfed and unsheared because the wool market had gone, wandered hungrily along the road verges and seashore, searching for anything to scavenge. Now that was a sight that would have roused the animal welfare lobby here in England!

We also visited a large dairy farm with some five hundred cows, all with their tails docked and unable to swish flies, standing on an acre of burning concrete waiting to be milked. We heard from the farmer how, to keep their calving pattern tight for management purposes, they abort any cows that are late in calf.

My thoughts kept going back to the high welfare standards we farmers in the UK have to maintain and how unfair it is that overseas producers are able to flood our markets with butter or lamb produced from systems which are clearly oblivious to our constraints.

Over the next few days we stayed on a mixture of sheep farms, deer farms and exquisite private country houses until we reached the 'adventure centre' of Queenstown in South Island. All the way down I was increasingly disappointed at the drought conditions; because everything I had ever heard about New Zealand suggested that it was ideal grassland. As a grass grower myself, I was looking forward to seeing how it should be done.

The roads were quite wonderful, largely empty of cars, and the scenery majestic. We spent one hot day on the beaches of the Able Tasman and listened as our skin actually sizzled in the sun. Another evening was spent being taught the rudiments of deer farming on an isolated holding near Mount Hutt by a charming fellow. Unfortunately, his lonely wife just couldn't stop talking, which became a little wearing. We left eagerly next morning and headed on south. Down the long ridge of the Southern Alps and the intermittent crystal lakes, such as Lake Tekapo, which unless you see it, you would never believe its colour. Every corner we turned presented another vista to burn in our memories of that route.

Queenstown was quite an eye opener. The whole place was full of adventure-hungry young people, their needs filled by a host of adventure sports with bungee jumping being the number one crowd puller. We watched but were not drawn to it. My most active day was spent rowing Tony, line dangling behind, from our lovely 'home-stay' around Lake Hayes in the hope of catching a trout. It was not successful but a bit of exercise that was needed.

We two took a small aircraft and were piloted over Mount Cook and down to Milford Sound, landing at two small isolated airstrips and watching as little commercial spray planes constantly came and went waging their incessant war against the Possums, imported some years before from Australia, which were destroying the forests of this lovely Country wholesale. The views from the air were quite startling.

After some four days in the resort we then moved on to Dunedin where, in weather more akin to Sussex in March, we walked out on the Otago peninsular to watch the Royal Albatrosses as they made land, to breed on the only mainland colony in the world. Truly magnificent creatures, fighting to survive huge periods at sea and 'deep sea fishermens' hooks.

A day or two later saw the four of us on the last leg, back up to Christchurch. There we visited a boy's public school, where Tony and Sue's son Tim had done a spell as a teacher a few years before, the idea being to meet his ex-headmaster and pass on news from the Old Country. Then with a final few hours to 'kill' we included a walk around the magnificent botanical gardens of Christchurch, before another reasonably early night ready for our next flight in the early hours.

We had been very impressed with the whole country, loved its warmth and its people, and wished it was just a little bit closer to home. Its great attraction being that it has a land area pretty much the size of the UK, with but only three million people, a third of them Maori's, a third living in Auckland and the remaining million spread thinly over the rest of the islands. What a change from home.

Our next flight took us across the Tasman Sea to Brisbane there to change planes for another short two hour hop to Cairns in the north east corner of Queensland. After an hour-long bus ride along the coastal road we finally arrived at our next stop, Port Douglas where the wall of heat we had last experienced in the Pacific Islands again hit us hard.

Our reason for going there was to take a boat trip out to the Great Barrier Reef, which we did the following morning when we boarded an impressive speed boat, *Quicksilver*, along with some hundred other tourists, for the 90 minute spin out to its mother raft, moored on the Outer Reef. The proximity of so many other people after our comparative solitude in NZ came as a bit of a shock. However by the time we had spent five or six hours exploring the reef, snorkelling, diving in a glass bottomed 'submarine', swimming and eating like lords we had forgotten all that and had all enjoyed an invigorating experience.

The next day we sweltered in the heat, too much for very long despite the closeness of a shoreline which is hardly safe to swim in. Stinging jelly fish or sharks, take your pick! We did briefly venture in the water where Mary thought she had been stung and quickly called for the services of the handsome lifeguard. It was a false alarm.

I managed to go in the sea with my wallet in my pocket and, trying to dry it out, left it on a seat and when the bus came, forgot it completely until we arrived back at the hotel! Fortunately, the natives were honest and a couple of calls from hotel reception located it and it arrived back intact within the hour. How very lucky.

It was also lucky that our plans meant we were moving on next morning. Despite the Reef we had found Port Douglas rather a disappointment, and further excitement beckoned on our journey.

By midday the following day we were being shown in to the most superb luxury apartment, 20 storeys up in an hotel between the Sydney Harbour bridge and the Opera House with an amazing view, looking out across the wide reaches of the glorious harbour with vessels of all sizes constantly passing across the picture.

This was to be a rather special evening, since we had arranged to meet two old friends for dinner who were wintering in Australia. This pair, Dick and Angela Graves, went back a long way with the four of us and we were all excited to be seeing them, although, knowing that Angela had been increasingly poorly for some time we were apprehensive as to her condition.

Dick had been a friend from the days of the A team at Middleton, where he often opened the bowling at the other end from me in the mid-fifties. Angela was an older friend still, being the girl with whom I had shared those distant days on horseback around the gymkhanas of Sussex even before cricket became a part of my life, and whose sister Sue and parents had always been so generous and friendly to me when I called at their house in Fontwell.

They had drifted away when they married and Dick's work took him to the midlands, but in the recent past had moved back to West Sussex and we had all 'taken up where we left off'.

So now here we were together again, some 12,000 miles from home on the other side of the world and we had a happy reunion over a couple of bottles of champagne, high up over Sydney. Angela was her usual vivacious self, but I was anxious at how much more frail she appeared since we had last seen her three months earlier. Afterwards, we went together to a popular open air restaurant close to the waterfront, where we shared another couple of happy hours of chatter, before the two of them decided they really had to go.

Tony and Sue afterwards agreed that Angela looked to have become much worse since the autumn and we all worried as to the outcome of her illness. It had been a lovely evening but Mary and I were filled with concern for our old dear friend but we little realised this was the last time we would see her. She died in England the following Summer.

When we awoke the following morning, the view from our room had been enhanced, for there, between the Opera House and the Sydney Harbour Bridge now rested the great liner *Queen Elizabeth II*, berthed alongside the quay where we had dined last evening. What an amazing sight those three great modern wonders of the world made.

This was our last day in Australia and we filled it with a walk round the city in heavy rain and a trip around the harbour in even heavier rain. Then, although the others were too nervous to join me, I took a trip to the top of the giant AMP Tower, high above the city, still in heavy rain. Consequently, the view was more akin to looking down on the clouds from Murren than what I had hoped for, but if these things are there they need seeing.

As we waited to leave our hotel that afternoon I noticed a succession of extremely fit looking young men in our hotel lobby. Half recognizing the odd face I nudged Tony.

"Isn't that one of the Waugh brothers." He was unsure. Then a few moments later the unmistakable hairstyle of Shane Warne, the Aussie spin bowler, appeared and suddenly the room was filled with the whole Australian cricket team in transit between a series of one day matches against, among others, England. We had been watching them playing on the TV in our rooms, not an hour earlier.

They all loaded up into a coach as we too took our leave of the Quay West Hotel and headed for the airport to make a flight which I was not looking forward to.

Some four hours later we landed for a refuelling stop at Perth, Western Australia and had twenty minutes to stretch our legs before taking off on a crowded plane for a ten and a half hour trip across the Southern ocean to Johannesburg South Africa.

When I think of that part of the world I think of cold deep seas, desolate rocky islands and Antarctica. There are not too many places to land in emergencies and for the whole flight, since I could not sleep in those seats, I imagined every unusual noise in the aircraft was the start of some terrible emergency! I am not a nervous passenger normally, but by that time we had done so many flights they were beginning to get to me. Home was starting to call. If, that was, we survived the night!

However we did. And at five thirty in the morning disembarked into a rather sad looking Johannesburg and began searching for our departure area for yet another flight. Unfortunately we had some five hours sitting around in the airport lounges, which after a night without sleep is hard going, but eventually the hours slipped past and despite the airport staff's hardest efforts to stop us, we boarded a small turbo prop aircraft for the Bush airstrip at Skukusa in the eastern Natal close to the borders with the Kruger park.

So began the most magical two days any of us had experienced. We were met at the strip by a young Game Ranger in a large multi-seated four wheel drive truck who then proceeded to bounce us for forty minutes across some of the most rutted and unmade roads I've ever seen. If any of us had any inclination to nod off it was soon dispelled.

Along the roads we had regular glimpses of antelope and other similar animals which seemed largely to ignore our passing. Then suddenly we were by water, the Sand River, and alongside us a collection of tidy buildings, set on a slight rise, just back from the river, with a panoramic view of some 90 degrees across the water and away into the distance.

Welcoming faces approached from all directions, we were introduced at once to our personal guide Finn and taken for a look at our rooms and given a welcome drink. This was Mala Mala, a private game lodge with some 24,000 acres of natural wild scrub running along the by now unfenced boundary with the famous Kruger National Park. The sights that greeted us were quite amazing.

As we sipped our drinks, all thoughts of tiredness faded away. We looked across towards the Sand River and could see a couple of Hippos submerging themselves in the fast flowing stream. To our left, doing their best to strip the lower fruit off some large marula trees were two huge Elephants, not fifty yards from where we stood and quite oblivious of our presence.

After lunch, under sunshades on the terrace, we decided that, as was the way of the English in Africa, we would take an afternoon siesta before setting out on what was, after all, the reason one goes to these places, the first evening game drive. At that stage I was actually thinking along the lines of letting the others go and sleeping, but I was forcibly dissuaded by Mary.

At four that afternoon, well smeared with anti insect spray to top up our malaria pills, we boarded a Land Rover packed with seats. Sue sat in the front with Finn and his rifle across the bonnet, two Italians sat next in front of Tony, Mary and myself at the back alongside a black tracker.

The next four hours were quite wonderful, as an experience that strangely I had been somewhat indifferent about beforehand, turned into the clear highlight of our trip. From the moment we set out, Finn and his tracker looked for and found the complete range of big game. Everything we had ever seen in books and films we could now observe around us, living out their own private battles for survival in what must be some of the harshest conditions for wildlife in the world.

Almost every animal we saw was in imminent danger of being killed by something bigger, yet apart from the nervousness of some of the antelope their fear was not obvious. At every turn in the deep grass and acacia scrub we would come across rhino, giraffe, buffalo or lion, and all the time we were assailed by the constant cacophony of sound from night birds, crickets and (most amazingly to me) frogs.

As we returned to camp for our communal evening meal some four hours later, we had to slow the vehicle to allow a porcupine and shortly after a pair of leopard room on the track. Quite stunning.

The meal was taken in something of a dream, since we were all four so tired, and shortly after ten thirty we departed for our comfortable cabins and a very welcome sleep, but with the clear understanding that we were to assemble promptly at 5:45am for the morning drive!

Amazingly, neither Mary and I or Tony and Sue had any difficulty waking and shortly after six we were loaded and off again. This time the fauna seemed quite different. Many of the same creatures were present, obviously, but not in the same numbers as on the night drive. Now the emphasis was more on birds, and the variety was stunning. Eight or ten species of kingfisher for example, hovering like humming birds, and darting in and out of the river. Eagles, hawks, vultures, birds which one had seen in books and marvelled at because of their shape and colours, flitted to and fro and posed for us.

The drive lasted four hours but was over too soon and after a leisurely breakfast we spent the morning at rest, mostly in the swimming pool not fifty yards from the biggest bull elephant we were to see. Then lunch and it seemed, before we could catch our breath we were out on our second evening drive.

This went much as before, except we stopped once for a quick break and were served with what Finn described as 'barbecued porcupine'. I challenged him that it was actually chicken and he had to give way! Then we went off in search of a pride of lions which he thought were hungry and about to make a kill. This hunt took some time.

With the use of radios the other two vehicles out that evening helped each other in the search. We would stop silently, waiting for a noise in the bush or a radio signal for direction. On one such stop we looked in wonder at the stars, so clear in the unpolluted sky. As we gazed Mary suddenly said, "Look... a shooting star!"

"No," said Finn, "It's a man-made satellite in orbit."

As we watched it, another similar light came up from the southern sky and the two paths crossed. The sky everywhere must, of course, be full of these communication satellites, but in our polluted northern skies they never show. We all gazed in wonder.

Suddenly there was a sound of excited running in the bush in front.

"They are in for the kill" said Finn. There was noise all around now, then a thud, like a rugby pack going down for the scrum. The engine started, other car lights came on in the surrounding scrub and we all raced at speed towards the sound of the impact. Then the Land Rover stopped.

"Impala," said the tracker.

On the grass not twenty feet in front of us lay five lionesses with heads together and jaws pulling against each other over the lifeless form of a small antelope. A lion lay expectantly beyond, watching.

Moments later we heard a sickening tearing sound and all five drew back with their now torn share of the carcase. The three vehicles sat quietly around, flashlights occasionally shooting as we watched the scene in awe. The male lion moved in to claim his 'percentage' and backed out again. Amazingly, none of these big game animals shows any inclination at all to attack us. They totally ignore us.

"So long as everyone stays seated in the confines of the vehicle," Finn told us, "You are in no danger. Get out and you will be dead in seconds."

We all sit very tight. Ten minutes later the lions are finished. They lick themselves and each other and begin to look drowsy. Us too. But what a thrill that night had been!

We followed the same routine again next morning. In all, over the two days we went on some sixteen and a half hours of game drives over virgin Bush that stretched unfenced perhaps as far as Ethiopia in the north to the plains of Namibia to the west. The animals were all truly wild creatures, roaming free. It had been a simply mind-numbing experience for us all.

By midday we were saying our 'farewells' and 'thank yous' and were on our way back to Skukusa and then on to Pretoria for the next part of our adventure. However, no two days could possibly match that experience at Mala Mala.

THE LAST LEG

When we arrived in Pretoria there was something of a shambles awaiting. We were taken to our hotel only to be greeted by the manager with the news that one of our bedrooms had a faulty bath and was being repaired. He told us he had arranged for us, all four, to instead be taken to 'another place' in town which he hoped would suit us'. It all seemed rather strange but we had no choice but to go along and if anyone reading knows Pretoria it is not a place to be on your own without accommodation.

The house we were then chauffeured to was something which I really don't have the words to describe. It was luxurious but a bit strange. A number of things stick in the memory, but I will tell of the two we most remember.

Firstly, we were greeted and shown around by a couple of black valets who had been assigned to attend to our every need. We were not allowed to pour a glass of water such was their attentiveness. When they guided us to our rooms much play was made of the fact that our room was where Nelson Mandela had slept with, hush, his girlfriend Gracia Machel but a few weeks past. We were indeed on hallowed ground. Unless one has been resident of Robben Island prison or the presidential suite in many of the top hotels in the world, which, respectfully, is unlikely, this is something unlikely to befall most people!

The second memory was of the garden, which was exotic and fell steeply away from the house with Pretoria University in the distance. All around us during daylight there was the most eerie shrieking from some most unusual birds, obviously Ibis, but we suspected they had been hand-reared such was their confidence around humans and particularly the numerous staff flitting around.

When I asked my 'valet' he assured me they were completely wild Hadejah Ibis, "just dropping in for the grubs they can find on the lawn." He could have been 'telling it straight' or it could have been a line, but I think they were probably being fed in the same way I used to feed ducks with grain when I was shooting them long ago. They certainly added something rather memorable to the place and I suppose it was better to tell the guests that they were wild.

Memorable as it was, we breathed a huge sigh of relief when we finally extricated ourselves from the clutches of the over attentive staff next morning and quickly found ourselves transported to the central station in Pretoria, just in time to catch the 'Blue Train' to Cape Town.

The Blue Train is something that anyone who has travelled in Africa, indeed travelled anywhere, will almost certainly have heard about. It is a luxury sleeper which travels sedately between Pretoria and the Cape, with a few extras added on; to Victoria Falls in Zimbabwe for example. It is considered to be the ultimate railway experience and we had thought about doing the trip since we were in Africa with the Don and June Hansford in 1983. Now we were here.

Settling in we quickly made our way to the saloon to see for ourselves if the stories about unlimited free drinks, champagne included, were true. Indeed they were. All this time the train was trundling through a collection of timber and tin shacks which I would barely have consigned my dog too. These were the 'townships' that may be seen continually for what seems hundreds of miles around Pretoria and Johannesburg and are, quite honestly, a disgrace.

They actually coloured my personal impression of that trip from the first hour. Why the authorities, who have done so much to improve the lot of the native workforce in South Africa, cannot bring themselves to tidy up this eyesore I cannot think. Surely they cannot really want visitors to have such a close up view of this awful situation.

Finally we moved away into the high veldt and settled into the rhythm of the journey. We had a fair lunch in the luxurious dining car, coffee in the saloon and by mid/late afternoon had arrived at Kimberley where we were advised we would be given a conducted tour of the 'Great Hole' of diamond mining fame.

When we alighted from the train the heat that hit us was quite phenomenal. This time a somewhat dryer heat than earlier hotspots and we all wilted. However there was no getting out of it and we were taken by old tram to the site of the museum alongside the vast hole.

It would indeed have been very interesting had it not been so darned hot, compounded by the fact that all the roofs were made of corrugated iron which, like our old barns of years ago were almost unbearable. We then had a tour of the old site looked down into the immense hole where hopeful white prospectors hand dug some 23 million tons of soil and wheeled the whole lot up from the lower levels, some thousand feet below. It was then distributed in heaps around the hole itself where it largely remains today.

Out of that mass of soil they actually found the equivalent of some two tons of diamonds. For that thousands of men gave up the best years of their lives and only a very few ever came away with a profit. Except Barney Barnato and Cecil Rhodes.

It was a memorable sight to see, but only slightly more memorable than our relief, when we got back inside the air conditioned coaches and set out south again.

That evening we again ate their best food and drank their finest wines before retiring to the extreme luxury of our individual sleeping compartments and settled in for a night on the move. In fact the train appeared to be stationary much of the night but regardless we slept well.

So the hectic trip went on. We rose and breakfasted in some style before again retiring to the saloon for a final round of Champagne as the vineyards of

Worcester slowly turned into the squatter camps of the Cape and the depressing vista again surrounded us for the remainder of the slow journey into main central station.

I have thought a lot about that journey. Doubtless had it been at the start of a holiday, or indeed the feature of the holiday it would have been a wonderful experience. However, at the end of a trip such as we four had just about completed, it was a bit of a let down. One doubtless becomes somewhat blasé with 'over-travel' and I think by now that was our situation.

Half and hour later we were in the Vineyard Hotel at Newlands. Not 150 yards from where, some seventeen years earlier, we had stayed in Lindsay's house at the start of the first trip. Now we were at the end, almost, of this one and home was beginning to loom large in my thoughts.

The Hotel was actually full of British people, most of whom appeared to be members of various golf clubs in Sussex! Mary and I felt somewhat out of place. Almost as I imagine one would feel on returning to civilization after a year in the jungle alone. It was rather like I imagine Butlin's must be, and we were uneasy.

The next day we took a trip round the coastline running down to Cape Point. The scenery we remembered was no longer there. Everywhere now were new homes and civilisation and it was rather sad. Even Cape point was crowded. Actually the highlight of that day was at the point where there is a long tradition of resident Baboons, animals which run riot, and will steal anything left unattended.

Walking back to our car we suddenly noticed a whole family of these creatures playing excitedly in the back of a new BMW convertible, which the owner, despite visible and numerous warnings, had left open. There was nothing we could do, as they showed no fear of humans, so as we left we took a photo or two of the group tearing the upholstery and going about their natural business over the open seats. What the owners reaction was when they returned we could only imagine!

Now we were really getting towards the end. Next day we drove to Stellenbosch and revisited the winery at Boschendal. The restaurant was just as we remembered it from our earlier trip and the heat too was just as intense. On the way home we called in at Stellenbosch Golf Club and watched hoards of hot people sweltering across the sun-drenched fairways. Mary and I at least were thankful we had sworn not to waste one day of the trip on a golf course and we didn't regret it at all. I think perhaps Tony and Sue regretted the lack of golf a little more than us.

Next day after a long hard spell under a sun umbrella by the pool we finally gathered up our cases for the last time and set off to the airport for the final leg. Another enthralling ten and a half hours of cramped discomfort was to follow, and the only thing to keep me going the thought that tomorrow we should be able to go to bed at Flansham. The journeys had become progressively harder to bear since we arrived in New Zealand. We had flown sixteen different trips and the thick end of 40,000 miles. All this had been done in some 35 days and we arrived home ready for another holiday!

All that said it had been a truly wonderful experience which we wouldn't have missed for the world. Well I suppose we couldn't have really! Tony and Sue and Mary and I had got along pretty well and all mutual or individual irritations were well enough overcome. It is sometimes hard work living so closely for such a period, but we had succeeded and had jointly enjoyed an experience of a lifetime.

But it was great to open the front door and be greeted by Tara and enough mail to burn Guy Fawkes.

MORE HARD DECISIONS

It is amazing how quickly one settles back into routine, and after that monumental trip spring work soon took over my thoughts. It was an early warm spring and by the middle of March all the grassland was rolled, chain harrowed and fertilized ready for the coming season. The fence contractors had been on their rounds and some of the stronger animals were out. Shortly after this, as things again slackened prior to silage making, I began to have some quite serious doubts about the direction of the joint venture at Black Barn Farm. My 'partner' was hardly ever to be seen, but there appeared to be a huge amount of expenditure instigated, with rather too little thought, on such items as new water tanks and electric fences. It appeared all the decisions were being taken by the herdsman in the boss's absence. He was there for perhaps an hour every two weeks and yet I knew how much time it actually took to keep on top of all the problems that arise on a dairy farm, however good the herdsman.

On top of these worries there were also some clear signs from the actual calving dates, in relation to the projected ones, that the cows were not calving as expected. Having spoken to the Vet and then all other parties involved, I quickly decided that things had gone far enough.

There was an added dimension too, in as much as the milk price, which had for three years been making the job profitable and worthwhile for the first time in anyone's memory, was taking a nosedive. My feeling now was that, if money was going to be lost (which would ultimately be my company's money) it would be better if I was responsible for it rather than a third party who, clearly, had too much on his plate elsewhere.

It all came to a head very soon afterwards in late May when the herdsman, realizing, I think, that I was onto him, gave in his notice. My 'partner' was terribly upset, but my reaction was 'good riddance'. I wondered what other skeletons would soon appear.

To keep things going, we arranged for the contractors, LKL, to set up interviews for a new man, and after six weeks were able to engage a cheerful young man who had already had a seven-year stint with one of the most progressive dairymen in the south east. His references were excellent and he was a bright personality.

Peter Brown started with us in the last days of July. Just as Mary and I returned from a short break in Scotland, where we stayed again with Tom and Sheena Hay for the Carnoustie Open.

As soon as we returned I went up to see that Peter was settling in OK and found him busy and confident. I was, to say the least, surprised that the man who was supposed to be running the farm for me, my 'Joint Venturer', had not yet been to the farm to see Peter and point out to him the many things a new man needs to know.

By the time I had seen him and returned home, my mind was now made up. The only solution was going to be for me to come out of my self-imposed semi-retirement and take up the reins again before Peter got 'turned' and before the by now obvious losses of the operation became too serious.

The next few weeks were indeed somewhat tense as the break was made. I think the other party knew in his heart that he had let things slip. Probably due to the recent drop in the milk price making it harder to make a profit from what had previously been an easy job. We gradually began sorting it out and by the start of September the business was again back in my control, with a substantial overdraft which had not been there two and a half years before when the Joint Venture was set up.

Though it was now my responsibility again and something of a new challenge, I took the job on with surprisingly renewed vigour.

1999 had been a really hectic year on all fronts. Apart from the holiday and the upset at Madehurst with the Joint Venture we had suffered at Flansham from the Environment Agency putting a major new sewer through the heart of the farm. We knew it was coming, but nothing, nor any amount of compensation, could cover for the stress and inconvenience it caused us, and this despite the agents feeling they had done a good job for us!

We had four rectangular meadows, in all some forty five acres, which suddenly became eight triangles. Through their centre ran an eighteen yard wayleave, which was being churned to hell by heavy plant, and in the middle, a trench some twelve feet deep which held the huge pipe.

This work went on for three months and despite a fair amount of goodwill on both sides initially, by the time we came to take the land back most of this had evaporated. By the end of October we had forced the contractors to give us the land back so it could be re-seeded for the next year's grazing. Unfortunately, as with any operation causing land to be disturbed and drains broken, the ongoing effects of this work still stick out like a sore thumb even two seasons later.

A little ironically, the catalyst for most of the events related over the preceding pages, i.e. those threats from the water agencies regarding nitrates and dirty water, still, as I write some five years later, have yet to be realised.

All in all I was really quite happy when the old century came to an end. Happy to be still farming, still in charge of my faculties and my business, despite some pretty trying times, and still able to enjoy the things about my life that have kept me interested and active for the past fifty years.

~ *Chapter Ten* ~

IS THERE A SOLUTION?

With such diversions as the bowls to fill our time, the reader can perhaps see how, as a 'slightly over middle aged' farmer, I intend to proceed into the new century. How I intend to control, and subdue, my frustrations at the state of farming in the deadly hands of bureauocrats, politicians and pressure groups with other interests.

A real problem nowadays is that there is so much EU and UK Government money sloshing around for environmental causes, leading to ever more pressure groups and lobbyists, all trying to get in on the action to create roles for themselves and their departments and claim these funds.

Duplication in this is nothing short of a scandal. Here in Sussex we have, in the last few years, had to suffer the creation of the South Downs Conservation Board (SDCB) whose basic function is to do what the County Council and individual landowners had been doing anyway.

They persuade a gullible local press and through their pages tell the public what a splendid job they are doing, and then go back for yet more funds, to employ yet more staff, for yet more scatty schemes.

As an example, they spent, in 1994-95 some £20,000 to £30,000 enclosing an area of traditionally open hillside close to our farm at Madehurst that had been enjoyed by the public since the Duke of Norfolk long ago gave it to the County Council.

The SDCB fenced and gated it, installed stiles and laid on a water supply at very considerable cost. They then designated it as a 'Local Nature Reserve'. The purpose of this, it transpired, was that they had decided that grasses and brambles were suppressing the natural wild flowers, in their words 'the Downland Flora' and to restore that ideal they planned to graze it.

One day they phoned me, and asked if, as the closest farmer, I would like to graze my cattle on the site. I suggested we meet on site.

Next day the warden arrived and again ran through his ideas. I replied that I had no sheep and since sheep were the creatures that created the traditional downland turf, along with rabbits, they were the ones to try and fulfill his dream. Secondly I said I felt the grazing in that spot was practically worthless.

"Oh, we didn't plan to use sheep," he said. "We were advised by the Ministry of Agriculture to put cattle in there." I thought quietly to myself that this was just about the quality of advice one could expect from the ministry advisers.

I tried to explain the different needs of sheep and cattle. Sheep create a close-knit turf but the hooves of cattle cause huge damage in wet conditions and that would destroy what turf was still there, and since the fodder was almost worthless they would require supplementary feeding.

"But the Ministry said..." He went on.

I stopped him. "If you want cattle in there I would want £8 a week per head for extra feed and a full indemnity against their roaming when gates were left open. I should also want the clumps of Yew fully fenced to avoid poisoning the animals."

This was clearly not the reaction he expected and he began to come round to the idea of sheep. He then asked me if I knew a grazier who could help. I gave him a couple of names, but later found out that they declined due to the risk of dog worrying.

Six months later there were a dozen horses in the enclosure "Up from the New Forest," I was told. They spent their time standing disconsolately by the road side, looking hungry. Within a couple more weeks they were gone.

The reason, so it transpired, was that one or two had been found dead with yew poisoning.

Since then the site has been empty, apart from rabbits. Another resounding success for the SDCB and their hangers on, and all paid for by money provided indirectly by you and me.

So much for experts. The only ones to gain have been their employees and the contractors who supplied the fencing and water supply... and yet a little later there was a report in the local papers from the annual report of the SDBC. It quoted the Chairman who, in glowing terms, reported 'the resounding success of their year's work' and 'excellent conservation policies', followed of course by a call for 'further funding' to pursue yet more of their fanciful dreams.

It seems that these politically appointed bodies know 'everything but nothing' and they don't appreciate that there are historical reasons for things being done in certain ways. They often come in with a narrow mandate, perhaps to protect cowslips on a hillside and then exclude all other considerations.

On the other hand, Landowners and country people take all these diverse aspects into account naturally, almost without thinking, simply because it is obvious. It needs no rules or assessments to cope with such situations.

There are certain jobs for certain seasons; routines which have evolved to take account of every season, and every aspect of our landscape. The only element that this routine fails to allow for is that of outside human activity, in the form of increasing visitors, residents and lawmakers.

Clearly the English countryside is going to have to adapt to accommodate this increasing problem. However if it is to truly succeed and continue to be the envy of the world, it is the incomers and officials who are going to have to adapt their perceptions even more.

Country people don't go to the cities to tell urban dwellers how to run the show, since they themselves certainly know their towns best. Yet for some strange reason they think they know what is best for the countryside too.

Our habits and traditions have evolved over centuries, as has the landscape but it seems that the outsiders fail to understand this. They also fail to understand all the lesser issues. Since they don't understand, for example, fox hunting, stag hunting or shooting they say its unsociable so 'ban it'. There is no acceptance of its place in the 'order of things'.

So it is, for reasons such as these, that we are in grave danger of losing what everyone purports to love, the English landscape.

This process is well under way, faster than anyone would believe and as I have said elsewhere, when its gone it will be gone for ever, if for no other reason than that the people who have the real skills to nurture it will be gone too.

These are not skills you can teach people from reading books and university courses. They are skills learned by countrymen and women from birth and are totally in tune with nature but sadly out of tune with 'policymakers' and 'experts'. (Definition of an expert: 'an ordinary man a long way from home.')

The future of my land, and, like most others in recent times, pessimism, clouds my outlook. For so long there was an unchanging aspect to the industry but now the old principles no longer apply.

My Father, brought up with his strict Victorian values, and in hard times, saw changes in the countryside that would have been unbelievable for one born even twenty years earlier. So little had changed in farming methods since the middle ages and the tools of the trade consisted of a few hand items, shovels, spades, hoes, rakes, brooms, axe, adze, crosscut and scythe. The only power sources were men, oxen or horses and even in his childhood, indeed till the years of the 39/45 war, it was nothing to see men cutting a whole fields of flattened corn with hooks.

He often told me of how as a child he watched men threshing grain from the heads of wheat by the use of the old flails. This was a hinged stick, with which the crop was spread on the floor and actually flailed, to knock the grain free in the same manner as the Egyptians did the job over two thousand years before!

This he saw done on the thick boarded floor of the Sussex barn we had recently converted into office space, and when we began that work, I well remember lifting those old boards and thinking of the sweat, use and history they had seen.

Then, in the last forty years of his life, he saw farming move on from that state to the now almost totally automated systems of the present time. In one lifetime, from the oxcart to sophisticated computer controlled sprayers that apply the correct but variable volume of chemical to a crop, from information supplied direct into the tractor cab from a satellite circling in space. Quite unbelievable changes in so short a time, yet change that he welcomed for what it did to ease the work of the farm staff and improve life.

In my case, following along some thirty years behind, I was still around in time to see the horse drawn plough, hand milking and a hundred other labour intensive chores, and from that time, things have moved on through a complete agricultural revolution. Happily, so far, without the bloodshed of many other revolutions.

I can now accept the sight of combines that can clear a hundred and fifty acres in a normal day's work, others that can strip raspberries from the cane with the touch of a feather; robotic milking parlours, and computers, that will in a second provide answers to almost any question man can ask.

I have watched my own small community, once occupied only by farming people whose only function was, like their forbears, simply to supply food for the town dweller, and tend their stock. In the past twenty five years I have lamented as this and many other small settlements, their original reason for existence taken away, have become satellite dormitories for urban workers and retired outsiders. It has not been an entirely happy conversion.

Not too many of us in the country remain in the same place we were born in days before the Second Great War. Perhaps even fewer appreciate what has gone from our lives. As we move on, so the spirit of such places disappears for ever.

In this small place there are now, at the end of this century but four residents over forty years old who have spent their whole lives here, all in farming, whilst there are now also some eighty who have no connection whatever with the land.

It is because of these dramatic changes in so short a time that I am now so pessimistic about its future. Farms amalgamate and more and more good land is stolen for development, to house the ever-growing and ageing population that seeks to move south to our warmer climate.

My land, which six generations of my family have tended and loved, is surely and steadily being encroached upon and much will soon be lost for ever as farmland, overrun by powerful forces that neither it, nor we as its present guardians, can resist.

I can say, without too much fear of contradiction, that what hasn't been built on by 2025 will be either leisure areas or some form of wildlife park, land uses to suit day trippers and holidaymakers on some of the finest arable and grazing land in the south of England.

You may well feel that such changes are for the good, and that farming should not take up subsidies and space in populated areas, but if you truly feel that way you don't have a feeling for the countryside; for it's carefully tended enclosures, its old buildings and its history.

Not that the land that is left to farming in the future will even resemble what the onlooker will consider today as the traditional English countryside. That is being taken care of by the rapid intrusion of the enforcement industry. With their new environmental controls, nitrate vulnerable zones, health and safety dictats, 'open space' policies and most ominous of all, Conservation Boards and National Parks.

A thousand and one outsiders coming in, bright eyed and bushy tailed, with their clipboards after a three-year course in 'rural sciences', which supposedly qualifies them to know what is best for those who still live in what's left of the countryside.

Suddenly, before anyone realises what has happened the damage will be irreparable. The English countryside which has been created by small family farmers and their sons, and by the Dukes and Earls on their big estates, will be gone for ever – and I mean *for ever*.

Here are three good reasons why:

Firstly, once the young farmers have seen how much they can earn in the towns doing a nine to five job, they will laugh at the working hours a farm demands.

Secondly, the cost of equipping a viable farming unit, which even today is out of the reach of all but a few, will be so formidably high as to make the prospect economic suicide.

Finally, because the public, who will have by now moved in and completed the conversion of every cow barn, hovel and farm cottage, will resist such things as smelly cattle and noisy tractors encroaching their new, prettified village territory.

So yes, I am pessimistic. Where my Father may have been concerned at the quality of his crops, I am concerned at the quality of life in the countryside I have known. The only blessing is that with luck I will no longer be here to witness its fate.

Lest you now think these are the inane ramblings of a jaundiced old rustic let me point out to you how many of our dairy and stock farmers have gone from just this one small area in the past 25 years; years in which there was no serious environmental pressure, and during which dairy farming usually made a fair return on labour and investment.

I well remember when almost every farm had a herd of cows. When you could more easily count those farmers without a dairy or beef herd than those with. There were in excess of twenty herds within five miles. Wherever you stood you could usually see cattle.

Five years ago this figure was down to eight. Then in three weeks during the Autumn of '97 three of those sold up and the farms ceased to be dairy farms for ever. For two of those, the blame fell on the environment agency, for the other on new urban neighbours who objected to every operation that went on around the farm. Those residents may soon regret their objections as cattle farming gives way to further residential development or perhaps open-cast quarrying.

LETS KEEP THE BALANCE

One is aware there are many people who may question the ethics of a person who can shoot birds on some occasions and yet fight to conserve them on others, yet as far as I am concerned there is no conflict at all.

During my whole life, ornithology has been by far my most enduring interest, since I first became fascinated by birds at a very early age, and this has stayed with me through everything else I have done. On the golf course I will stop and watch reed warblers or skylarks, a darting sparrowhawk or the rare kingfisher and many of my companions have learned much about the birds around them from observation during our games. In the Alps, during, and around the exertions on the snow and ice, golden eagles and ravens vie with the tumbling alpine choughs, for my attention. And in the other more exotic places there have been equally exotic species to admire. Frigate birds, long tailed tropic birds and albatross and even penguins.

Former times: Jack and Alan hand-cutting flattened wheat with hooks, the only way to harvest a crop in that condition in the labour-intensive 1940s.

At home in Sussex is, however, where most of my interests and observations lie and the farm is to a large extent, always managed and tended with the view to the benefit of the myriad species which, despite common belief, still live in the area or visit us each year.

One of the few winter chores that I still do regularly, is the annual trimming of the miles of thick hedges that surround every meadow on the farm. My motivation is almost as much to provide secure and adequate breeding sites for the coming year, as to tidy the hedges themselves, both equally vital work.

The job is always aimed at the period between Christmas and the beginning of March, to strike a balance between destroying the late berries for winter feed and to make certain the work is finished before the first blackbird begins her nest building.

A few of the hedges are shaped into inverted Vs to create a natural barrier for the cattle and maximise a protecting screen of spring vegetation. This also creates a corridor for numerous other creatures like hedgehogs, to traverse the farmland in privacy, and in more safety than would be found in open country during daylight hours.

It does have one setback in as much as it also provides a safe breeding area for the rabbit population and this problem can only be overcome by shooting. That problem too could be overcome in a short time, were I to adopt the more common trimming fashion of 'straight back and sides', since then the land could be cultivated tight to the roots and rabbit holes dealt with. However that would destroy the value of these hedges as nest sites so it is a price I am prepared, but not happy, to pay.

The bigger farm hedges are treated in the same manner, only in as much as they are always lightly trimmed. Any trees or branches threatening to damage the barbed wire fences beneath are cut with a chain saw and removed before they fall, since the prime objective of the operation is to ensure a stock-proof boundary around the whole farm.

People have asked me why I bother to trim these hedges at all, so pretty do they think they look, but I have to point out that, left alone for too long, they become quite unmanageable. Many of the more vigorous species, ash, elder, hawthorn will grow up to five feet in one season and therefore need controlling annually. Dog roses are the one species that, if I can, I leave to mature because they are so beautiful in June.

This trimming is a satisfying task, with the shape quickly reformed by the whirring flails as I pass back and forth along the hedge. As I work I often think back to those early days in the fifties when I left school and Johnny and I would spend the winter, armed with hand saws, axes and long handled hooks, struggling to trim back a hedge that had not been cut for twenty or thirty years, perhaps more. Over the course of a winter we could cut and burn the distance of perhaps three hundred yards. Put into acreage terms, the hedge around maybe a three or four acre field. Today this would take me perhaps an hour, with no subsequent tidying up to do since the vegetation is shredded into a mulch by the flails. The whole farm, some three hundred acres, can easily be trimmed to the standard that a good gardener would accept in about a forty hour week. The 'good old days' my foot!

THE EASIEST JOB OF ALL

Saying that hedge-trimming is one of my only winter chores is really to over simplify, since, as any farmer knows, there are always a thousand little jobs asking to be done. One that takes most of my time throughout the year is, in the eyes of an outsider looking in, no job at all, since it requires no physical effort. This is the task of looking at animals. It may be done simply by leaning on a gate. Other times I do it sitting on a stile, and on other occasions I stand still amongst the animals and let them come and inspect me.

It is probably the most vital job a stockman can do and is never time wasted. The fact that our regular stockman, Wally Elvin, sees the animals once or twice a day is neither here nor there, since he usually sees them during feeding time; when they are usually jostling around feed troughs, and are not always easy to inspect.

When they are grazing, lying quietly in the meadows, or on their straw yards, there is a far better chance of good relaxed observation, and that is where I do my quiet work.

There are, as I have explained earlier, basic things to look for and all vital. There are usually cows close to calving, needing almost constant watching, until one is sure the calf is firstly presented correctly and then born, and finally nuzzling round its mothers udder and taking its first drop of milk.

There may perhaps be a cow with foul in the foot, a case of bloat, or a young animal with a 'cloudy' eye which most likely signifies 'new forest eye', and this, like all the other afflictions needs urgent treatment.

It may be an animal with a digestive upset, one away on its own in a quiet corner with no obvious problem other than just the fact of its self inflicted isolation, telling the experienced stockman there is something wrong.

Twenty minutes leaning on that old gate, quietly looking at a bunch of animals may well seem, to the casual observer, the luxury of wasting time; yet it seldom is. There is bound to be something useful to see and learn. Very often it is just to discover that the little owls have returned to nest in the old hollow willow tree in the corner of the little brook, across from where I am watching. Now that too is interesting.

A very strange thing that I found out long ago about this watching 'game' is that animals will come up and 'tell' me that they are unwell.

It is almost certain, as my stockmen will vouch for, that if I go to a gate, or enter a compound full of stock, any animal that is not 100% will show me within a very few seconds. This is something I discovered a long time ago and remains true to this day. It has caused several of my stock tenders over the years considerable embarrassment when I have noticed something that they should have spotted earlier, but on the whole I blame nobody, and am thankful for this extra sense that helps me spot a problem.

As I come close to them the first thing I do, as any stockman would, is to cast my eyes round the yard or field. To subconsciously sum up the picture. Count them, look at the food situation, and for anything else that is not quite right. It may indeed be a fence slack or a water tank dripping. It may be, and usually is, nothing at all.

By the time this inspection is done, perhaps half a minute later, if there is a problem, one of two things will have occurred. Either an animal will have approached me or alternatively, will be standing or lying away from its group, alone.

Why, I don't know, but it will be short odds that one of these two cases, probably the one that has come to me, will be not quite right. Don't ask me why but it's a fact. Perhaps the animals themselves somehow recognise me as their 'protector' and so reveal their problem in this manner.

When Wally first came to work for me in the early nineties, he grew quite upset when at times I would point some problem animal out to him after he had spent time bedding or feeding them perhaps only an hour before. I had to assure him that so long as he looked carefully he should not take it too personally. But it keeps him alert.

Recently he has come around to accepting this and welcomes it as a backup to his own observations although he can never quite understand 'how he didn't see it first'. Of course, by spotting these things early there is a much better chance of a full and speedy recovery.

For example, a weak calf, left untreated for six or eight hours because its birth wasn't noticed, could well be dead by morning, particularly during long cold winter nights. So with Wally feeding twice a day, and me looking at them during the day and last thing at night not much passes.

There are the obvious signs of trouble which every countryman recognises; bellowing is a sure sign, indicating animals out of water, out of food or roaming free. Never ignore the noise of 'mooing' cattle without checking. They might be in your garden!

There are times when this mooing is less sinister, however, such as when calves have been weaned from their foster mothers after six months of being teat fed or when a bull wants to get at a nice bunch of bulling heifers, shut away for safety across the farm. When sex then rears its head all hell can be let loose; beware if the fences are poor!

Often during these out of hours visits I run into the local owl population. Lately a barn owl is visiting the lit stockyards at night and his ghostly form flits silently away as I approach. Their eerie shrieking call echoes around the buildings regularly and sends an involuntary shiver down the spine. It is a noise to match the thin bark of the fox on a cold January night. Both make me pull the duvet tighter around my ears.

A pair of tawny owls are always resident here and hoot endlessly during the winter months around the gardens of the quiet settlement, whilst we always have a considerable number of little owls living and breeding in the old hollow trees around the farm.

Foxes are a huge problem to the likes of wildfowl, game birds and domestic fowl. They are a problem that the local shooting fraternity struggle to control but it is an uphill effort. The fox is such a clever opportunist, and the best hope is that the overall population can be controlled. They will never be eliminated.

The latest 'safe haven' they have discovered is amongst the huge stacks of half ton Hesston bales that we store around the buildings each autumn, and in the early spring we regularly spot a vixen sneaking round the buildings, at any time of the day, as she sets out in search of food for her growing and hungry cubs.

They are enchanting little devils but sadly there is no way we can leave them alone and regularly with guns and terriers we try to thin out the numbers. This may seem heartless but vermin have to be contained. That being said, we always struggle to outwit 'Reynard' and foxes remain numerous.

Speaking of the Little Owls reminds me of one evening when I was cutting grass one May in Little Brook. There is an old willow tree there, once a huge specimen and, as far back as I can remember, hollow. This has always been the nest site for these birds and even today, standing as barely a stump the owls still manage to nest and rear young there, so they are always around the little meadow. On this occasion I watched in amazement as the parent bird suddenly dived into the ground close to the hedge in front of the tractor wheels. It seemed completely oblivious of the machine and within a split second again became airborne; only now it had a full grown rat struggling in its talons.

Having seen pictures of Osprey rising from the water with large salmon, I know what power these creatures have but to see this example, in real life, was spellbinding. Despite the resistance of the impaled rat the small owl carried it across the meadow some hundred yards to the old willow stump and delivered it to its greedy youngsters.

The old tree is really now on its last legs since these past few summers the big Simmental bull has used it as a rubbing post and it is quite loose. It should probably be removed but I hesitate since it really has been the hereditary home of this small family since before my childhood. Perhaps I should rebuild the base with concrete to ensure it lasts me out!

Alternatively an old telegraph pole with a good private nest box would be better. However, I think I will probably wait till the willow stump gives up the ghost.

Twenty years ago we also had a resident colony of Long Eared Owls in a small spinney west of the farm on Langmead's land. It probably was only a family but there always seemed to be five or six birds there whenever we visited and they would rise and with their huge wings silently flap off round the surrounding brooklands.

Some shooting days we would surround the spinney and the beaters would drive it for pheasants. On these days the owls would usually sit tight and watch us with their huge ears cocked, and show not the least concern or fear.

Sadly they have now moved away, driven off finally I think by the hurricane of '87, although I have a feeling there may again be a pair across the brooks to the north.

Funnily enough, these owls were replaced at the same time by a couple of pairs of herons who lost their nesting tree, a huge solitary conifer, in the same storm. Looking for an alternative they settled in the little spinney, and despite some vandals shooting all the young birds one year in the early nineties they have now grown into a strong colony some thirty in number.

Interesting birds, but not the best friends of owners of well stocked fishponds within a considerable radius! However it is yet another success story of birds living with an increasing human population.

Another such success, but not a popular one for real bird lovers, who know what is happening, is the increasing number of sparrowhawks. Even ten years ago one would not see these birds, but gradually they have made a strong recovery and now pose a serious threat to the songbird population. A threat to match that of magpies and crows.

Without fail, if we sit in our sun room at twilight, Mary and I will see a hawk rocket through the garden at almost ground level as it attempts to flush and then catch a late feeding blackbird or thrush.

Its success rate becomes obvious when walking round the garden next morning, one invariably finds a pathetic pile of freshly plucked feathers where it has prepared its meal.

The sad thing is that so often its victims have been brooding hen birds, off their eggs for a few minutes to clean up and feed before night sets in.

The sparrowhawk is not selective and will kill anything between a blue tit and a pigeon, indeed I recently saw one kill a yaffle (a green woodpecker). Every time it takes a bird with eggs or young in the nest, the whole brood is lost in short time, either to the cold or to the persistent corvids as they scavenge early next morning and hear the hungry plaintive cheeping of the orphan nestlings. Despite the denials of the blinkered RSPB, the effects are showing and songbird numbers are dwindling very significantly.

The society would rather blame this on the countryman than on the truth, and indeed even if they did acknowledge it privately, it is most unlikely they would admit it publicly, lest donations dry up.

Any observant countryman and gardener can see what is happening. The case against sparrowhawks, crows and magpies is an open and shut case and unless the RSPB ends its hypocrisy very soon there won't be many wild songbirds for anyone to see.

The migrating birds already have to contend with European 'sportsmen' who trap these little travellers in their millions as they struggle across the continent. To survive 'mist netting', shooting and evil traps to then be killed by the protected bullies in our urban areas seems a pretty hard fate.

In their own space these hunter/killers are superb specimens, they are agile intelligent and spectacular hunters, yet I will not hesitate to kill them and in turn if someone were to take a sparrowhawk in my sight he would not be reported to anyone.

The life of all small birds, mammals too, is a constant struggle, not so much from man as from these natural predators whose numbers and variety in our local district, despite the encroaching urban sprawl, are increasing.

With killers such as these on the increase, man has to help balance nature. There is after all no other balance. The only thing that will lower their numbers is when they no longer have songbirds to kill for food. In the unlikely event that we see the sparrowhawks and corvids becoming rare again, the decrease in the songbird population will perhaps tell the RSPB something that they may take on board. But probably not.

The time has come, I believe, when those country people who agree with this analysis have to stand up and be counted. And if a shot across the bows of the local sparrowhawk population is required, the justification for it is easy to find. Not perhaps in law but certainly in fact, which again unfortunately, makes the law something of an ass.

Too much of the countryside and the lives of the creatures that inhabit it, is being taken over by sincere, soft hearted and misguided zealots who know next to nothing about the real natural world.

Too often these days, politicians are guilty of short-termism, influenced by the likes of the RSPB, RSPCA and other numerous groups, with more money and power than is healthy. Their constant public utterances about the countryside and its evil countrymen carry far more weight that they deserve and within a very short time gullible but influential sections of the public, and then our populist leaders, take up the cry. "Ban this" "Ban that" "No" to everything, "Stop the..." Every week we hear of some new cause. This is quickly followed by the unerring support of the BBC front men, who with their glum faces and mournful voices exaggerate the stories. Closely followed then by some publicity seeking MP, even a minister to promote a private members bill in the House, and yet another bad law is thrust on us.

It is sadly only a matter of time before these busybodies get their way over Hunting. It won't be many years before fishing and shooting follow suit. Yet, as I have said elsewhere, do not these people ever stop to consider who it was, and indeed still is, who made and continues to keep the British countryside what it is?

Who it is that nurtures and still strives to maintain the beautiful landscapes we see all around us? Sadly it is the same group of people who will soon be trodden under by the green-wellied brigade of self-appointed evangelists. People paid for by public taxes, who will soon be running our fields, moors and woods.

I hesitate to go on because it actually distresses me as much as it probably does other country people, however these things need an airing. Where is the difference, say, in killing a sparrowhawk that kills our songbirds, killing a fox that eats our chicken, taking a trout from a chalk stream or killing a fat bullock?

To my simple countryman's mind you either accept them all, if done, in say, the case of the sparrowhawk, for the right reasons at the right time, or you accept none.

We must live, and let others live, their own lives. Or if you must regulate, apply a blanket, honest and unhypocritical policy across the whole population. It is grossly unfair to pick constantly on countrymen. We are not perfect in the countryside but we've made a pretty good fist of it, unregulated for centuries. Nor are we total idiots, heartless or needlessly cruel. If the day comes when the control of our wild and natural places is taken from us countrymen, and placed in the hands of the RSPCA, RSPB, CIWF, Greenpeace, FoE, and the thousand other pressure groups, the countryside will, within a couple of years, be as lost and sick as most large urban centres.

That would be a disaster of unmitigated proportions, and its progress can only be halted, if it is to be, by the silent majority exercising their brains and coming urgently to the rescue. The whole issue, of the matters I have spent so long pontificating on, community, countryside, farming and our natural world is intrinsically interwoven. To disturb one small block, as was seen in the incompetent handling of the BSE saga, brings the whole house down.

I am one of many independent 'voices in the wilderness' calling for the countryside to be returned to the care of the only group who will really continue to care for it. Not talk about what should be done in an ideal world. Actually continue to do the job.

That group is the people who tend the farms, forests lakes rivers and moorland. Tenant Farmers, landowners, what used to be known as 'yeoman farmers' even, I reluctantly admit, the wealthy but absentee 'businessmen-cum-sportsman' who want to make their mark. Many have, and some have made mistakes, but the few mistakes are outnumbered a million times by the success stories.

We have a wonderful asset in the varied countryside of the British Isles. Present policies and opinion shifts are coming very close to losing it for ever. In a small way I hope these chapters have given you a small glimpse of what the next generations are in grave danger of losing.

DECLINE AND FALL

Since my childhood, the decline of stock farming, particularly cattle, in West Sussex has been relentless. Clearly, the effect of this shift from stock to arable farming, hastened by European Grant aid under the CAP, has had a dramatic effect on farming patterns, manifesting itself not simply in the obvious disappearance of stock from the fields, but in the switch from traditional grasslands to the culivation of wheat, rape, legumes and the biggest evil, 'set aside'.

That switch persuaded arable farmers that hedges and ditches needed removing to accommodate increasingly large machinery. With fewer turns, more work could be done in a day, by fewer men.

All farming systems have been shedding labour since the fifties and that trend is irreversible, despite the protestations of some daydreamers who cling to romantic celluloid visions of the countryside, without ever having had to suffer the work.

In turn, farmers no longer need so many farm cottages for staff. They don't require, either, the old barns and hovels, most of which long ago became too small for modern equipment and have spent a quarter of a century falling into disrepair.

Too often, before one can say 'planning consent', the result is that all the old cottages and most of the surrounding buildings have been turned into quaint residences and country people replaced by ex-town dwellers with no interest in village businesses, and thus the heart of most rural settlements has rapidly been removed.

Apportioning blame to any particular issue has become a media inspired sport in recent years and really achieves nothing positive. What has happened to our villages and our countryside was always going to happen once mechanisation took hold – a sort of mechanised version of the 'highland clearances', right across the country. Even were we able to agree on the causes, it would not stop the destruction, which still continues apace.

In France the government has, dare one say, its faults, but it recognised long ago the need to retain the structure of its small rural communities. It introduced measures to ensure that people stayed, lived and worked where they always had, on the land. It also ensured that the population balance was retained and the land cared for. This is a lesson the British politicians seem not yet to have learned, and its getting late.

Some one hundred and fifty years ago, the French Republic passed the 'Law Napoleone', whereby the descendants of a landowner shared equally the holding on a death. Despite the fragmentation of land the wily French have made the system workable; and more to the point have retained a hugely influential rural foothold.

The result is that with so many landowners, however small, their interest in rural matters is ongoing, and the government is inclined to take notice when the rural populace rumbles. At the last count it was estimated that close to 50% of the French still had a rural interest of some kind. At the same time only some 2% of British people were involved in agriculture in any way, not just ownership of land. It is pretty clear why our countryside is in the mess it now is.

Not only are we losing our cattle, our meadows, our hedgerows, the rural nature of our countryside, our countrymen and our traditions. We are also losing our old buildings and our quiet country lanes to three and four car families and we are being disenfranchised to boot.

Black Barn Farm, Madehurst after a winter snowstorm.

The gulf between the country people who struggle on and the 'new villagers' continues to grow apace, and because of such wide and diverse backgrounds and priorities, the gap is now unbridgeable.

ITS BEEN GREAT FUN

So what have I achieved over these past forty odd years? Measured in whose terms and by whose yardstick? For the physical effort I have put in I would maybe have to say that the returns are pretty pathetic. I have friends who worked in the City and made fortunes in a few short years without ever needing to get out of their beds at some ungodly hour on a cold winter's night to tend to their business. Others can afford holidays on an almost monthly basis and yet never seem to have done a week's work in their lives. Some have worked as hard as a man can and yet still have nothing substantial to show for it. Others who started out with prospects and a good job have perhaps through no fault of their own seen the whole lot go to rack and ruin.

One thing I have learned is that everyone has their own yardstick. They have made up their minds that they want to lead their lives in a certain way and have gone out and done so. If in the process they have fallen on hard times, like Father's brother Alan, who is to say their lives have not been just as satisfying as the lives of those who have worked hard for their long term security and yet lived dull lives?

Life is surely for living, and living how the individual wishes. All I can say is that I have no regrets and would do very few things differently given another chance. Luck and good timing have played a huge part in my life. Being in the right place at the right time and seeing the odd opportunity has helped a lot.

I married a wonderful wife who has spoilt me almost to a point of cruelty (I almost burn water if I make coffee!) and I should have been lost without her constant good humour and support.

So after all these years I can now spend time leaning over the farm gate, or sitting on a shaded stile in summer heat, and watching a group of contented cattle growing up. I can pick and choose which work I wish to do, and call in a contractor for that which I would rather not.

I have seen the farm business grow strong, diverse and as secure as anything can be in these modern times and indeed it could be a powerful launching pad for, where it here, the next generation to push forward and build a strong commercial operation. An operation which, unlike in the family's past, would not be hindered by the need for constant borrowing, but only by the politics of food production

And then I think to myself that if I had a son to follow on he might well want a quite different lifestyle. He could be idle, or lack drive and blow the whole lot, like dear old Buckle. God forbid, he might have got into the drug scene. On the other hand he could have become a sportsman and made his fortune in a few short seasons. We shall never know, which is a shame, yet it has not until now, nor will it, spoil the rest of our lives. It is called fate, and overall the fates have been kind to me. What is to come is to come and, as a country lad who has stayed at home, whilst not being complacent, I am quite content with my lot.

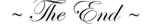

~ *The End* ~